THE VOICE OF THE PEOPLE

THE VOICE OF THE PEOPLE

HAMISH HENDERSON AND SCOTTISH CULTURAL POLITICS

◆ ◆ ◆

COREY GIBSON

EDINBURGH
University Press

For Siobhan, and for my parents, Joyce and Wallace

Edinburgh University Press Ltd
The Tun – Holyrood Road
12 (2f) Jackson's Entry
Edinburgh EH8 8PJ

First published in hardback by Edinburgh University Press 2015

www.euppublishing.com

Typeset in 10/12.5 Sabon by
Servis Filmsetting Ltd, Stockport, Cheshire,
and printed and bound in Great Britain by
CPI Group (UK) Ltd, Croydon CR0 4YY

A CIP record for this book is available from the British Library

ISBN 978 0 7486 9657 4 (hardback)
ISBN 978 1 4744 2849 1 (paperback)
ISBN 978 0 7486 9996 4 (webready PDF)
ISBN 978 1 4744 0367 2 (epub)

CONTENTS

ABBREVIATIONS

AM	*Alias MacAlias*
BW	*Ballads of World War II*
CPS	*Collected Poems and Songs*
EDC	*Elegies for the Dead in Cyrenaica*
PL	*Prison Letters*
TAN	*The Armstrong Nose*

ACKNOWLEDGEMENTS

This project would have been impossible without the generous support of Edinburgh University Press, the Carnegie Trust for the Universities of Scotland, the Department of English Literature and the Institute for Advanced Studies in the Humanities at the University of Edinburgh, and the US-UK Fulbright Commission. I would like to thank Dr Alex Thomson for the great gift of his time, patience and insight as I researched and wrote this book. Dr Sarah Dunnigan has been immensely helpful and supportive. I would also like to thank Dr Scott Hames, Professor Penny Fielding, Professor Ian Duncan, Professor Eric Falci, Professor Janet Sorensen and Dr Margaret Mackay for their thoughtful advice and their support.

I am very grateful for the support of Hamish Henderson's family, in particular, Katzel and Janet Henderson. The attentive and accommodating staff of the National Library of Scotland, the Department of Celtic and Scottish Studies and the many libraries of the University of Edinburgh, the Hamish Henderson Archives Trust, the Dulwich College archives, the British Film Institute, Pelicula Films, and Scottish Television, also deserve a great deal of thanks for their friendliness and efficiency. I am very appreciative for the recognition bestowed on this research by the Universities Committee for Scottish Literature and The Scottish Arts Council, with the G. Ross Roy Medal for 2012. Pino Mereu and Amletto Micozzi showed me great kindness during my research in Rome. Timothy Neat, Steve Byrne and Alec Finlay have also been very forthcoming with help and advice.

Without the hard work and compassion of my parents, Joyce and Wallace, I would never have been in a position to undertake this project. My brother, Fife, and my sister, Ione, and my mother and father-in-law, Rosemary and Patrick, have also given me an enormous amount of encouragement. Finally, I want to thank Siobhan, my wife, for her love and support, and for lending me some of her own brilliance and intelligence.

INTRODUCTION

The full life-course of a folksong is essentially unknowable. We might know the name of its author; we might have a stack of published versions available for consultation; but we will only ever get glimpses of the role of oral tradition in its perseverance. In new contexts, songs find new incarnations. In every performance a given song is presented with the opportunity to persist and proliferate, lodged in the minds of those who hear it. And, as people sing to one another, the complex network of tiny moments of cultural transference soon becomes both too vast and too transient to follow. A song might be reduced to its melody, motifs, lyrical features and basic plot structures. This helps the folklorist to recognise its relations and measure their distance from one another. When folklorists scrutinise a particular song, they pull on it like a thread and trace those connections that the nomenclature and methodology of that discipline make visible. Very quickly, however, the folklorist comes to infer a system that has no discernible beginning or end. Therefore, in a process distinguished by its boundlessness, the evidence with which the folklorist works can seem arbitrary: simple accidents of circumstance and history. When we look at a singular folksong version, we only know that there exist many more tributaries feeding into it, and many more distributaries flowing out of it, which have left no apparent trace. The little that we can know always invokes the greater part of the tradition, which lies beyond our knowledge.[1]

Hamish Henderson (1919–2002) called this the 'folk process', and its presence can be felt in every aspect of his long polymath career, not only as a folklorist and folk revivalist, but as a poet, songwriter, political activist, translator, public intellectual, and latterly, as folk hero. As a folklore scholar, Henderson set out to chart this immense and immersive terrain; as a revivalist he sought to actively intervene on its behalf. He envisaged the role of the artist in society as one caught between an absolute submission to the collective tide of human experience and the need to absorb and recreate this collective force according to an individual or personal credo. Henderson tried to overcome this tension by suggesting that it might be possible to reconcile the self-conscious directives of political theorists, poets or cultural commentators, with the unchecked, transcendent processes of the oral folk tradition. In his war poetry and army balladry, for example, he experimented with the lyrical form, attempting a politically engaged art that might represent the soldier without patronising or alienating him. In the life and works of the Sardinian Marxist philosopher, Antonio Gramsci (1891–1937), he found a theoretical framework that both emboldened the vitality of folk culture, and diminished its political expediency. Henderson tracked a careful path through the obfuscations of the Scottish literary tradition: through issues of form, language, national identity, and the various ideological hues of his peers and predecessors, in search of a genuinely popular and politically conscious literary culture for twentieth-century Scotland.

In her 1984 study, *Burns and Tradition*, Mary Ellen Brown set out a similar tension between the individuated 'author' and the collective 'tradition'. Conceiving of tradition as a 'constant process across time and in time', she describes continuity and dynamism, and the 'elusive but preserving culture' that binds people, and quells our common fear of 'isolation and insularity'. Brown deploys this notion to locate The Bard in two reciprocal fields: in his use of tradition, both intuitive and self-conscious; and in tradition's use of him: his works and his legend. Burns becomes both agent and conduit. He is 'explicitly' the National Poet and, 'implicitly', the 'anonymous voice of Scotland'.[2] Henderson, too, becomes both subject and object in his relationship with folk culture. He is a 'tradition bearer', receiving songs and tales and passing them on, individually insignificant but contributing to the cumulative power of the collective. But he is also an active and original agent for change, especially in his efforts to incite a popular folk revival tied fast to particular political ideals.

In Burns and Henderson, as with other authors embroiled in the vast 'folk process', the relationship with this tremendous cultural force is characterised by a strange synthesis of submission and appropriation. To make assertions about the cultural or political value of this tradition is to simultaneously diminish the authority of the individual author, and award a great deal of influence to those who mediate this tradition through their own songs and poems or through their collections. Henderson used 'tradition' both by instinct and by design. Though he is acknowledged for his wartime poetry, his public disputes with Hugh MacDiarmid and his status as the 'father' of the modern Scottish folk revival, Henderson has nevertheless remained on the margins of modern Scottish literary history. This might be explained, in part, by the scattered and relatively scarce publication of his poetry and songs, especially during his most productive period, in the 1950s and 1960s. Henderson, and latterly his supporters, account for this dearth with his preference for the anonymity of the 'folk process' over the renown of the named author. If he decided to eschew publication in favour of the anonymous byways of the oral folk tradition, and if this was part of a calculated strategy, the parameters of his influence become as elusive as the life-course of the folksongs he studied.

The facts of Henderson's own life are more easily verified. Born in Blairgowrie on 19 November 1919, he came to see his generation as one born out of and for war. As a child in Perthshire, the gateway to the North-East, he was exposed early to the 'anonymous song poetry of Scotland' and regarded this, alongside the 'comradely solidarity of the anti-Fascist struggle' that defined his young adulthood, as his two great formative influences (*AM*, p. 454). Henderson did not know his father, and after his mother's death when he was thirteen, he won scholarships to study at Dulwich College in South London, and later, to read modern languages at Cambridge. He served in the North African and Italian Campaigns during the Second World War. After his demobilisation he published *Ballads of World War II* (1947) and *Elegies for the Dead in Cyrenaica* (1948). He then set out for Italy to translate Gramsci's *Lettere dal Carcere* (1947). On his return to Scotland, Henderson began his professional career as a folklorist, becoming one of the first full-time staff at the School of Scottish Studies in the University of Edinburgh, in 1952. During this period he co-founded the Edinburgh People's Festival (1951–4), a forerunner to the modern Edinburgh Festival Fringe. Over the next four decades Henderson worked collecting and cataloguing folk culture and was rewarded in his later years with a symbolic status: as a representative of the School and its mission, of the academic study of Scottish folk culture, and of the modern popular folk revival.[3]

On 27 March 2002, less than three weeks after Henderson's death, Members of the Scottish Parliament (MSPs) engaged in a debate on his life and work:

> in appreciation of his lifetime devotion to international solidarity, peace and socialism, his many contributions to Scottish culture and politics, including his role in gathering traditional songs, his support for other artists and his authorship of the song that many believe should be Scotland's (inter)national anthem, 'The Freedom Come All Ye' [sic].[4]

Henderson was the first cultural figure to be given this honour by the young Parliament. Members from all major parties contributed anecdotes and personal reminiscences, celebrations of his politics, his scholarship, and his achievements in poetry and song. In the closing exchanges, the Scottish National Party's Mike Russell and Labour's Elaine Murray proposed that the new Parliament Building be a place where people like Henderson, 'a Scot who came before us and who helped us to attain the Parliament', are commemorated. Now, on the Canongate Wall of the Parliament Building, lines from 'The

Freedom Come-All-Ye' are carved in stone alongside quotations from figures as disparate as Hugh MacDiarmid and Andrew Carnegie, Mary Brooksbank and Charles Rennie Mackintosh. 'The Freedom Come-All-Ye', Henderson's rallying cry for a post-imperial, post-racial, non-nuclear, egalitarian Scotland, reconciled with its history in its commitment to a radical future, is perhaps his best-loved song. In the summer of 2014, it was performed by the South African soprano Pumeza Matshikiza at the opening ceremony of the Glasgow Commonwealth Games. Only two days later the song was evoked by its melody – 'The Bloody Fields of Flanders' – which featured as the backdrop to Chris Dolan's one-man play *The Pitiless Storm*. David Hayman plays a trade unionist and tribal Labour supporter experiencing a crisis of conscience on the eve of Scotland's independence referendum. These performances took place in very different contexts: one on the world stage, the other in Rutherglen, Glasgow, Bo'ness, and Edinburgh; one to mark the beginning of a sports and athletics event founded on the community of former British colonies, the other, theatre in the tradition of agitprop, describing events as they unfold; one explicitly celebrating the anti-apartheid and internationalist thrust, the other, tangled in the detail of an individual's lifelong political struggle. However, together, they help to articulate something of the diversity of Henderson's legacy and the importance of the political traditions his work has come to embody.

The earliest critical responses to Henderson's work were reviews of his wartime *Elegies*. It was not until the late 1960s that his work as a folklorist and folk revivalist began to attract critical attention in publications like *Chapbook: Scotland's Folk-Life Magazine* (est. 1964). In the 1980s critics started to address his cultural-political agenda more broadly, analysing his poetry, song and prose works in conjunction with the events of his own life: his experience of the War and his leading role in the folk revival. Henderson's reputation as a polymath, whose significance could not be gleaned from his sparse list of published works, grew gradually into the 1990s, though he was still principally associated with Scottish Studies and, more generally, with the preservation and promotion of Scotland's folk culture. In the 1990s and 2000s Henderson's work was given much wider exposure with the publication of *Alias MacAlias: Writings on Songs, Folk and Literature* (1992), *The Armstrong Nose: Selected Letters of Hamish Henderson* (1996) and *Collected Poems and Songs* (2000). A more comprehensive picture of his interests and expertise began to emerge, and since then, his legacy, and his importance in Scotland's cultural and political history in particular, have been widely discussed.

From the obituaries, the parliamentary debate, and more recent accounts, such as Timothy Neat's two-volume biography, *The Making of the Poet* (2007) and *Poetry Becomes People* (2009), and Eberhard Bort's series of essay collections, *Borne on the Carrying Stream* (2010), *'Tis Sixty Years Since* (2011), and *At Hame Wi' Freedom* (2012), the only consensus on Henderson's legacy is that it is genuinely multifarious. Alec Finlay, the editor of Henderson's collected essays and selected letters, reminds us that 'we have . . . to account for the influence of his informal pedagogy and the manner in which his natural conviviality was in itself a cultural force' (*AM*, p. xvii). The difficulty in mapping Henderson's influence is perhaps inevitable if his 'cultural force' is seen as predominantly 'informal', undocumented, and *oral*. The greater part of his achievements are often mooted as that of a kind of nexus connecting innumerable singers, scholars, students, poets, editors, publication boards and political campaigners. This might be partially traced in his correspondence and Neat's biography achieved a great deal in this regard. However, as with the 'folk process', much of this undocumented influence is essentially unknowable, only apparent in the memories of those involved and in the stories they tell. The range of tributes offered by the MSPs speaks of the same difficulty, as Henderson's accomplishments are diffused in biographical fragments and projected onto competing perspectives of Scotland's recent social, political and cultural histories. The only common factor is the folk-hero figure: a loose constellation of cultural and political principles wide open to interpretation.

The idea of Henderson as a focal point where various strands of cultural and political life meet is complemented by the notion that his 'conviviality' was in fact an important part of his armoury, consciously deployed to promote his cultural-political agenda. Though this aspect is impossible to measure, it sits alongside his written corpus, and is very near the surface in any panegyric on Henderson. In one sense, this legacy will be short-lived if it relies on personal reminiscences and kind-hearted sketches of a tall, ambling, slightly shabby intellectual, gregarious, opinionated, always ready to burst into song, holding court in the unofficial headquarters of the Scottish folk revival, Sandy Bell's Pub in Edinburgh's Old Town. In another sense, Henderson cannot simply be cast as a folk hero whose value is in his absorption of a variety of political and cultural concerns. The purpose of this book is to consider what Henderson's legacy might be if it is to be drawn solely from his writings. My intention is not to dismiss out of hand the fond, anecdotal, familiar picture, nor to overlook the range of Henderson's interests and talents and, therefore, the variety of roles in which he might be cast; it is, instead, to show how his life's work is underpinned by an ambitious moral-intellectual programme to reconnect and reintegrate the artist within modern society.

The title of this book, *The Voice of the People*, is not an unqualified declaration of Henderson's accomplishments. Rather, it is a name for the ideal he consistently pursued. It captures the familiarity of Henderson's aim, but also its elusive, ambiguous, and contradictory qualities. Neither 'voice' nor 'people' are straightforward signifiers. Henderson gave this same title to his 1989 *Sunday Mail* piece on the history of the modern folk revival and its eighteenth- and nineteenth-century precedents, but he also described MacDiarmid, the totemic poet of high-modernism in Scotland, as 'the voice of the people from which he sprang' (*AM*, pp. 1–4, 316). This 'voice' can, therefore, be found in both the collective 'tradition' and the individuated 'author'.

'The Voice of the People' is also politically efficacious shorthand for one of the central tenets of romantic nationalism. It is an anglicisation of one of Johann Gottfried Herder's key terms, and the title of his ground-breaking collection of world folksongs, *Stimmen der Völker in Liedern* (1778–9) (Voices of the People in Songs). An invocation of Herder's *Volk*, a communal political and cultural consciousness aligned with the nation, also conjures up the long-established elision between the *Volkgiest*, the 'spirit of the people', or the 'National character', and the literary and folk traditions that are said to be its source. In *The World Republic of Letters* (1999, trans. 2004), Pascale Casanova grounds her overarching theory of literary capital and its relationship with the national struggle for legitimacy and power, on the fallout of the 'Herderian Revolution': 'all the "little" nations in Europe and elsewhere were able, on account of their ennoblement by the people, to claim an independent existence that was inseparably political and literary'. The 'soul' and 'genius' of the people, extolled by Herder, allowed the national cultural tradition and its attendant origin myths to reach further and further back into their 'oral heritage' for validation.[5] While Henderson subscribed to these romantic ideals, the body of his work also describes a complex, often strained, relationship with the national paradigm and its connection to 'the people'. Terry Eagleton captures the political dimension of this dilemma:

> The Enlightenment and its Romantic aftermath gave birth to two doctrines distinguished only by the letter *s*. The first was that people had the right to self-determination; the second was that *peoples* had such a right. The former belief is the keystone of modern democracy, and indeed of socialism; the second is a piece of romantic mystification, a fact which has not prevented a good many on the political Left from endorsing it.[6]

This tension, between the universalism and internationalism on which socialism is founded, and the 'romantic mystification' that underpins the national paradigm, is continually played out in Henderson's writings. In this sense, his place in Scotland's literary history can be regarded as spanning both Romanticism and Modernism. He was convinced that the 'folk', whose cultural inheritance reproduced and sustained the nation, could also be the source of an autochthonous socialism and, therefore, a deep-rooted and far-reaching internationalism. Like the poets of the early twentieth century he despaired at the isolation of the artist in modern society, yet he promoted the return to a distinctly romantic model – a literature imbued with the influence of popular folk culture – to redress this condition.

This is not a comprehensive study of all that Henderson wrote, recorded or otherwise produced in his lifetime; it is an analysis of the ways in which he developed his cultural politics. Henderson stood with MacDiarmid in challenging the ascendency of English literature; he contributed to the protracted debates over poetry in Scots; he wrote war poetry that sought to reconcile the whole of the living with the whole of the dead; he smuggled Antonio Gramsci's cultural Marxism into Scottish public life; and he advocated a cultural-political project that would reconcile art and society by channelling the durability and pervasiveness of the folk tradition. In all of these endeavours Henderson provides us with an alternative narrative in understanding the political and ideological upheaval of the twentieth century and its consequent expression in literature – all through an emphatically Scottish framework.

Finlay's extended Afterword for *The Armstrong Nose*, 'The River that Flows On', is an important foundation for this project. It is perhaps the only comprehensive overview of Henderson's career that makes connections with wider developments in literary, intellectual, and political history, and scrutinises Henderson's cultural-political agenda in a way that is sensitive to its deficiencies, and to its development over time. The present study expands on Finlay's project by moving away from a biographical approach to address particular phases in Henderson's writings, and profile the struggles that he was engaged in, in his attempts to articulate and enact his cultural-political principles. The texts that Henderson produced, including reams of poems and songs, essays, newspaper articles, public and private correspondences, and literary translations, are the primary sources of this study. I draw from all of his published works, and, to a lesser extent, from unpublished archives in the National Library of Scotland, Edinburgh University Library, and Dulwich College. Though the bulk of Henderson's working life was spent recording thousands of hours of songs, tales, tunes, oral histories and testimonies, his findings, in the archives of the School of Scottish Studies, will not be the primary focus of this book. Instead, I will emphasise the ways in which Henderson conceived of this material, and the lessons he drew from it. My approach, focusing principally on the texts themselves, and inferring an underlying theory from them, has also led me to eschew more personal, or biographical readings. Henderson is, for example, widely known to have been bisexual. Also, he was brought up in the Episcopalian tradition. Though he did write about issues of sexuality, religion and ecclesiastical history, they were not the most prominent features of his work, and are not so explicitly integrated in his cultural politics as other factors, which are dealt with in more detail in this study. My textual-analytical approach is the foundation for my central thesis, which describes Henderson's overarching cultural-political theory and his efforts to reconcile the artist and society.

Chapter One is concerned with Henderson's public 'Flytings' with MacDiarmid, which appeared in the opinion columns of *The Scotsman* between the late 1950s and the late 1960s. These exchanges demonstrate, in form and content, the perpetual and irresolvable nature of the underlying debate between the doyen of the Scottish Literary Renaissance, and the 'father' of the modern Scottish folk revival.[7] Chapter Two addresses Henderson's efforts to connect with the lived experiences of the soldiers of the Second World War in his own *Elegies* and in his collected army ballads. While these publications belong to drastically different modes, this chapter shows how they share a commitment to a politically and culturally engaged art that might represent the soldier without the gloss of homogeneity, or the retreat of the personal and confessional. Chapter Three examines Henderson's relationship with the life and works of Gramsci: the martyr, and the political philosopher, whose holistic view of the politics of culture would help to inform the modern folk revival. Gramsci both validated Henderson's conception of folk culture by celebrating 'the creative spirit of the people in its diverse phases', and forced him to consider the theoretical foundations of this 'folk culture' by admitting into his analysis all of these 'diverse phases'. Chapter Four is an account of Henderson's place in contemporary discussions on the form and content of Scottish poetry. It addresses Henderson's perceived 'turn' away from art-poetry towards folk-song and considers his negotiations with the legacy of the interwar literary Renaissance. Finally, Chapter Five sets out Henderson's conception of the folk tradition, and its manifestations in his work as a folk revivalist and as a folklore scholar. Federico García Lorca's comments on the *duende*, and the vital folk culture of Scotland's travelling people helped Henderson to glimpse the unbounded reach of the folk tradition and, consequently, the limited scope of the folklorist-revivalist.

Notes

1. Throughout this volume 'folk-song' denotes the mode of cultural expression, and 'folksong', any given song or ballad.
2. Brown, *Burns and Tradition*, p. xii, 81.
3. See Neat, *Poetry Becomes People*, pp. 1–16; and Bob Chambers, *The Carrying Stream Flows On*.
4. The debate was secured by Labour MSP, Cathy Peattie. See 'Official Report Debate Contributions', Scottish Parliament's 'Parliamentary Business' site: http://www.scottish.parliament.uk/parliamentary-business.aspx, last accessed 25 November 2014.
5. Casanova, *The World Republic of Letters*, pp. 77, 80.
6. Eagleton, 'Nationalism and the Case of Ireland'.
7. I have chosen to capitalise the 'Scottish Literary Renaissance' throughout because, though its proponents varied greatly, Henderson and his peers seem to have acknowledged it as a distinct movement. In comparison, the modern folk revival, in Henderson's own estimation, was less willed, and had a more ambiguous and less prescriptive relationship with those who campaigned on its behalf.

CHAPTER

1

THE FLYTINGS

It is perhaps ill-mannered for a visitor to intervene in a debate between two such masters of 'flyting' (surely a folk-art in itself) as Mr Henderson and Mr MacDiarmid. (Thomas Crawford, letter to *The Scotsman*, 25 January 1960) (*TAN*, p. 99)

From late 1959 through to early 1968, Hamish Henderson and Hugh MacDiarmid engaged in a series of public debates on Scottish literature, folk art, and politics that were to become known as their 'Flytings'. They comprised three separate disputes: 'The *Honour'd Shade* Flyting' (1959–60), 'The Folksong Flyting' (1964), and 'The 1320 Club Flyting' (1968). Though other contributors were involved, Henderson and MacDiarmid were the most prominent participants, and their particular conflicts provided the debates with their most dynamic and resonant episodes. Other notable parties included academics and authors such as the Marxist literary critic, David Craig; the nationalist, classicist, and poet, Douglas Young; the critic and pioneer of modern Scottish literary studies, Thomas Crawford; the poet, Stewart Conn; and Scots language poets, Tom Scott and Sydney Goodsir Smith. Yet this series of impassioned debates has garnered almost no critical attention.[1] Existing material on the 'Flytings' comes substantially from those whose remit is simply to survey Henderson's long and varied career. As such, the 'Flytings' are approached, straightforwardly, as the public dimension of his complex relationship with MacDiarmid. The debates have become part of Henderson's reputation as a 'folk-hero' and are seen – like most of Henderson's creative and critical work – in biographical terms, as context for the political and cultural vision of this 'father' of the Scottish folk revival.

Given this critical lacuna, the 'Flytings', their contributors, and their principal concerns, deserve clarification. The immediate contexts of the 'Flytings' ought to be understood; in particular, the cultural movements MacDiarmid and Henderson came to represent: the Scottish Literary Renaissance and the popular Scottish folk revival. An in-depth analysis of the 'Flytings' affords the most direct access to Henderson's cultural politics in the absence of a manifesto or *magnum opus*. In challenging him, MacDiarmid took to task a political-cultural programme that had been inspired by, and partially founded on, his own poetry and public persona. The 'Flytings' were performance pieces whereby the folklorist sought to publicly co-opt the poet to his cause. The support of a writer whose poems, to Henderson at least, constituted 'the operations of a radical surgeon on the rotten flesh of contemporary society', would lend critical and intellectual substance to his popular folk revival, which during this period, was increasingly identified with the commercial commodification of traditional song-cultures (*AM*, p. 316).[2]

The 'Flytings' were originally published in the 'Points of View' columns of *The Scotsman* as open letters 'To the Editor'. Though these columns were a common setting for public debate, they seldom hosted disputes as prolific or volatile as the 'Flytings', which constituted a series of fundamentally irresolvable conflicts over the relationship between art and society, scattered throughout these pages, over almost a decade. The letters of the 'Flytings' were interspersed among other episodic disputes on various issues: from local interests to geo-politics and economics. Although this format meant that the debates gained an air of urgency, which may not have translated in an edited collection or a less-frequent cultural magazine, the momentum of the discussion was fragmented. Contributions appeared days, sometimes weeks, after the letters to which they responded. Ripostes were sandwiched between advertisements and unrelated, miscellaneous text, often under column headings that referred to other popular topics of the day.[3]

Heated public debates on Scottish culture and history were commonplace during this period, and remain so. In late 2009, the historian T. M. Devine and Neil Oliver, presenter of the BBC's 'History of Scotland' series, engaged in a series of exchanges over the historiographical credentials of this popular television series;[4] in February 2010 short articles by Paul Henderson Scott and David Greig were published in *The Scotsman* setting out their opposing views on the national aspect of the work of the National Theatre of Scotland (25–6 February); and in November 2011 the *Scottish Review* was, according to its editor Kenneth Roy, the site of a personal 'flyting', quite consciously in the tradition of MacDiarmid, on what constitutes a 'Scottish writer' (14 November).[5] The years and months approaching Scotland's independence referendum saw an explosion of such 'flytings', from the chat-room to the debating chamber, the comments thread to the high-wire presidential-style debate. In recent years, the established cultural and political debates to which these periodical clashes belong have become a more explicit part of their performance. In addition to old-fashioned intertextual referencing, hyperlinks have allowed these exchanges – through online editions of print publications, blogs, comment threads and tweets – to cohere, and become part of a single trajectory, supported by the momentum of online trending and search-engine algorithms. Debates gather and accumulate others without becoming unwieldy. This has also enabled commentators, professional and amateur alike, to banish data and supporting evidence to the paratextual level, freeing up their prose for rhetorical acrobatics. The range and specificity of cultural references in Henderson and MacDiarmid's 'Flytings'; the highly stylised language and carefully cultivated tone; the self-conscious performance; the length, focus, and intensity of the debates, sets them apart from many of these more recent disputes. However, they do share one aspect. The mutual exclusivity of the two opposing views portrayed is not in itself the point of interest; rather, it is how this opposition over one – often, carefully circumscribed – problem, intersects with broader assumptions: about the function of art in society, the tensions between the academic and the popular, or the motivations behind, and consequences of, constitutional resettlement.

This exploratory function of the flyting was forefront in the minds of the 'National Collective' – an online forum of 'artists and creatives for Scottish Independence' – when they proposed, in March 2013, that Henderson and MacDiarmid's 1964 'Folksong Flyting' be a model for the movement. They envisaged this aspect of self-reflexive debate as that which distinguishes a movement from a mere campaign:

> The creative side of National Collective is the side that eschews party politics; we attempt to appeal not to ideas of the Scottish state or nation but to the more human ideas of creativity, individual and collective potential, and creative autonomy.

Though the vituperative side of the flyting project seems not to have had the same appeal, the proposal put forward by the 'National Collective' did include a degree of performance: independent meetings between supporters in locales across the country were to receive questions from others, and respond in any format they thought appropriate ('photographs, films, pictures, writings, drawings, or anything else'). The questions included: 'What are the main components of "Scottish Identity"?'; 'What is meant by "social justice"?'; and 'What are the best ideas from "Freedom Come A Ye" [sic]?'. The principal focus of this project was to explore the ways in which the question – 'Should Scotland be an independent country?' – cuts across more substantial ideas about the kind of country or society that might be imagined, and the role the artist has in this task.

The first dispute, the '*Honour'd Shade* Flyting' of 1959–60, saw the emergence of the Henderson-MacDiarmid polarity that characterised later exchanges. The debate took its name from a 1959 anthology of contemporary Scottish verse selected and edited by Norman MacCaig. Published to mark the bicentenary of the birth of Burns, the dust jacket proclaimed that it was to present 'a picture of the widely various ways in which Scottish writers find it natural to express themselves'. The title of the collection was taken from Burns' 'Address to Edinburgh'. Praising the city's 'palaces and tow'rs' and its status as the former seat of sovereignty, Burns describes his sheltering in the 'honour'd shade' of Edinburgh as kin to that beneath the boughs 'on the banks of Ayr'.[6] While it is Burns' (and by inference, Scotland's) 'honour'd shade' that is explored in the anthology, the ensuing debates were concerned with a coterie of established poets strongly associated with Edinburgh. An anonymous reviewer from *The Scotsman* noted the absence of Henderson, Alan Riddell, T. S. Law and David McEwan, and suggested that on the basis of this neglect the collection might simply have been named 'The Muse in Rose Street', given its editorial bias towards the poets identified with that part of Edinburgh (*TAN*, p. 79).[7] MacDiarmid responded with typical recalcitrance, stimulating a debate on how a representative selection of Scotland's 'best' contemporary poetry should have been determined (*TAN*, p. 80). Inevitably, the correspondents gave voice to various criteria that might inform the selection of a 'truly representative' anthology, and the discussion looked likely to descend into a tedious reflection on the tyranny of taste. However, another provocative interjection from MacDiarmid focused on the issue of popularity as a determinate factor in, or signifier of, literary quality. The folk revival was then examined as a forum for testing these ideas, after Henderson wrote of his vision of a progressive popular literature tied closely to the oral tradition. It was only in the final few exchanges that this first flyting condensed into the Henderson-MacDiarmid antithesis that was to become the central thread of the later 'Folksong Flyting'.

The intensified fervour of the 'Folksong Flyting' was immediately apparent, and as Henderson and MacDiarmid's private correspondence shows, this was due in part to the fact that they had anticipated the revived public debates. In March 1960, Henderson wrote to MacDiarmid:

> Travelling in various parts of Scotland, I have become aware – as you probably have too – of the widespread interest in our recent flyting. Some time this year I intend to write a lengthy article about the whole question of literature and the oral folk art, so no doubt you will be emerging from your corner for the second round! (*TAN*, p. 102)

This article never materialised but Henderson deployed his research in the flyting that followed (*TAN*, p. 102n). The controversy was this time initiated by a letter from the literary historian David Craig lamenting the under-representation of traditional song by the Scottish Home Service and the recent depreciation of the idiom by some of Scotland's well-known poets. He directed his disapproval at MacCaig in particular, who had, in Craig's words, ended his Third Programme comments by saying that 'folksongs might be good enough for berry-pickers and steel mill workers, but not for him – he had read Homer' (*TAN*, p. 117).[8] Again, MacDiarmid responded incredulously, and by describing folk-song as inherently antithetical to the demands of modern literature, he lit the touchpaper of another more vigorous and drawn-out dispute (*TAN*, pp. 118–9). Picking up the impetus of the *Honour'd Shade* controversy, Henderson and MacDiarmid were quickly established as the central combatants. The primacy of their particular disagreements was further emphasised by the titles for the 'Points of View' column: Henderson alone provided the editor with 'Full-Blooded Folk Poetry: More and More Becoming Known' (3 April 1964), and 'Why Does MacDiarmid Despise Folk Arts? Apostle of a Kind of Spiritual Apartheid' (15 April 1964). Gradually the discussions centred on a broader consideration of how art, and particularly literature, ought to relate to society as a whole. In this context, the history of interaction between 'folk' and 'art' literature was scrutinised, as was the figure of the genuinely popular and yet distinctly 'literary' poet. Both men reflected on the nature of literary endeavour, and each accused the other of opposing forms of philistinism. Once MacDiarmid left the conversation, Henderson and Douglas Young continued on a tangential discussion over Young's editorship of the collection *Scottish Verse 1851–1951* (1952) (*TAN*, pp. 136–40). Henderson accused Young of neglecting folk-song, and the altercation soon became tangled in semantic fine-tuning. Compared with the vitality of the Henderson-MacDiarmid opposition, this confrontation was merely technical, and lacked the responsiveness and flexibility that characterised earlier exchanges.

The '1320 Club Flyting' of 1968 was a brief scuffle by comparison. It primarily dealt with the political strategy of the Home Rule movement, with which both Henderson and MacDiarmid were attached, rather than aesthetic concerns. MacDiarmid was a founding member of the 1320 Club, which took its name from the year of the signing of the *Declaration of Arbroath*, and had originated as a think-tank on independence. By the time of the 'flyting' it had become an extremist branch of the nationalist movement, even advocating militarism. Though Henderson supported Scottish Independence, he sought an outwardly democratic route, as opposed to the initiative of what he called the 'self-elected elect' of the 1320 Club (*TAN*, p. 164). These discussions, though not directly concerned with conceptions of literary value, reflect an opposition similar to those of the '*Honour'd Shade*' and 'Folksong' flytings. Henderson again countered MacDiarmid's promotion of an intellectual elite with his belief in the wisdom and autonomy of the 'commonweal' (*TAN*, p. 166). Each of these flytings addresses its own distinctive set of concerns, yet a deeper opposition between Henderson and MacDiarmid informed all three. The turbulence of these 'Flytings' was not due to the fact that their fundamental beliefs stood in stark opposition, in fact they agreed on a great deal, fought for common ideals, and shared many enemies, yet their cultural-political visions appeared incompatible.

The popular Scottish folk revival was well established by the time the first public flyting began in 1959, and by the mid 1960s it was clear that this constituted the national branch of a larger movement of traditional music revivalism flowering all across Western Europe and North America. The revival was also becoming increasingly visible. The School of Scottish Studies had been established at the University of Edinburgh in 1951, and Henderson joined the Gaelic scholar Calum MacLean as one of its first full-time staff in 1952. Edinburgh University Folk Song Society was founded in 1958 and many similar associations appeared across Scotland in subsequent years, followed in the 1960s by the rapid spread of resident folk clubs.[9] Enthusiasts like Norman Buchan MP, and Morris Blythman held folk-song workshops in Glasgow schools. Even the BBC, which had been perceived as unfairly dismissive towards the traditional arts, began to broadcast some populist folk-song performances. In 1962 a collection of political songs that had emerged around protests against the docking of American Polaris-equipped nuclear submarines in the Holy Loch was published as a pamphlet and recorded and released for Moses Asch's 'Folkways' label. The next year, 1963, saw the establishment of annual folk festivals in Aberdeen, and in the following year Arthur Argo published the first *Chapbook*, which was to become the leading Scottish folk music magazine of the period.[10]

Outside these channels of folk revivalism – in which Henderson was instrumental – the movement fuelled a huge commercial market. Taking full advantage of developments in mass communication, traditional songs were broadcast widely. As a consequence, many politicised founders of the Scottish and British revivals, like Henderson and Ewan MacColl, found only a parody or, at best, a thinly veiled artifice of genuine folk culture in the contemporary folk music market. Naturally, MacDiarmid saw the commercial aspect as a convenient brush with which to tar the entire movement in his contributions to the 'Flytings' (*TAN*, p. 120). As folk clubs arose in all major towns and cities, the revival made inroads into urban centres with an art form traditionally associated with a rural, even pastoral, setting. The major redistribution and recontextualisation of traditional folk-song was an undeniable reality by 1964.

This year also marked forty years since the French scholar Denis Saurat's heralding of a new movement in Scottish literature, in his essay 'Le groupe de "la Renaissance Ecossaise"'. It has been noted that the Literary Renaissance, beginning in the inter-war period, passed through a 'second wave' in the 1940s and 1950s, which saw the emergence of poets like Goodsir Smith and Norman MacCaig.[11] However, in the late 1950s, and certainly by the early 1960s, a new generation of Scottish writers was beginning to reject the poetic models of the so-called Renaissance 'establishment'. Poets like Ian Hamilton Finlay and Edwin Morgan sought out new forms that were not directly influenced by those older poets.[12] In fact, in lieu of the *Honour'd Shade* controversies, and in response to the editorial bias towards Lallans poets in the anthology, a group of young poets expressed their distance from the established literary coterie by releasing a recording of their readings under the title *Dishonour'd Shade: Seven non-Abbotsford Poets*, in February 1960 (*TAN*, p. 80n).[13]

This generational fracture among Scottish writers was put into sharper relief by incidents like MacDiarmid's infamous rejection of Alexander Trocchi's 'spurious internationalism', at the International Writers' Conference of 1962.[14] In the same year MacDiarmid published a pamphlet titled *The Ugly Birds Without Wings* (1962): a concerted attack on the 'concrete poetry' of Finlay. MacDiarmid also became embroiled in another dispute in *The Scotsman*, defending the 'renaissance establishment' from the attacks of the 'Teddyboy Poetasters' of the younger generation.[15] MacDiarmid's predilection for controversy is well illustrated by a host of other oft-repeated anecdotes. Two of the most common examples are his rejoining the Communist Party of Great Britain (CPGB) in 1956 after the Soviet invasion of Hungary, and his listing of 'Anglophobia' as a hobby in his *Who's Who* entry. By the late 1950s the greater part of MacDiarmid's poetry, and all of his most celebrated work, had been published. As the final chapter of Alan Bold's biography testifies, though these later years were not dedicated to poetic production, his active engagement in Scottish culture was sustained, and he was almost continually embroiled in controversy of some kind.[16]

A Festschrift for the poet was published in 1962, which was followed in 1964 by Duncan Glen's monograph *Hugh MacDiarmid and the Scottish Renaissance* and Kenneth Buthlay's *Hugh MacDiarmid*. From this period onward, book-length studies of MacDiarmid's *oeuvre* began to appear more frequently, and in publishing terms the early 1960s represents the beginning of an on-going discourse on MacDiarmid's poetics and politics. In the period of his flytings with Henderson, discussions on how MacDiarmid's work should be read, and how it should be placed in a national literary tradition were being extricated from the poet himself, and recentralised as an issue of national concern among literary critics. The *Collected Poems* (1962) won the William Foyle Poetry Prize in 1963, which bolstered the process of public appropriation. Interpretations of his poetry were, and continue to be, complicated by the persistence with which he sought to divulge his aesthetic project in different forms at different points in his career: from *Albyn; or, Scotland and the Future* (1927), through *Lucky Poet* (1943) to *The Kind of Poetry I Want* (1961). Contradictions and inconsistencies are never far away in MacDiarmid's corpus and these provided fodder for Henderson in the 'Flytings'. Indeed, MacDiarmid's opponents tried to make his own work undermine the position he professed to take. Henderson, and his ally Craig, capitalised on the opportunity to disentangle the poetry and the poet.

MacDiarmid's vision of a Scottish Literary Renaissance prompted controversy over the use of 'synthetic Scots', over the appropriate subjects for poetry in modern Scotland, and over the political principles that ought to inform such poetry. Public disputes in print were not uncommon and, in the 1940s alone, MacDiarmid contributed to, and was often the subject of, debates in the pages of the *Daily Worker*, *The Scotsman* and the *Glasgow Herald*. The bitter altercation between MacDiarmid and Edwin Muir following the publication of Muir's *Scott and Scotland* (1936) is perhaps an equivalent example of the way in which timely debates on the national culture can be embodied by the opposing views of two cultural figureheads.[17] Henderson's 'Flytings' with MacDiarmid, though not well documented, represent a more constructive conflict, circumventing the language question and the national paradigm, in favour of the continuum between the literary, and that romantic construct, 'the people'.

Henderson's collected writings and selected letters testify to the fact that he was also no stranger to public debate. Early essays like 'Enemies of Folk-song' (1955) show a carefully constructed argument directed at a public who needed to be woken to the suppression of traditional folk arts under the authority of the 'high' arts. His regular contributions to publications like *Saltire Review*, *Our Time*, *Daily Worker*, *Conflict*, *The Scotsman* and the *Glasgow Herald* demonstrate an acute awareness of contemporary cultural and political debates. Henderson defended the 'Lallans Makars' throughout the 'plastic Scots' debates of the late 1940s, and continued in later years to incite lengthy exchanges on a variety of subjects in the 'Points of View' columns of *The Scotsman*. For example, in 1966 Henderson and John Prebble engaged in a brief 'flyting' of sorts over inaccuracies in the historian's recent work, *Glencoe* (1966) (*TAN*, pp. 146–9); a few weeks later he debated with the playwright Bettina Jonic over her understanding of the circumstances around the death of Federico García Lorca (*TAN*, pp. 149–52); and in early 1984 he swapped blows with V. T. Linacre over the need for 'rapprochement between the West and the Soviet Union' (*TAN*, pp. 248–52).[18]

The dearth of critical material on Henderson and MacDiarmid's 'Flytings' is perhaps a reflection of the problem they present as a series of exchanges both highly polemical and utterly sincere. Eleanor Bell has, for example, referred to Henderson's 'famous "flytings" with MacDiarmid'.[19] However, this 'fame' cannot be understood as the type that is sustained by scholarly work and critical appraisal. The 'Flytings' are remembered in anecdotal terms, as entertaining episodes that demonstrate the thorniness of the poets of the period. In this sense, the 'Flytings' can be added to the already swelling store of oft-repeated MacDiarmid-isms, and to the long list of fond remembrances so often attached to the cult of personality that has grown around Henderson.

In two retrospective pieces for *Cencrastus* (1994): 'Tangling with the Langholm Byspale' and 'Flytings Galore: MacDiarmid v. The Folkies', Henderson recounts these public debates, quoting extensively from the original letters, and setting them in an autobiographical context (*AM*, pp. 381–404, 405–26). In the first, he describes his schoolboy discovery of the poet; his early experiences 'jousting . . . on the subject of folklore and the oral tradition' (*AM*, p. 384); the relationship he enjoyed with MacDiarmid in the years after the War; and the emerging divide between the 'Rose St Poets' and the 'Folkies' (*AM*, p. 396). In the second, he details his relationship with Allan Riddell, the poet and founder of *Lines Review*, who promoted the work of writers like Trocchi, Morgan and Finlay; those who had at various points found themselves the object of MacDiarmid's ire. By providing the 'Flytings' with these pretexts, Henderson encouraged particular interpretations of the debates and fostered their growing reputation as the 'muckle flyting' (*AM*, p. 409), an event that was to gain currency in the collective memory almost like a folk tale.

MacDiarmid did not share Henderson's view on the importance of their public disputes. In fact, outside the debates themselves, and his private correspondences with Henderson, MacDiarmid barely mentioned them. The relative significance of the 'Flytings' is reflected in the subsequent criticism: in Bold's biography, *MacDiarmid* (1988), for instance, Henderson is entirely absent. The '*Honour'd Shade* Flyting' and the 'Folksong Flyting' appear as two examples among many, of MacDiarmid's much-relished newspaper controversies. In this instance, the 'Flytings' are lost in the hull of a greater narrative of 'travel, cultural controversy, political engagements and public speaking' in these later years of the poet's life. Henderson's commentators award the 'Flytings' more prominence, though this might be explained by their attendant panegyric tone. The character-led portrayals that celebrate the folklorist-poet, through all his various interests and endeavours, always retain the image of 'Big Hamish, Seumas Mór . . . his eye twinkling and his fists swinging in time to the chorus of "Tail Toddle"' at their centre.[20] Andrew R. Hunter's article, 'The Odyssey of a Wandering King' (1987), reads like an obituary, and records the 'Flytings' as simply another episode reflecting Henderson's personal and creative development.[21] Henderson's holistic approach to academic and creative work, making no distinction between poetry and song, and engaging directly in the 'folk process' while seeking to understand it, has perhaps encouraged his admirers to adopt a similar approach. As a result, a body of text like the 'Flytings' is homogenised into this rendering of Henderson as 'folk-hero', battling for his political vision and its foundation in the radical folk tradition. This public debate becomes Henderson's attempt to identify the folk revival as the true inheritor of MacDiarmid's early poetic promise. Arnold Rattenbury notes that Henderson colluded in cultivating this version of himself: 'around such a figure myth and legend quite naturally swirled and, sometimes with his own help, stuck'.[22]

Raymond J. Ross, in his article 'In the Midst of Things' (1985), though writing principally of Henderson's poetry, draws on the interconnectedness that is apparent in his various interests, and makes concise yet illuminating use of the 'Flytings' to reflect upon the humanitarianism of his poetry and song, as opposed to the elitism that seemed to inform MacDiarmid's attitudes.[23]

Henderson and MacDiarmid embarked on their 'Flytings' at a time when the folk revival was already well established; a younger generation had emerged who were rejecting the poetic models of the inter-war Renaissance; and MacDiarmid was beginning to be sequestered by literary historians and fellow poets. Neither figure was new to public debate, yet these discourses were to expose, with remarkable self-consciousness, the tension between two opposing cultural dimensions of a common political agenda: the appeal to the 'common-weal', and an extension of the perceived cultural heritage of the many; and the narrower, pioneering work of the avant-garde; the intellectual elite.

Negotiating MacDiarmid

In one of Henderson's later contributions to the '*Honour'd Shade* Flyting', he revised one of MacDiarmid's attacks and turned it back on the poet:

> There is a witless philistinism of the streets which can be very galling. But there is also a philistinism of the boudoir (and even of the Rose Street pub) which can be considerably more dangerous, since it more often than not camouflages itself as a protective interest in literature and the arts.
> (*TAN*, p. 93)

This strikes at the heart of Henderson's struggle with the idea of the 'poet'. Here, Henderson situates himself between two apparently opposing positions: first, the dismissal of cultural forms due to preconceptions of their high-mindedness or elitism, and second, due to their apparent populism, or popularity. However, Henderson's inclusive conception of literary value extends to both the 'monumental' and the 'epic', which MacDiarmid champions in his contributions, and to the 'crambo clink', or bucolic poetry, which the poet maligns (*TAN*, pp. 127, 89). While this brings us no closer to a concrete conception of literary value, beyond the fact that work cannot be dismissed on the grounds of either its intended audience, or its actual audience, it does demonstrate the 'creative clash of contradictions' that comes out of Henderson's negotiations with MacDiarmid.[24] From Henderson's point of view, open conflict with MacDiarmid was the supreme testing ground for his ideas on art and society. Arriving at the position whereby neither extreme of philistinism can be forgiven, Henderson is forced to accept neither 'impenetrability', nor 'accessibility', as terms by which literature can be evaluated. This in turn means that his commitment to reconciliation between the artist and society is not necessarily to be achieved directly, by consciously appealing to the people's tastes, nor by seeking to elevate the audience through the difficulty of the material. If the 'value' of artistic practice is to be judged by Henderson's own terms, in its capacity to appeal to 'the people', then this is no more or less achievable by patronising the people and pandering to what you imagine their tastes to be, or by self-consciously cultivating 'high-art' that is defined as such precisely because it excludes the majority. The 'genuine people's culture' that Henderson envisaged would, like the work of the folksinger, connect with the 'people' without being populist; and embody resolute political principles and a 'revolutionary humanism', without retreating into 'self-gratificatory elitism'.[25]

Early in his career Henderson subscribed to MacDiarmid's infamous tenets. He acknowledged the threat of an English cultural imperialism; he was wilful and confident about the capacity of Lallans for great art-poetry; he demonstrated a consciousness of the need to reconcile the new movements within Scottish writing with national political and cultural traditions; and, like MacDiarmid, he believed that the currents of Scottish cultural practice could and should be concentrated on broadly socialist, nationalist and internationalist perspectives. These positions were, in fact, largely inspired by MacDiarmid. Later, Henderson wrote of his teenage discovery of the poet's work and 'the exact moment I first read this amazing poem ['The Bonnie Broukit Bairn'], and antisyzygy first took me by the thrapple' (*AM*, p. 381). In this instance, the 'antisyzygy' ought not to be understood in terms of G. Gregory Smith's rendering, as an abstract notion of the contrary nature of the Scottish people and their culture(s). Instead, it can be appreciated in a more technical sense, as a structural aspect of these early lyrics. MacDiarmid describes this approach as like nightingales' song, cognisant of its contradictory impulses:

> . . . whose thin high call
> And that deep throb,
> Which seem to come from different birds
> In different places, find an emotion
> And vibrate in the memory.[26]

In the lyric Henderson had in mind, the beautiful neglected child at the parade of dignitaries, and the tragic figure of the earth among the planetary gods, describe two such voices 'in different places' chiming in the mind of the reader. MacDiarmid's influence was invigorating. His early lyrics offered positive proof of what could be achieved, where his prose was directed with unremitting precision at what must be overcome.

In a 1948 survey of contemporary Scottish writing, Henderson asserted that MacDiarmid's 'most positive service' was not, however, his work with the Scots language, rather his 'furthering the great cause of the proletariat in Scotland' and his 'clarifying the relation of the cultural revival to the political struggle':

> He [MacDiarmid] realised clearly, and stressed over and over again that no literary revival is worth a damn if it fails to identify itself with the *present* difficulties and tasks of the people. And conversely, that no poetry which desires to be actual

> can afford to neglect the ramifications of exploit and dream in the people's past. In short, that Scottish poetry, if it is to contribute anything of value to the international complex, must first of all throw off the alien mummy-wrappings we have heard of, and recover its true identity. (*AM*, p. 376)

In the late 1940s, Henderson was in awe of MacDiarmid's seemingly unassailable position. The quality of MacDiarmid's poetry and the remedial, restorative effect of his public attacks and proclamations on national cultural and political life set him up in Henderson's view as one '[towering] in rugged monolithic eminence above the contemporary Scottish scene' (Ibid.). While Henderson joined his peers in celebrating MacDiarmid's early Scots lyrics, accolades like the one cited above were reserved for the poet's role as an outspoken critic, facilitating the search for 'true identity' by clearing the path of obfuscations. It is in this capacity that Henderson was a committed convert both to MacDiarmid's project, and to the discarding of those interpretative frameworks (or 'alien mummy-wrappings') that would obscure the present conditions of the people by misappropriating and misrepresenting their inherited histories and folk-beliefs (those 'of exploit and dream'). MacDiarmid encouraged Henderson to explore the precarious conceptual terrain between the political and philosophical reaches of poetry, and the actuality of the lives of the people.

In 1951, Henderson began editing a volume of selected poems by MacDiarmid to be published by the Scottish Committee of the Communist Party. Though it was never printed, the selection exhibits something of Henderson's view of the political-philosophical value of MacDiarmid's poetic voice. Henderson gives prominence to many of the poems that would feature in his own writings, such as the three *Hymns to Lenin* and 'The Seamless Garment'.[27] He heralded the *Hymns* as 'a landmark in European literature of the period between the wars' (*AM*, p. 378), and compared the effect of this work on the Scottish poets of his and Sorley MacLean's generation to being in the basement of a house being shelled (something he had experienced during the Italian campaign): 'It was like receiving a giant's blow between the eyes, and still retaining consciousness' (*AM*, p. 444). He agreed with the critic John Speirs, who suggested that 'Second Hymn to Lenin' was perhaps the 'only really *contemporary* poem in Scots for many generations'.[28] Henderson recommended 'The Seamless Garment' to anyone 'wishing to see how perfectly colloquial speech and fifty-fathom profundity can be blended in the best of MacDiarmid' (*AM*, p. 378).

These poems helped Henderson to express, in vivid poetic descriptions, *his* understanding of the 'folk process' in which songs can be picked up, adapted and passed on (*AM*, p. 430). To this end he cited the sixth stanza from the 'First Hymn to Lenin': 'Descendant o' the unkent bards wha made / Sangs peerless through a' post-anonymous days . . .'[29] Henderson also quoted the 'Second Hymn to Lenin' ('*Are my poems spoken in the factories and the fields?*') in the 'Folksong Flyting' (*TAN*, p. 124), and concluded the extended introductory essay to his translation of Antonio Gramsci's *Prison Letters* with a considerable portion of 'The Seamless Garment' (*PL*, p. 21). While these uses of MacDiarmid's poetry are calculated to support particular discursive points, the terms in which they are couched and the frequency with which they appear, suggest that Henderson's perceived alliance with MacDiarmid as a poet was more than simply tactical.

These poems held a particular appeal for Henderson because they all feature a pronouncedly reflexive poetic voice and demonstrate an awareness of the task of the poet and of the potential of poetry to achieve something vast, inclusive, unitary and absolute. Of 'The Seamless Garment', Henderson wrote: 'he moves effortlessly from . . . a tweed mill in his native town . . . to a philosophical discussion concerning the nature of fully achieved poetry like Rilke's and the unremitting relentless unity of Lenin's revolutionary thought and praxis'.[30] 'Second Hymn to Lenin' also addresses the philosophical reach of poetic and political endeavours and the challenges they represent: 'Ah, Lenin, politics is bairn's play / To what this maun be!'[31] Henderson's conception of poetry was therefore informed by his appreciation for the balance between this highest of artistic disciplines that must have the capacity to express all of human knowledge and experience, and the impulse to give voice to the lives of the people – as exemplified in MacDiarmid's poetry.

MacDiarmid offered the young poet-folklorist a literary surface on which to project himself. Not only was Henderson inferring an alliance with a poet he considered to be one of the greatest living poets of the day and perhaps Scotland's greatest ever (*AM*, p. 427); he was also setting in motion a more calculated process of appropriation. Henderson wanted to square his cultural-political project with that of *his* MacDiarmid. The well-documented excesses or 'extremes' of MacDiarmid's thought need not be reconciled if the 'MacDiarmid' you choose to draw out from his work is one that consistently undermines or transcends the flippant sound-bites that have frequently come to characterise his 'anti-humanist' or 'elitist' positions. In expressing his own cultural-political agenda Henderson cited particularly contemplative lines, empathetic passages and abstracted philosophical verses from MacDiarmid's corpus. In doing so he gave the impression that MacDiarmid's poetry constituted an endorsement of his ideas, even if the poet himself disapproved: he appealed to the poetry to refute the poet. In his later, retrospective pieces, Henderson often referred to MacDiarmid as the 'Langholm Byspale', which is both personalised and eulogistic.[32] 'Byspale' can denote a parable or a proverb, as well as a person of rare or wonderful qualities. Given the poet's well-documented relationship with his native Langholm, it might also have been intended to evoke the role of an 'outcast' or an 'illegitimate child' (*OED*). An epithet such as this allows for the ambiguities and difficulties in Henderson's appreciation for MacDiarmid.

As Alec Finlay has confirmed, by the 1940s Henderson had positioned himself securely on MacDiarmid's side of those polarities that the poet had himself fostered in Scottish cultural life (*TAN*, p. 306). In an article titled 'Scotland's Alamein', Henderson demonstrated not only his political alignment but also his rhetorical affinity with MacDiarmid, echoing the journalistic hyperbole that typified the poet's prose. Published in MacDiarmid's *The Voice of Scotland*, it details the symbolic currency of the Highland 51st Division throughout the North African and Italian campaigns, and goes on to compare this 'picture of Scotland at war' with 'the spectacle of our country-men in peace-time'.[33] The comparison culminates in Henderson's explanation of the 'Alamein': the strategic battle that might determine the outcome of an on-going war, a scenario that, apparently, Scotland still faced. The article should be read in the context of the National Assembly of the Scottish Convention, which took place on 22 March 1947, and the editorial line of the publication in which it appeared, which was forcefully pro-independence. Henderson confidently sketches the details of this metaphorical 'Alamein' in robust and proclamatory language. He attacks 'pious platitudes', especially those of the Kirk, reasoning that 'spiritual uplift is no substitute for earthly élan', and asserts that forms of cultural distinctiveness (like the Mod, or programmes to encourage the use of the Gaelic language) are toothless and 'pathetic' if detached from direct political objectives, such as the establishment of a Scottish Parliament:

> The fight to maintain and develop a distinctive Scottish way of life must be invigorated and sustained by political action. Without the latter the former is – in the last analysis – only an elaborate form of shadow-play, which in time must become inept and meaningless.

Henderson recognises that the writers of the Renaissance, 'MacDiarmid, Young, Maclean and the rest', are among the few who had 'maintained some kind of superstructure of Scottish culture over the gutted desolation of the national like [sic] in this century'.[34] The defence of the Renaissance is an extension of those accolades Henderson consistently awarded MacDiarmid: 'He is the man who has sacrificed everything to purge Scotland of its deadening Philistinism and who – in John Speirs' words – "still stands for health and life and sincerity in Scotland against complacency and indifference"' (*AM*, p. 390). Henderson attributes the apathy and ignorance that MacDiarmid railed against to a lazy self-satisfaction common to the comforts of peacetime and to the depoliticised discourses of a community that does not feel threatened. The language suggests an embattled position on the national question, though Henderson avoids identifying the 'enemy' in this formulation. There is no mention of the 'English imperialist Ascendancy', 'consolidated . . . with the full acquiescence of the Scottish bourgeoisie' of which he also wrote elsewhere during this period (*AM*, p. 374).

Though he is careful with his terms, Henderson invokes a committed and resolute campaign. Couched in the language of military strategy, he acknowledges that one cannot afford to be discouraged by the possibility of defeat:

> Scotland's national situation to-day is fully as perilous as the Eighth Army's when it faced the defensive battle of El Alamein . . . It was necessary to check the Axis army, and then throw it back – nothing else would do. For Scotland, here and now, the same alternative presents itself. If this nation does not forthwith rally and hurl back once and for all the forces which for two centuries have been encompassing its obliteration, it will henceforward be fighting nothing but a forlorn rearguard action. It will have had it.
>
> [. . .]
>
> One cannot exclude the possibility that they ['the Scots'] will be defeated. But they had better not be. History does not pardon the defeated. She seldom even provides them with a gravestone.[35]

The dramatic strokes of his rhetoric are similar in tone to MacDiarmid's on this subject. Structured around a basic metaphor the article pre-empts various counter arguments. Henderson is emphatic: spiritual platitudes must be rejected, apathy must be rooted out and the cultural must be tied fast to the political if it is to be of use. While he notes that the Highland 51st Division is a valuable symbol *despite* the 'cheap propaganda which stuck in the Jocks' gullets', this is justified by its use as an image of absolute resolution and of the 'perfervid spirit of our ancestors' – which seems no less propagandistic.[36] The structuring thought is then not only historically evocative and romantic; it also allows for the exacting language of military strategy and elicits a programme for change that would cut through 'sentimentalisms' and drive aggressively at the ultimate aim: political self-determination.

After the War, Henderson was a regular contributor to MacDiarmid's *National Weekly*. Towing the editorial line, he wrote on the state of the nation, Irish Republicanism, James Connolly – 'Ireland's greatest Marxist and revolutionary leader' – and Scotland's place at the World Peace Congress of 1949.[37] Like other contemporary Scottish writers such as Alexander Scott, Douglas Young, Goodsir Smith and Maurice Lindsay, Henderson was part of MacDiarmid's publicity machine in the post-war period. Like these figures, he was never wholly subsumed into MacDiarmid's project, though he did share in the poet's ambitions for cultural and political life in Scotland and presented himself as a disciple to the poet's cause. Henderson conscribed to some degree to what Goodsir Smith described as 'the gospels [MacDiarmid] bears witness to . . . those seeming irreconcilables, Scottish Nationalism and Communism'.[38] However, Henderson's position was one marked by its humanism and, as it transpired, by a commitment to the '*democratic* muse' of folksong. Henderson looked back on MacDiarmid's membership of the CPGB (a 'Stalinist' organisation as he saw it) and placed himself, instead, in 'the Dubcek wing, in all this' (*AM*, p. 443).[39]

Henderson carried *A Drunk Man Looks At The Thistle* with him through the War and at this point still looked forward to the day when he might meet its author. Even at this early stage, he expressed some of those tensions that would be publicly performed in the 'Flytings' more than a decade later. In northern Italy, in the autumn of 1945, Henderson composed a response in verse to MacDiarmid's autobiography. He later explained:

> I read *Lucky Poet*, and sat reflecting on MacDiarmid's bewildering poetic and political career, and all the paradoxical and self-contradictory things I had heard about him, which seemed to me not so much a fruitful interplay – or clash – of opposites as hopelessly disparate ideas and contentions collapsing into an incoherent jumble. (*AM*, p. 385)

In the poem, which became 'To Hugh MacDiarmid: On Reading *Lucky Poet*', Henderson praises the incisive criticisms his subject had made of the 'blubbing company' of the 'Scots burghers'. 'If there were just two choices . . .' writes Henderson, 'mine would be yours' (*CPS*, pp. 119–20). However, he goes on to detail those 'maladies of Scottish, not of English making', lamenting the easily bought loyalties of the Scots, and their taste for 'the jackal's pickings' of empire. While MacDiarmid's achievements in showing 'the shame of our idiot Burns Suppers' are celebrated, those truly damaging elements in Scottish society, 'the meanness, the rancour, / The philistine baseness, the divisive canker', are regarded as internal issues. Henderson writes, 'If we think all our ills come from "ower the Border" / We'll never, but never, march ahead in "guid order"', and in this light, he struggles to make sense of MacDiarmid's 'tortured logomachy'. The poem ends: 'Just what *do* you stand for, MacDiarmid? I'm still not certain. / I don' wanna step behin' dat tartan curtain . . .' Henderson is frustrated by the medium of MacDiarmid's political and cultural project, suggesting that vicious hyperbole achieves certain aims but neglects to offer positive solutions to the nation's various 'maladies'. The potency of Henderson's suspicions even brings him to fear that there may be a vacuum beneath MacDiarmid's staged persona, behind the 'tartan curtain', where there ought to be an ideological foundation and a plan for its implementation. The complex of intertextual references in *Lucky Poet* and the density of its prose no doubt contributed but Henderson's concerns were established early and would deepen in the following two decades. In a collection dedicated to the poet on his seventy-fifth birthday, in 1967, Henderson's contribution was set apart from the fawning of some others. Adapting Maurice Lindsay's 'somewhat lightweight effort of 1943', '*The English see you as an angry eagle / Who tears at them with sharp and furious claws*', Henderson's rendering is '*The English see you as an ancient beagle / That limps along on mangy calloused paws*' (*AM*, pp. 387–8).

In an article on MacDiarmid published in *Edinburgh City Lynx* just weeks after the poet's death, Henderson included a photograph of MacDiarmid cutting peat in Whalsay. It is a double-exposure image and shows two figures, one standing upright and the other stooping over. The two appear on the same spot, sharing the task and the landscape, though the standing figure's horizon is a shadowy copy of the darker, more clearly defined one below it, which belongs to the crouching man. Henderson notes that the dedication reads 'To Hamish, Hugh MacDiarmid and Chris Grieve at the peat in the Shetlands'.[40] While many who have written on the poet have qualified their use of 'MacDiarmid' and 'Grieve', delineating between these identities as and when the poet did, Henderson's inclusion of this image speaks to something more personal.

The potential interpretations of this photograph are many, particularly for the student of modern Scottish literature: the duality of the man and the poet perhaps lies closest to the surface, especially given MacDiarmid/Grieve's inscription. Furthermore, the image brings to mind G. Gregory Smith's familiar visualisation of the 'Caledonian Antisyzygy': a 'grinning gargoyle at the elbow of a kneeling saint'.[41] It shares aspects of its composition with another double-exposure image of the divided self said to embody Smith's concept: that of Richard Mansfield crouching in front of himself as both Dr Jekyll and Mr Hyde.[42] Henderson showed his awareness of the currency of such an image and extends this sensitivity towards the difficulties of interpreting MacDiarmid's work in the text of the article. Writing in 1978, Henderson concludes with something of an understatement: 'it will be a long time – possibly years – before MacDiarmid's gigantic *oeuvre* can be seen in perspective and appraised properly'. He continues, 'for all his savage arrogance in controversy, MacDiarmid is revealed by the greatest of his poetry (and by the testimony of many friends) as a very different kind of being'.[43]

The challenge that MacDiarmid presents to those who try to negotiate with his writings and with his political and aesthetic principles is central to Henderson's tribute. Having briefly outlined his own sometimes strained relationship with the poet, Henderson closes his article with a passage from the poem 'Depth and the Chthonian Image', including the lines, '*Ein Mann aus dem Volke* – weel I ken / Nae man or movement's worth a damn unless / The movement'ud gang on withoot him if / He de'ed the morn'. By centralising the contradictory elements of MacDiarmid's *oeuvre*, voicing his frustrations with *Lucky Poet*, and his admiration for *In Memoriam James Joyce*, Henderson was to maintain MacDiarmid's legacy and the 'movement' that he promoted. The demand for the poet to be '*Einn Mann aus dem Volke*' emerges as one of Henderson's chief concerns, and one of the major battle lines in *The Scotsman* disputes.

The 'Flytings' as Flytings

The designation of the flytings *as* 'Flytings', by contributors at the time and by subsequent commentators, affiliates them with a literary tradition particular to Scotland. Flyting is generally associated with Scottish poets of the sixteenth century, and with *The Flyting of Dunbar and Kennedie* (c.1503) in particular. Dunbar and Kennedy's contest is widely recognised as the earliest example of a model of flyting in Scots verse, which was revisited with David Lyndsay's *Answer to the King's Flyting* (c.1537) and *The Flyting of Montgomerie and Polwart* (c.1585). In this context 'flyting' denotes a formalised bardic contest, distinguished by its show of virtuoso versification and powerful invective. In deference to this literary tradition, the term 'flyting' has become synonymous with the period, and with these defining characteristics. *The New Princeton Encyclopedia of Poetry and Poetics* states that 'Scottish flyting is marked by its vivid language, hyperbolic slander, and underlying playfulness'.[44] However, as Priscilla Bawcutt has suggested, the etymological implications ought not to be overlooked and, in fact, this literary-critical sense is a comparatively recent conceptualisation. Bawcutt explains that there was a common usage of the word in Scots (with variations in Old English) in the medieval period, which corresponded more simply to terms like 'dispute', 'quarrel' or 'scold', and did not necessarily refer to literary endeavour but to any such publicly expressed disagreement.[45]

In a late interjection in the *Honour'd Shade* disputes, Thomas Crawford was the first to use the term 'flyting' to describe the debates, and in doing so he taunted MacDiarmid with the remark that this was 'surely a folk-art in itself' (*TAN*, p. 99). Throughout the controversies the various participants show a clear awareness of the terms of their debates as being rooted in an oppositional format that is synonymous with a flyting and not necessarily associated with the newspaper's 'points of view' page. The language of contestation is apparent whenever the correspondents reflect directly on the nature of their discourse: MacDiarmid refers to Henderson and Craig as his 'opponents' (p. 134), Henderson talks of their 'controversy' (p. 131) and Douglas Young repeatedly laments Henderson's 'renewed attacks' (pp. 134, 138). Of all the correspondents in the three 'Flytings', Henderson is most vocal in his recognition of their participation in a kind of modern-day flyting. He thereby establishes himself as one side of the opposition that is implied. In this sense, the 'Flytings' are something of a self-fulfilling prophecy: as the discourse is increasingly recognised as a flyting, both Henderson and MacDiarmid distinguish themselves as the two conflicting voices that define it as such. This differentiates them from those who intervene in an effort to mitigate the conflict, often by pointing out that both sides set out arguments that are not necessarily mutually exclusive. William Smith's contribution is a prime example. In his letter in the 'Folksong Flyting', he calls attention to the 'spuriosity of applying to folksong the criteria employed in the appraisal of formal literature' (*TAN*, p. 129). By interjecting in this manner Smith displayed his fundamental misunderstanding. Henderson and MacDiarmid were under no illusions as to the most apparent differences between folk-song and art-poetry. Smith's reductive reasoning had no place in the performance of the 'Flytings', where broader conceptions of art and its function were under discussion, and not the fact that a song is sung and a poem is not. In response to an onslaught of particularly barbed comments from MacDiarmid, and in framing his own invective response, Henderson took note of the 'bold figures of speech in polemical correspondence' (*TAN*, p. 96). Later in the 'Folksong Flyting' he writes of how 'the correspondence is taking on with every letter more and more of the high mottled complexion of a Celtic flyting' (p. 124). Furthermore, in a particularly fervent climax, Henderson makes a show of his efforts to account for MacDiarmid's position:

> Some readers may have put Mr MacDiarmid's growlings down to mere testiness, or regarded them as understandable excrescences on a flyting which in the nature of things may tend to get a bit inflamed. In my opinion it goes much deeper than that. (p. 132)

Henderson goes on to explore the fundamentally 'unresolved contradictions' in MacDiarmid's outlook and identifies what he calls an anti-humanist 'kind of spiritual apartheid' (Ibid.). As this example illustrates, the tendency of participants towards hyperbole, and various other rhetorical strategies, are to be expected in this context. Though quotations are unburdened by context, opponents are rendered as caricatures, straw men appear at every juncture and the intellectual and imaginative limitations of each are invoked with snide remarks from the other, this performative aspect is crucial. Personal attacks and lofty intellectualism are bundled up together and spat onto the opinion columns of *The Scotsman*.

Both Henderson and MacDiarmid were well aware of Scotland's flyting heritage. MacDiarmid famously drew from one of the original innovators of the form in his call to go 'back to Dunbar' and his most celebrated work, *A Drunk Man Looks at the Thistle* (1926), opens with the claim that his '. . . *flytin'* and scaltrie sall be / . . . / As the bauch Earth is wi' the lift / Or fate wi' mankind!' (emphasis added).[46] Furthermore, in an editorial for *Voice of Scotland* in 1948 MacDiarmid described contemporary debates over the poetry of the Scottish Literary Renaissance under the title 'The Flytin' o' the Makars'.[47] Henderson wrote an extended song-poem of his own called 'The Flyting o' Life and Daith' (*CPS*, pp. 144–5) which revises the 'playful' element of the traditional flyting, transposing the form onto the seriousness of an internalised verbal contest between 'Life' and 'Death', where each makes competing claims on 'the warld'. Bawcutt asserts that flyting is 'one of the few poetic traditions that survived, unbroken, from the time of Dunbar to that of Allan Ramsay'.[48] Kurt Wittig, in *The Scottish Tradition in Literature* (1958), projected the 'flyting spirit' onto

Fergusson, Burns, Scott, Byron, Carlyle and, finally, MacDiarmid.[49] Kenneth Simpson's essay 'The Legacy of Flyting' (1991), though it focuses on the vernacular revival of the late eighteenth century, includes a note on the west-coast tradition of 'sherracking / shirracking' – as it appears in the novel *No Mean City* (1935) and in Edwin Morgan's poem 'King Billy' – which is described as a descendant of the flyting tradition.[50]

There has, however, been a tendency to find evidence of the 'flyting spirit' in any example of stylised polemical writing by a Scottish author. Signifiers of the flyting form become part of the apparatus of critics who inadvertently reduce the rich variance of Scottish literature to a handful of recognisable tropes, themes and techniques. In *Scottish Literature and the Scottish People: 1680–1830* (1961) Craig notes that such 'forced Scotticising' 'runs amok' in Wittig's book, and relies on a narrow conception of the 'truly Scots', with 'no word of either the practical needs which threw up such features or of the quite other cultures in which they also occur'.[51] This same danger is apparent in attempts to understand the heritage of flyting in Scottish literature, and it cannot be allowed to colour our consideration of the relationship between *The Scotsman* 'Flytings' and the literary mode to which they allude. In this respect, it is important to note that Henderson and MacDiarmid's is a conscious parallel with this medieval literary tradition and not necessarily part of an instinct or state of mind that the Scottish writer has no choice but to function within.

The political wing of the folk revival found an important place for the flyting tradition in conceiving of their programme for cultural renewal. Writing in the sleeve notes for *Ding Dong Dollar* (1962), a collection of 'Anti-Polaris and Scottish Republican Songs Recorded in Scotland' and written and performed by various revivalists, folk poets and songwriters, Henderson describes the parallel traditions of 'literary' and 'sub-literary' satire in Scottish cultural history.[52] From the literary flytings of early 'Celtic' society, through 'partisan and often scurrilous satirical verse and song' these traditions are said to have 'cross-fertilised', converging most famously in Burns and, in the twentieth century, in MacDiarmid. As the modern-day inheritor MacDiarmid had reasserted 'with all the power of faith, passion and intellectual ferocity, everything that is most important in this tradition'. Henderson then claims that the 'new direction' of younger poets towards a 'Scottish Folksong Renaissance' was inevitable, and that the establishment of a 'new metropolitan folk-song corpus' is part of the direct inheritance of this satirical vein.[53] Politically minded revivalists, therefore, seem to have endorsed Henderson's vision of the descent of the modern movement and considered themselves part of a continuum of literary and folk-based interaction, of which the medieval flytings were an early example. The modern 'Flytings' also validate Henderson's thesis by having staged debates on the place of folk culture in Scottish society: the folk revival and the 'Folksong Flyting' then belong to the same tradition, as Crawford insisted in his observation ('two such masters of "flyting" . . .').

Many of the defining characteristics of flyting are apparent in *The Scotsman* debates. Simpson posits that flyting is informed by paradox as 'apparently spontaneous expressive energy is channelled through a form and a mode suggestive of ritual and formality'.[54] Besides the 'ritual' element, which is presumably a feature tied to the poetic form of the traditional flyting, this is also true of the later 'Flytings'. The carefully structured arguments presented by Henderson and MacDiarmid in particular, often appear impulsive and almost conversational. Both enlisted a strategy whereby they would nonchalantly disregard the other's argument before expressing their own in altogether more forceful and precisely articulated terms. MacDiarmid's response to Henderson's suggestion that he was 'the apostle of a kind of spiritual apartheid' is a good example:

> How silly can Mr Hamish Henderson get? Everybody in some degree practices what he calls 'spiritual apartheid' if he or she likes one thing and dislikes another, prefers to associate with certain people and not with others, and so forth . . . But all this has little or nothing to do with the essential argument . . . At the present stage in human history, there are far more important things to do than bawl out folksongs, which, whatever function they may have had in the past, have little or no relevance to most people in advanced highly industrialised countries today. (*TAN*, pp. 133–4)

These comments precede MacDiarmid's own assertions on the progressive force of literature, which, due to his apparently tenable disregard for Henderson's accusations, can be presented in sharp relief, as a model of rationality. This introduces another technique employed in the 'Flytings': the purposeful misinterpretation of the other's arguments. MacDiarmid's reading of the 'spiritual apartheid' is, for example, not the same as that which Henderson intended. A highly qualified statement on the poet's marked 'anti-humanism' in some of his early work and under 'one of his persona' (*TAN*, p. 131), is thereby transformed into an absurd and indiscriminate pronouncement made by a desperate antagonist. Bawcutt asserts that Dunbar and Kennedy's famous flyting is 'a quarrel, not a reasoned argument'; that it has a 'pattern less of argument than of accusation and rebuttal'.[55] It is the kind of exchange that goes on forever and gets nowhere. It invites ingenuity and dynamism but not necessarily in the pursuit of truth, only perseverance: outlasting your opponent, always ready with another rebuttal, another accusation.

Simpson recognises the reductive juxtaposition of formal and vernacular diction as another prevalent technique used in flyting, and again this can be seen throughout Henderson and MacDiarmid's debates, even in the excerpt cited above.[56] The informal language – 'how silly can Mr Hamish Henderson get' and 'bawl out folksongs' – has the desired effect: portraying the ease with which MacDiarmid can dismiss his opponent's 'silly' comments, especially in light of the altogether more eloquent presentation of his own views:

> Folksong, and other folk-arts, may be the root from which all else has sprung, but a root is best just taken for granted, if the tree or plant is flourishing . . . It does not matter one iota if we never see the seed (or root), nor would it matter if we just failed to realise there is one. (*TAN*, p. 134)

Though these modern-day flytings do not demonstrate the complex versification, metrical ingenuity, alliteration and rhyme schemes that are paraded in the traditional form, they are nevertheless characterised by their 'display of rhetorical skills'.[57] At times, they also demonstrate biting invective, as in MacDiarmid's tirades against folk-song as 'a wallowing in the mud-bath of ignorance' and a 're-emersion in illiterate doggerel' (*TAN*, p. 94). The performance of the medieval flyting and its apparent standing as court entertainment, has encouraged literary historians to question the sincerity of the poet's animosity in these exchanges. Bawcutt suggests that few readers seem to have taken the participants' anger seriously, and Simpson refers to the 'joke' that some of the audience would interpret such insults literally.[58] In reference to the 'Folksong Flyting', Angus Calder remarks that MacDiarmid had only 'pretended to believe that folksong was intellectually worse than insignificant'.[59] However, it would be a mistake to see the exchanges of *The Scotsman* debates as merely performance. Henderson and MacDiarmid's quarrel also harboured genuine disagreement over the fundamentals of artistic production.

In a 1958 essay for *Lines Review*, 'The Flyting Scotsman', W. A. Gatherer traced a 'peculiarly Scottish sin . . . Ire' and the virtue made of it among the nation's writers. Having followed the transformations of the flyting form through Scottish literary history, Gatherer identifies a hiatus of 'flyting' that only ended with MacDiarmid's *A Drunk Man Looks at the Thistle* (1926) and *To Circumjack Cencrastus* (1930). He explains that in these works the poet rediscovered the 'true force of poetic flyting'; that is, not as mere 'scolding' but as 'the working-out of an argument in terms of passion and sarcasm'.[60] Writing in the following year for the same publication Morgan cited *The Battle Continues* (1958) – MacDiarmid's response in verse to Roy Campbell's pro-Franco poem *Flowering Rifle* (1936) – as an example of a particular 'branch' of the 'Scotch flyting tradition' that is less comedic than its sixteenth-century precedents, and more purposeful and 'hortatory'. Morgan emphasises the palpable anger, and even hatred, that MacDiarmid harnessed in this long poem. While MacDiarmid does not betray such 'hatred' in the modern 'Flytings', it might still be argued that 'amusement is subservient to political zeal', as it is in *The Battle Continues*.[61] Certainly, any given flyting contributor need not choose between the impulse to entertain and the desire to emerge victorious from their debate; both compulsions are evident in Henderson and MacDiarmid's contests.

The poet's power to 'satirise' is recognised as a prominent factor in the historical practice of flyting and Henderson and MacDiarmid sustained this climate of ridicule in their public debates.[62] It is not enough to dismantle an opponent's argument, to expose contradictions or inconsistencies in their position: a flyting participant must also belittle the contributions of their opposition and render them unworthy of considered response. In another of MacDiarmid's controversies, this time with Hamilton Finlay, he published a pamphlet outlining his views, which began with the following passage:

> The instance of this pamphlet . . . serves for a final word on a recent bewildering exchange of public addresses which, in truth, do not really affect the answering poet. On the contrary, it is hoped that it is only an opportunity to clarify further his system of immediate reaction to a situation he would regard as extraneous nonsense.[63]

Flytings in the Middle Ages are thought to have been a form of 'court entertainment', to be performed publicly, or else written on manuscript and passed around, or displayed in a public place, for instance, pinned to a church door. The monarch, or another patron, then named the triumphant poet on the basis of their skill in versification. Among a professional class of poets these contests had an important function, determining the future of art-poetry in that court or principality. As Bawcutt describes, 'the combat is envisaged as part of a judicial process, in which the contestants put their own veracity and their opponents' lies to the test of battle'.[64] Similarly, these mid twentieth-century flytings were public discourses set in the opinion columns of a national newspaper, perhaps a modern equivalent of the church door. Although no victor was declared, two aesthetic programmes were set at odds, in open discussion, exposed to the scrutiny of the Scottish public. Subsequent generations of poets and poetry readers were perhaps to be the ultimate adjudicators. However, the 'Flytings' did not begin and end with this small selection of letters 'to the Editor': the core issues are critical to the worldview of any creative artist. As such, everything Henderson and MacDiarmid ever wrote can conceivably be interpreted as an extension of this series of debates, especially in Henderson's case. He frequently revisited the 'muckle flyting', and, perhaps more than any of his peers, wrestled with the contradictions of MacDiarmid's project as though they were his own.

Core Issues

The Scotsman 'Flytings' are difficult texts to analyse precisely because of the characteristics they share with their medieval antecedents. The complex of tactical arguments, reductive readings and flamboyant rhetoric, make an interrogation of the core issues of the 'Flytings' problematic, as they are inextricably bound up in, and often obscured by, the self-conscious performance of the flyting form. Indeed, Bawcutt's conception of flyting as simply a process of 'accusation and rebuttal' is perhaps the only framework within which the diverse subject matter of the three debates can be fully understood.[65] Beneath the complexities of form, it is possible to identify four major issues that are most extensively, or most emphatically, discussed. These are: first, the problem of the prescription of literary 'value'; second, the problem of the 'popular' in literary production; third, the disputed dichotomy of 'high' and 'low' arts; and finally, the guiding principles of the 'individual' and the 'communal' in the pursuit of a progressive literature. Each of these issues represents a different aspect of the interface between literature and society.

These four principal issues do not function in isolation. They give shape to the debate, and articulate the grounds on which Henderson and MacDiarmid built their disputes. The problem of the appraisal of literary 'value' is made immediately apparent in the '*Honour'd Shade* Flyting' with arguments over which poets should have been represented in the 1959 anthology (*TAN*, pp. 79–91). It is also clearly an issue for the 'Flytings' as a whole, as Henderson and MacDiarmid establish themselves as the spokesmen of two opposing conceptions of how literature in Scotland should advance. Where Henderson extols the advantages that could come of a synthesis of folk-song and art-poetry (p. 95), MacDiarmid reasserts his belief in the contemporary demand for 'higher and higher intellectual levels'; a pursuit that is, he assures us, incompatible with Henderson's vision (p. 119).

The 'Flytings' are awash with competing value judgements and claims made, particularly by MacDiarmid, on unequivocal terms. MacDiarmid refers to the folk-song so passionately promoted by Henderson as 'the simple outpourings of illiterates and backward peasants' (p. 128) and smugly informs his opponents that 'a preference for the inferior is one of the commonest disguises of envy' (p. 84). In regard to the *Honour'd Shade* disputes he defends the progressive impetus of the 'Abbotsford Poets' as a literary avant-garde (derisively reworded as a 'clique' by other correspondents) (p. 80), and dismisses other contributors' views as 'the kind of contention and conception of poetry that has bogged Scottish verse in ruts of worthlessness so long' (p. 85). In this context, MacDiarmid imagines himself 'protecting literary and artistic *value*' (emphasis added) (p. 94). He prompts his opponents to question how much authority is afforded to MacDiarmid due to his standing as a poet, or due to the forcefulness with which he asserts his criteria for literary greatness. Other commentators, including Henderson, are far less categorical in their claims. Indeed, in response to MacDiarmid's outspoken attitudes Henderson charges him with 'that very same self-centred provincialism which he is forever and a day claiming to combat' (p. 90). For Henderson, the most damning charge is that of provincialism, as it speaks of a narrow, regressive perspective, which is precisely the national malady that both figures propose to remedy. Such disputes over objective literary 'value' are invariably informed by subjective analyses and are, in this sense, inherently irresolvable. As Young states in one of his letters in reference to a short series of exchanges on the matter of linguistic choices in Scottish poetry: 'it is a matter of taste' (p. 89). This is not to say that the discourse is simply a turgid, unproductive affair where stubborn contributors refuse to develop their arguments; the contributors provided *The Scotsman* readers with an investigative dialogue that compels us to question the constitution of literary value, though they do not come close to reaching a consensus on the issue.

The problem of the 'popular' in literary production pervades the 'Flytings'. In response to Henderson's insistence on the virtues of folk-song, a mode 'in the idiom of the people' (*TAN* p. 88), MacDiarmid declaims 'the philistinism that attacks literature and the arts for not appealing to the big public, but does not expect science to do anything of the sort' (p. 94). In comments like these MacDiarmid expresses his disregard for the need for popular endorsement and reaffirms its irrelevance in determining 'literary quality'. In another of his eloquent retaliations he writes:

> In all literatures there is a vast undergrowth of doggerel and mediocre versifying, but it is a remarkable instance of *trahison de clercs* if Dr Craig would have us believe that this is to be valued as equal to or better than acceptably great poetry simply because, thanks to their minimal literacy and because it corresponds to their ignorant tastes and reflects the sorry condition of their lives, it is more popular among the broad masses of the people than the poems of, say, Shakespeare, Dante, Goethe, Rimbaud, Rilke, Pasternak, Montale, etc, etc. (p. 118)[66]

MacDiarmid explains the basis of these attitudes in a quotation from an early essay on his work, 'The Poetry of Hugh MacDiarmid' (1938), by Nan Shepherd:

> The actuality . . . [is] that men are obtuse, dull, complacent, vulgar. They love the third-rate, live on the cheapest terms with themselves . . . they refuse to explore the largeness of life. This refusal he [MacDiarmid] sees as a cowardice. If for the mass of men this picture is true, he believes that human society is wrongly ordered. Therefore the poet demands a political change that will give men such living conditions as may make the finer potentialities actual. (p. 97)

MacDiarmid's endorsement of this analysis suggests that he writes for a society that has already passed through the political reordering he sought. It also implies that the 'popularity' of a literary work, in this context, is in fact a mark of its betrayal of the writer's creative duty. The 'mob ignorance' that he laments is, in another contribution, ascribed to failures in popular education and to the class-structure of modern society (p. 122). Nevertheless, MacDiarmid refuses to let extenuating circumstances like economic base and socio-political superstructure diminish his determination not to pander to 'popular' taste.

Though his is an incisive critique of the cultural landscape of twentieth-century Scotland, and the increasingly sophisticated and pervasive channels of mass culture that emerged, MacDiarmid must also concede that he requires nothing less than revolution if his poetry is to find the society for which it was written. Where Henderson tries to excavate and re-popularise traditional arts that have survived, in isolated pockets, into the present day, MacDiarmid demands that the whole of society transform itself to accommodate his art.

In his account of Scottish Labour and their conceptualisations of 'popular culture', Angus Calder describes the same theoretical tensions explored by Henderson and MacDiarmid in their flytings. Calder recounts debates over whether the party ought to encourage '"proactive" rather than "reactive" cultural expression', and whether it should support, or initiate, 'challenging work which, because of innovative forms and new ideas, may begin to puzzle audiences and be, in one sense, "unpopular"'.[67] As with Henderson and MacDiarmid, elements in the Labour movement shared political ambitions, but differed on the role popular culture might play in realising these aims. In a direct response to this resolute opposition between the 'popular' and the 'literary', Henderson drew upon the figure of the simultaneously popular and distinctly literary poet. He contested MacDiarmid's revulsion for the Burns cult, insisting that Burns' popularity was maintained 'in spite' of the cult rather than because of it. He drew from his experiences fighting with the *Resistenza* (the Italian Resistance) during the Second World War, where partisans recited whole passages of Dante by memory (*TAN*, pp. 123–4). In *Scottish Literature and the Scottish People: 1680–1830* Craig sought to establish a 'social history' of literature in Scotland:

> [tracing the] particular facts and particular passages of poetry or fiction in which the life of the people seems to reveal itself most genuinely, and hence to give actuality to themes such as community, society, class, speech-idiom, tradition – which are so apt to remain vague.[68]

In the 'Flytings', he was therefore well placed to make claims for the grass-roots popularity of Burns. He also suggested that Arnold Wesker's 'Centre 42' movement and Vladimir Mayakovsky's poetry represented examples of successful artistic engagement with the 'popular' (*TAN*, p. 126). Both Henderson and Craig cited MacDiarmid's poetry, allegedly showing his own 'attempt to bridge the modern cultural gulfs and to reach the people with his work' (p. 122):

> *Are my poems spoken in the factories and fields,*
> *In the streets o' the toon?*
> *Gin they're no', then I'm failin' to dae*
> *What I ocht to ha' dune.*[69]

While MacDiarmid deemed 'popularity' under the contemporary political and social structures a mark of failure, Henderson sought to harness it by bringing about the kind of class-consciousness and public politicisation that both poets desired. In this movement towards a 'popular poetry' Henderson saw folk-song as the best hope for 'communication across the apollyon chasms' between the artist and the people (*TAN*, pp. 96, 125).

The rhetorical devices and discursive strategies employed by the correspondents can lead to confusion over the precise nature of their arguments. At certain points in the debates it seems that, for Henderson, the 'popular' poet and the art-poet indebted to folk-song became interchangeable: to be popular is to invest in the creative potential of the folk tradition and to invest in this tradition is to be popular. MacDiarmid's original attacks on folk-song were largely based on its appeal to popular taste. Therefore Henderson and Craig considered a defence of either as a defence of both: that is, folk-song and the autonomy of the people in determining their own forms of cultural self-expression and artistic appreciation. Cultural terms are frequently co-opted or conflated and both Henderson and MacDiarmid, in their efforts to undermine one another, frequently fail to delineate their terms clearly, presenting instead a torrent of argumentation that conflates, for example, the idea of the duty of the poet to write for the people, with an appreciation of the artistic value of traditional Scottish folk-song. This can be explained in part by the tactical decision to purposefully misrepresent an opponent's position and respond to a simplified or parodied version of their argument.

In this context the issue of the 'popular' becomes a determining factor in the division of 'high' and 'low' arts, or more precisely, 'literature' and 'folk-art' – a dichotomy that Henderson explores frequently in his early essays. Henderson and MacDiarmid both felt that their cultural interests were under attack; Henderson's from the world of 'art-poetry' and its associated 'culture vultures', and MacDiarmid's from 'ignorance and apathy . . . the greatest enemies of mankind'. The division ran along the lines of two opposing forms of philistinism that Henderson and MacDiarmid were eager to put to one another: a 'witless philistinism of the streets', that MacDiarmid saw in the propagation of the folk arts, and 'a philistinism of the boudoir (and even of the Rose street pub)' which, in Henderson's view 'can be considerably more dangerous, since it more often than not camouflages itself as a protective interest in literature and the arts' (*TAN*, pp. 93–4).

Henderson sought to bridge this perceived division between the 'high' and 'low' arts by extolling examples of the fruitful exchanges between folk-song and literature, a task that Crawford supported in his contributions to *The Scotsman* disputes (*TAN*, p. 99). However, MacDiarmid interpreted such instances of the influence of folk arts in accepted 'literary' art, not as a synthesis of the two forms but as the utilisation of folk sources by the literary artist. In his estimations folk-song could, at best, only be a 'springboard for significant work' (p. 121). It does not matter whether the 'great writers, painters and composers of Europe have owed anything decisive to folksong', the real measure of their quality is in 'what they did with the influence in question' (p. 134). This contention was based on MacDiarmid's understanding of the nature of folk-song, which was typified by his relegating it to the confines of history and to a form of society that had not existed since before the Industrial Revolution (p. 122). This assessment of folk-song, as an archaic and moribund form, sits in stark contrast to Henderson's concept of a process free from constraint to any particular historical period. He was convinced of the role of folk-song as an expressive and instinctive reflex of 'the people', flexible enough to adapt to societal changes throughout human history. These conflicting conceptualisations of folk-song are in turn based on divergent views on the nature of 'authorship'.

Alec Finlay prioritised this aspect in his coverage of the 'Flytings', distinguishing between the arguments of MacDiarmid and Henderson in terms of their respective commitment to the figure of the literary poet as an individual, and to the 'communal' nature of the art of folk-song (*TAN*, pp. 322–6). Indeed, the principles of the 'individual' and the 'communal' can be used to explore MacDiarmid and Henderson's ideas about the nature of the relationship between poetry and society and therefore the basis of their 'Flytings'. More precisely, these models of authorship provide a framework within which to analyse their proposals for the prospective character of a progressive political literature. In an effort to clarify his position in the '*Honour'd Shade* Flyting' MacDiarmid cites Lenin:

> Communism becomes an empty phrase, a mere façade, and the Communist a mere bluffer, if he has not worked over in his consciousness the whole inheritance of human knowledge . . . made his own, and worked over anew, all that was of value in the more than two thousand years of development of human thought. (*TAN*, p. 95)

MacDiarmid's understanding of the purpose and function of poetry relies on the individual's relationship with the sum of human history, science and culture. In contrast, he sees those 'who insist that the level of utterance should be that of popular understanding', like Henderson with his proposed synthesis of folk art and literature, as part of a 'parasitical "interpreting class" . . . who are the enemies of the people, because what their attitude amounts to is "keeping the people in their place", stereotyping their stupidity' (p. 127). Scott Lyall notes that MacDiarmid likely lifted his notion of the 'interpreting class' from John Buchan who, in his autobiography *Memory Hold-the-Door* (1940), used the term to describe those who were 'by profession atomisers, engaged in reducing the laborious structure of civilised life to a whirling nebula'. Lyall describes MacDiarmid's disapproval of 'the managerialist cultural brokers who professionally create the artificial, academic divisions between the high culture of the educated few and the mass culture suitable for the ignorant many'.[70] MacDiarmid concludes that 'the interests of the masses and the real highbrow, the creative artist, are identical, for the function of the latter is the extension of human consciousness' (p. 127). On an individual basis, any one of the 'masses' can therefore engage in 'highbrow' art, and thereby expand their consciousness as part of an individuated but potentially universal process of poetic realisation.

Where MacDiarmid draws on Lenin to express his 'guiding principle', Henderson looks to Antonio Gramsci and his concern with the 'creative spirit of the people in its diverse phases' (*TAN*, p. 131). Henderson believed that a reinvestment in the folk arts was not the work of a 'parasitical interpreting class', who shored up artificial divisions in the provision of culture, but the hope for a revived, collective mode of self-expression for 'the people', on their own terms (pp. 139–40). MacDiarmid's unremitting commitment to the 'extension of human consciousness' fuelled Henderson's accusations of a kind of 'anti-humanist' 'spiritual apartheid' in the poet's work. In these attacks Henderson drew upon direct quotations from MacDiarmid's earlier works, including this one, from his essay '"Lewis Grassic Gibbon" – James Leslie Mitchell' (1946): 'I . . . would sacrifice a million people any day for one immortal lyric. I am a scientific Socialist. I have no use whatsoever for emotional humanism' (*TAN*, p. 132). Indeed, this aspect of MacDiarmid's worldview can be traced on a personal level as well as on a political one. In a letter to David Daiches in 1975 he explains that in relation to 'the men and women who have interested me most I only have my idea of what their interests and affiliations were – that is, my own idea of them, and never any ordinary human understanding'.[71] George Davie pointed out the essential difference between the two projects represented in the 'Flytings' when he explained MacDiarmid's argument:

> There is . . . a struggle between the elite, the intellectual few who do the discovering, and make possible the progress, and the anti-elitist many, who are not equal to participating in the general argument, and who seek [to impose] egalitarianism, of which the Burns international is for [MacDiarmid] the great example.[72]

The 'individual' and 'communal' emphases can also be seen in action in the later part of the 'Folksong Flyting' where MacDiarmid's promotion of the Communist model of 'monumental' and 'epic' art, aiming for a 'grand syntheses' for the 'grandeur of the times', is challenged by Craig and Henderson's support for a renewed investment in 'communally shared and developed folk arts' (*TAN*, pp. 127–9, 132). Where MacDiarmid imagined himself at the vanguard, dragging the people into class-consciousness and revolutionary fervour; Henderson sought to dissolve himself in a vast, anonymous resurgence of collective political (and poetical) action. The 'Flytings' asked how political action is taken: in the minds of individuals, or through a collective consciousness.

These four central issues of *The Scotsman* 'Flytings': the problem of the prescription of literary 'value'; the problem of the 'popular' in literary production; the disputed dichotomy of 'high' and 'low' arts; and the guiding principles of the 'individual' and the 'communal' in the pursuit of a progressive literature, are a crucial part of the dynamism and intensity of the debates. They do not, however, provide a comprehensive account of the importance of the 'Flytings' between Henderson and MacDiarmid. Without situating them within the distinctive formulation of these modern-day flytings, they cannot be wholly understood.

Dialectics

In his article on the legacy of flyting, Simpson emphasises the mutual respect and friendship that is presupposed by such 'contests of vilification'.[73] On the basis of this familiarity, the combatants of traditional flytings are said to have used the poetic model as a 'liberating device' for their dramatic invective, allowing for exchanges that could not otherwise have been openly expressed.[74] This dynamic is equally applicable to Henderson and MacDiarmid's 'Flytings'. By the time of the disputes they were well acquainted, as Henderson's autobiographical essays record (*AM*, pp. 381–426). The strength of their relationship combined with the forum of debate made available in the 'Points of View' columns contributed to their own 'liberation device', facilitating the free debate that followed. The debates may even have been orchestrated with the purpose of bringing issues of great national cultural concern to a wider audience. Though it seems unlikely that this was their primary motivation, it is clear from their resolve that both men were alive to the seriousness of their subject matter.

Neill Martin, in his study of ritual dialogue in Celtic marriage traditions, compares the oration in Celtic marriage ceremonies to the literary tradition of flyting:

> [There is] both interdependence and opposition in these events; as the dialogue proceeds, the two adversaries are continuously collaborating in a joint course of action to which they are both committed. As the poet puts forward a new insult, or opens an allegorical allusion, he is offering his opponent the opportunity to display his ingenuity at his expense; the principle of concord is as important as that of contest'.[75]

The exchange and interchange between Henderson and MacDiarmid functions in a similar way. Though any kind of resolution is effectively impossible, as it would require a concession from one or the other, they both participate in a kind of mutual reliance whereby neither MacDiarmid's aesthetics nor Henderson's can be fully articulated except within this adversarial framework: if agreement were possible, the debates would never have begun.[76] In the self-awareness of their performance, it becomes a more honest investigation: impartiality and objectivity are not staged, but rejected outright. The cynicism of gesture politics is dispelled with and replaced with something more provisional, equivocal, and inquisitive.

In *Lucky Poet*, MacDiarmid described his conception of the 'Caledonian Antisyzygy' in terms that might also apply to the relationship between his cultural-political position and Henderson's: 'It is not an easy relationship. It entails unceasing conflict, a conflict not of extermination, but rather akin to that state known in biology as "hostile symbiosis"'.[77] Their debates represented deep-running conflicts within Scottish literary production in the post-war era. These conflicts could not be expressed in any single-perspective format, but required argument and discussion by their very nature. In the sense that they investigate truth through discussion, the 'Flytings' signify a dialectical relationship between the two combatants, one inherent to the depth and consequence of the issues at hand. It is a process akin to that described in MacDiarmid's poem 'Utterly a Creator':

> A poetry that takes its polish from a conflict
> Between discipline at its most strenuous
> And feeling at its highest – wherein abrasive surfaces
> Are turned upon one another like millstones,
> And instead of generating chaos
> Refine the grist of experience between them.[78]

The reciprocal 'wearing-down' of more acerbic points streamlines their arguments, producing a cleaner sense of the opposition that is expressed. Points are made and countered, absorbed and responded to on both sides. Consequently, the seeming irreconcilability of Henderson's humanism and MacDiarmid's intellectual elitism is put into stark relief; their common purpose and mutual reliance is revealed. Most importantly, the precepts of literature that are at stake in these debates – its habitat and its audience – are explored in a public discussion and placed explicitly in several historical and national contexts at once.

As Finlay has noted (*TAN*, p. 342), Henderson extended the 'Folksong Flyting' by publishing a rejoinder in his article, 'McGonagall the What' (1965) (*AM*, pp. 265–85). Besides cruelly comparing some of MacDiarmid's less successful verse to that of 'the supreme practitioner of the art of the belly-flop', Henderson interrogates the work of William McGonagall (1825–1902) as inhabiting a 'debatable land' between art-poetry and folk-song:

> The hard truth is that folk-song becomes poetry – or has a chance of becoming poetry – as and when it gets rid of McGonagall. He is, as it were, the sump into which all that is least creative in folk-song is bound to drain.

In other words, this 'anti-hero of the un-folk process' drew, perhaps unconsciously, from the detritus of folk-song and balladry in an effort to achieve art-poetry, though he failed spectacularly (*AM*, pp. 280–1). For Henderson this represented an inverted equivalent of all those who had successfully produced a confluence of art and folk poetry; poets like Burns and Lorca (*AM*, p. 281). This 'debatable land' is essentially the same territory occupied by the 'Flytings'. As Henderson and MacDiarmid swap blows, it is in fact poetry itself with which they are most directly engaged in debate. Though they do not approach any kind of reconciliation, they bring life to the connecting principles of the dialogical relationship between art and society. Drawing from various sources, often the same ones, Henderson and MacDiarmid construct their opposing conceptions of what literature is, and how it might advance, all the time perhaps doing more to explore the problems inherent in such a task than actually achieving it.

Analysing *The Scotsman* 'Flytings' within the context of the cultural movements to which Henderson and MacDiarmid were respectively attached lifts them out of the anecdotal margins to which they have been confined. The significance of the allusion to the literary tradition of flyting also contributes to this re-contextualisation by providing an opportunity to explore how the forms of these debates are as relevant as their core issues. The distinctive marriage of form – the dialectical nature of the modern-day flyting – and content – the 'debatable land' of poetry and its relationship with 'the people' – is crucial to the expressive and investigative power of the 'Flytings'. Though the controversies discussed here were the only direct flytings between these two figures, Henderson's writings, from the post-war period through to his death in 2002, perpetuate this dialogue with MacDiarmid and the aesthetics and politics he promoted. Henderson's various writings on folk-song, literature, culture and politics consistently anticipate the kinds of attacks that MacDiarmid made real in the 'Flytings'. In his manuscript, George Bannatyne added a short postscript to the 'Flyting of Dunbar and Kennedy': '*Juge ye now heir quha gat the war*'. It is an invitation to the reader to evaluate the performance, not the truth of the combatants' attacks (whether one was pox-ridden or the other incontinent). Similarly, Henderson and MacDiarmid invite us to judge who 'gat the war' in their 'Flytings'. It is no good to ask who is *right*, when the effect of the debates is to enact, through collaboration and altercation, a series of contradictory truths.

Though the dialectical nature of their relationship ought to be emphasised, Henderson had more invested in these conflicts than the firebrand he faced, as subsequent writings by and about these figures indicate. MacDiarmid's contribution to these debates was partly informed by his appetite for controversy, whereas for Henderson there seems to have been more at stake. The 'Folksong Flyting' was essentially an interrogation of Henderson's model of revivalism, and of his conception of its political potential. Before his interjection in the '*Honour'd Shade* Flyting', the discussion was wholly concerned with the arbiters of literary value in relation to the editorial remit of the anthology; afterwards, it turned to more substantive issues like the social dimension of literary production. Henderson endowed the 'muckle flyting' with enormous significance: these melees were the intellectual testing ground for his cultural politics, developed over half a lifetime. In his piece on the flyting tradition, Gatherer wrote: 'It might be said that few Scottish poets have not also been preachers: that the true Scot is dicephalous . . . That the two heads should be on the same shoulders is surely monstrous – but that is the doom and the delight of the nation'.[79] Flyting, and all that comes with it – the performance, invective, and dialogue – was an appropriate form for Henderson to set out the foundation for his folk revival strategies, and his own work as a poet and song-maker. The collusion that is required in this mode of public dialogue, and the dialectical relationship it represents, are in keeping with Gatherer's image of the two-headed poet. Though Henderson synthesised the work of many figures in his writings, MacDiarmid was his most persistent and resilient influence. In working through his vision of the revival and his conception of the role of literature in society, Henderson found himself embracing MacDiarmid as his dicephalous other. To proceed, he had to negotiate with that part of the task that the poet represented. Despite his viciousness, this was a man who '[had] sacrificed everything to purge Scotland of its deadening Philistinism and who – in John Speirs's words – "still stands for health and life and sincerity in Scotland against complacency and indifference"' (*AM*, p. 390). Though Henderson could not give his unreserved support to MacDiarmid's cure for the national malaise, the poet had correctly diagnosed it, and had, in turn, inspired Henderson to look for his own solutions.

Notes

1. The only direct references to the 'Flytings' in recent surveys of twentieth-century Scottish literature appear in Bell, 'Old Country, New Dreams: Scottish Poetry since the 1970s', p. 189; and Watson, *The Literature of Scotland: The Twentieth Century*, p. 120.
2. An earlier version of this chapter appeared as 'The Folkniks in the Kailyard: Hamish Henderson and the "Folk-song" Flyting'.
3. For a representative sample of the 'Flytings' in the original format see *The Scotsman* throughout April 1964.
4. See Horne, 'Highbrow v "Highlander": the feud'.
5. The dispute began in response to an article by the novelist Sophie Cooke and included contributions from Tessa Ransford, Catherine Czerkawska, Stuart Kelly, Scott Hames and James Robertson.
6. *Burns: Complete Poems and Songs*, pp. 135–6.
7. 'The Muse in Rose Street' is also the title of a poem in the anthology by Goodsir Smith.

8. Craig went on to insist that 'Scotland's lays are the ballads, and thus it is not exaggeration but the sober truth to say that in Jeannie Robertson [a 'tradition-bearer' and singer 'discovered' by Henderson in 1953] Scotland has her Homeric-type singer' (*TAN*, p. 117).
9. Munro, *Democratic Muse*, pp. 20–48, 168–72.
10. *Democratic Muse*, p. 45.
11. Watson, *Literature of Scotland*, pp. 8–9.
12. See Morgan, 'The Beatnik in the Kailyard'; Finlay, '"A River That Flows On": A Critical Overview of Hamish Henderson's Life and Work'; and Nicholson, *Edwin Morgan*, pp. 38–41.
13. The poets involved were Ian Hamilton Finlay, W. Price Turner, Tom Wright, Stewart Conn, Shaun Fitzsimon, Anne Turner and Tom Buchan. The Abbotsford was one of the pubs in Edinburgh's New Town favoured by MacDiarmid and many of the poets featured in the *Honour'd Shade* anthology.
14. Bold, *MacDiarmid*, p. 417.
15. *Letters of Hugh MacDiarmid*, pp. 811–15.
16. Bold, *MacDiarmid*, pp. 402–31.
17. See MacDiarmid and Muir, 'For the Vernacular Circle (*The Bulletin* January 1938)'.
18. See *The Armstrong Nose* on anti-apartheid demonstrations (p. 185); on the marches of the Orange Order (pp. 198–202); on Christian attitudes towards homosexuality (pp. 209–10); on Scottish Labour Party policy and independence (pp. 227–8); on *Private Eye* and their brand of satire, particularly as directed against a young MP, Gordon Brown (pp. 255–6); on the 1820 Rising (pp. 265–9); and on Thatcher and the Poll Tax (pp. 272–8).
19. Bell, 'Old Country, New Dreams', p. 189.
20. McNaughtan, 'Hamish Henderson: Folk-Hero', p. 2.
21. Hunter, 'The Odyssey of a Wandering King', p. 118.
22. Rattenbury, 'Flytings', p, 27.
23. Ross, 'Hamish Henderson', pp. 14–15.
24. This is a phrase used by Henderson to describe Gramsci's methodology, though it also applies here to the expressive and incisive quality of Henderson and MacDiarmid's disagreements (*PL*, p. 15).
25. Henderson, 'Freedom Becomes People', p. 1.
26. MacDiarmid, *Complete Poems*, p. 1053.
27. He also chose 'To the Immortal Memory of John Maclean', 'The Dead Liebknecht' and 'The Skeleton of the Future (at Lenin's Tomb)'.
28. Speirs, *Scots Literary Tradition*, p. 159.
29. MacDiarmid, *Complete Poems*, p. 298.
30. 'Hugh MacDiarmid: The Langholm Byspale', p. 21. Henderson lifts his terms directly from the final stanza of MacDiarmid's 'Second Hymn to Lenin'.
31. MacDiarmid, *Complete Poems*, p. 328.
32. See 'Tangling with the Langholm Byspale' (*AM*, pp. 381–404).

33. Henderson, 'Scotland's Alamein', pp. 3–4.
34. 'Scotland's Alamein', p. 4.
35. 'Scotland's Alamein', p. 4. 'History does not pardon the defeated': Henderson perhaps adapted this sentiment from Auden's 'Spain', which ends: 'We are left alone with our day, and the time is short, and / History to the defeated / May say Alas but cannot help nor pardon' (*Selected Poems*, p. 57).
36. 'Scotland's Alamein', p. 3.
37. See 'Problacht na H-Eireann: Irish Republic Proclaimed' (1949) and 'Scotland at the World Peace Congress' (1949).
38. Goodsir Smith, 'MacDiarmid's *Three Hymns to Lenin*', p. 144.
39. Alexander Dubček (1921–92), Slovak politician, communist reformist and leader of the Prague Spring.
40. Henderson, 'Hugh MacDiarmid', p. 22. This image is reproduced in volume two of Neat's biography, *Poetry Becomes People*, pp. 316–17.
41. Smith, *Scottish Literature: Character and Influence*, p. 35.
42. The photograph was taken by Henry Van der Weyde around 1895. It appears in the Norton Critical Edition of *Strange Case of Dr. Jekyll and Mr. Hyde* (p. 175).
43. 'Hugh MacDiarmid', p. 22.
44. *Princeton Encyclopedia of Poetry and Poetics*, p. 416.
45. Bawcutt, *Dunbar the Makar*, pp. 222–3.
46. MacDiarmid, *Complete Poems*, p. 82.
47. MacDiarmid, 'The Flytin' o' the Makars', pp. 43–8. MacDiarmid's editorial was written in response to an on-going dispute in the pages of the *Daily Record*, in which W. D. Cocker retaliated against Douglas Young's arguments in his pamphlet *Plastic Scots* (1946) and denigrated the Scottish Renaissance Movement.
48. Bawcutt, *Dunbar the Makar*, p. 222.
49. Wittig, *The Scottish Tradition in Literature*, pp. 173, 208, 229, 241, 242, 287.
50. Simpson, 'The Legacy of Flyting', pp. 503–4.
51. Craig, *Scottish Literature and the Scottish People*, p. 310.
52. Henderson is not acknowledged as the author of these notes on the record itself, however, Neat makes this assertion in his biography (*Poetry Becomes People*, p. 97). The style and content of the piece is certainly consistent with Henderson's other writings on the folk revival from this period.
53. *Ding Dong Dollar*, pp. 1–5.
54. Simpson, 'Legacy of Flyting', p. 505.
55. Bawcutt, *Dunbar the Makar*, p. 227.
56. Simpson, 'Legacy of Flyting', p. 506.
57. Bawcutt, *Dunbar the Makar*, p. 228.
58. Bawcutt, *Dunbar the Makar*, p. 225; Simpson, 'Legacy of Flyting', p. 505.
59. Calder, 'Scottish Language in Transition', p. 70.
60. Gatherer, 'Flyting Scotsman', p. 4.
61. Morgan, 'MacDiarmid Embattled', p. 20.

62. Wittig, *The Scottish Tradition in Literature*, p. 123; Bawcutt, *Dunbar the Makar*, p. 244.
63. MacDiarmid, *Ugly Birds Without Wings.*
64. Bawcutt, *Dunbar the Makar*, pp. 233–4, 226.
65. Ibid., p. 227.
66. MacDiarmid's evocation of Julien Benda's *La Trahison de Clercs* (often translated as the 'treason' or 'betrayal' of the 'intellectuals') (1927) was no doubt intended to add critical and intellectual weight to his stance. However, MacDiarmid cannot be sure that Benda would not also dismiss his own work as a betrayal of the dispassionate pursuit of Truth that is, and should be, the sole concern of the intellectual, or *clerc*.
67. Calder, *Revolving Culture*, pp. 229–41.
68. Craig, *Scottish Literature and the Scottish People*, p. 11.
69. 'Second Hymn to Lenin', *Complete Poems*, p. 323. Henderson and Craig both cite passages from this poem with similar intentions throughout the '*Honour'd Shade* Flyting' and the 'Folksong Flyting' (*TAN*, pp. 95, 122, 125, 126).
70. Lyall, *Hugh MacDiarmid's Poetry and Politics of Place*, pp. 172–3, 178.
71. *Letters of Hugh MacDiarmid*, p. 743.
72. Davie, *Crisis of the Democratic Intellect*, p. 111.
73. Simpson, 'Legacy of Flyting', p. 505.
74. Simpson, 'Legacy of Flyting', p. 513; Bawcutt, *Dunbar the Makar*, pp. 226–7.
75. Martin, *Ritual Dialogue*, p. 362.
76. The friendship that Henderson and MacDiarmid enjoyed in the decade preceding the 'Flytings' does seem to have soured in conjunction with the acrimony of these debates. However, after MacDiarmid's death Henderson challenged descriptions of their 'desperate enmity' with accounts of the long personal correspondence they enjoyed in later years (*TAN*, pp. 141, 236).
77. MacDiarmid, *Lucky Poet*, p. 372.
78. MacDiarmid, *Socialist Poems*, pp. 73–4.
79. Gatherer, 'Flyting Scotsman', p. 5.

CHAPTER

2

WAR POETRY AND SOLDIERS' SONGS

Henderson's poem series, 'Freedom Becomes People', was published in 1985 with a brief passage explaining 'the idea of the poem'. This 'idea', dated 1968, set out the themes of an extended sequence of 'art-poetry' that was to be the first Henderson had published since his *Elegies for the Dead in Cyrenaica* (1948). It begins with a quotation from Heinrich Heine: 'Freedom, which has hitherto only become man here and there, must pass into the mass itself, into the lowest strata of society, and become people'. Henderson insists that what Heine says of freedom applies also to poetry: that it has the potential to *become* everyone, and indeed, that it has, like freedom, a moral imperative to *become* everyone. The simple present form – 'becomes' – invokes the sense in which both liberties and lyrical self-expression must be continually sought out and reaffirmed; this is a universal, timeless truth. To ensure that this democratisation of poetry is realised is, writes Henderson, 'our most urgent task'.[1] This ideal is articulated as an enterprise for the collective, and as an aspiration not only of Henderson's creative work but one that ought to be pursued by any poetry worthy of the name.

The 'idea of the poem' is not simply an exposition of Henderson's views on the responsibilities of the creative artist in contemporary society; it is a heuristic device offered to the magazine's readers. Henderson's ideas about how the 'isolation' of the artist in modern society might be overcome provide a distillation of his cultural politics and a blueprint for their suggested aesthetic forms. The purpose of this chapter is to explore some of the early manifestations of this search for a poetry that 'becomes people'. Henderson's most productive period, in terms of poetic output, coincided with his military service and with the remaining post-war years of the 1940s. Indeed, Henderson's experiences of war constituted a vital formative influence on his political values and on the cultural forms through which they were to be conceived and pursued.

Douglas Gifford suggests that Henderson was perhaps the greatest Scottish poet of the Second World War. He was also one of the most prolific. As Gifford noted, almost two-thirds of his *Collected Poems and Songs* are 'war-related'.[2] Though this collection is not exhaustive, Henderson's concern with the War is palpable in most of his poetry and in a considerable proportion of his songs. The immediacy of his experience of war, its landscapes, and its human causes and consequences, are ever-present in this material. The roots of the cultural-political position Henderson was to arrive at by 1968 can be traced in his work from the period during and immediately following the War. This war poetry and these soldiers' songs should be understood as concerted efforts to reconcile theory and practice, to imagine a lyrical mode that neither patronises nor alienates the soldiers whose voices are represented. In this way, Henderson's early works foreshadow his writings about the folk revival, which was to reconcile the artist with the voice of that romantic ideal, 'the people'.

The desire for a poetry that 'becomes people' had early expression in Henderson's notes for a Workers' Educational Association lecture entitled 'The Role of the Artist in Society' (1949): 'Artists must try to reach completeness . . . the poet and the community must be threaded together again'.[3] The re-engagement of 'poetry' and the 'people' must then include the poet's reconciliation with the 'community'. In his 1968 manifesto of sorts, Henderson proposes that we 'go to school with the folksingers . . . because in the past, and breenging into the present, it is their work which has "become people"'.[4] The aim of the poem, writes Henderson, is to argue for the reconciliation of the artist and society: 'it would no longer (like my desert war *Elegies for the Dead in Cyrenaica*) be a poem of endurance, of in the main passive suffering; it would rather represent the moment of *resolve*, of *transformation*, of *insurrection*' (emphases added).[5] Though Henderson does not elaborate in his description of this 'moment' that his poetry – and 'poetry' in general – should address, he does provide us with some clues. If 'resolve' is read in its musical application to refer to the movement from discord to concord; if 'transformation' is thought of in terms of linguistics: as the conversion of an element of the underlying, logical, deep structure of a sentence, into an element of the surface structure; and if 'insurrection' is taken explicitly, as a committed uprising against authority, the character of this 'moment', and its relevance to a poetry that 'becomes people', becomes a little clearer. Extending the metaphorical reach of Henderson's description we can see that his poetic project aims for a kind of harmony; a consensus or unity that can emerge from previously obscured places to present its true character openly and honestly. It also suggests a revolutionary act, pushing against the domineering discourses of officialdom. Henderson's 'poetry' seeks to address the world from among 'the people', redefining their relationship with art and promoting a sincere, direct form of collective self-expression. Folk art offers a visceral, unrefined, unpretentious form sustained by the anonymous agents of oral transmission. It is this notion of folk culture that Henderson seeks to find a setting and a subject for in his 'idea of the poem'. As Finlay has also noted, this moment occurs 'whenever a song is shared, for in the sharing the song is reborn. This moment is a proving ground for all emotional and political truths. It gifts us our common humanity, our insurrectionary awareness that "freedom becomes people"' (*AM*, p. xxxi).

Henderson explains that the symbolic movement away from the desert of his *Elegies* must be towards a 'likelier landscape [of] Italy and Scotland combined, as in "Banks of Sicily" [his song "The 51st Highland Division's Farewell to Sicily"]'. The poem would celebrate the '"vulgar" Italy so hated and despised by its bourgeoisie – its bounding voracious popular culture, its secrecy, its turbulence, its victorious gaiety, and above all its unbeatable lust for life'.[6] The 'vulgar' – from *vulgus*, the 'common people' – is another term for the popular lived culture that Henderson saw as a source for new poetic forms. The passage implies that this unbridled human expressiveness is common to parts of Scotland's cultural landscape and that these elements should be unearthed and celebrated. Such work could offer the possibility of a genuine 'people's culture' that would heal the division between the artist and society. The movement away from the landscape of the wartime elegies also suggests that there is an outlook that was forged, for Henderson at least, in the struggle against Europe's fascist regimes, but which had to evolve for peacetime and, in particular, for Scotland's place in post-war Europe. Informed by his experiences of the War, and negotiating with the difficult issues of how to represent the dead and how to speak for the whole community of soldiers, Henderson's poems and songs provide us with an account of his intellectual movement towards the folk revival and the folk-literary synthesis he proposed in conjunction with it.

Henderson's War

Henderson is generally remembered for his songs rather than his poetry. His folksongs, 'folk poetry', or 'song poems', as they were variously referred to, had almost totally supplanted what might be termed his 'art-poetry' by the 1950s. Though we know that he worked sporadically on literary poetry during this time, it was rarely published. His *Elegies for the Dead in Cyrenaica* (1948) was the only volume of poetry widely available until the *Collected Poems and Songs* (2000). The Henderson archives feature some early lyrical experiments and the collected volume contains some work from the period before his active service, however, the first published volumes, *Ballads of World War II* (1947) and *Elegies* the following year, are, in effect, Henderson's first great pronouncement on the role of the artist in society.[7]

Before the War Henderson studied modern languages and literature – German and French – at Downing College, Cambridge. He was active in political societies and debates, and, following a speech on fascism at the Cambridge Union, a Quaker group running a secretive anti-fascist programme in Nazi Germany approached him. Under the guise of a trip to Göttingen to read Hölderlin, Henderson was tasked with sending letters and messages for the resistance from within Germany. He returned, along with a child of the Jewish family with whom he had been staying, days before the invasion of Poland. Though Henderson tried to enlist, he was originally refused on the basis of poor eyesight. In 1940 he was drafted into the Pioneer Corps and spent the winter constructing anti-tank defences in East Sussex. He later joined the Intelligence Corps and was sent to Egypt in late 1941. Throughout the remainder of the War, Henderson was attached to various divisions, most famously, with the 51st Highlanders. He was involved in the North African Desert Campaign, and witnessed the Battle of El Alamein, before joining the invasion of Sicily and the subsequent advance north through Italy.[8] Henderson's duties included the interrogation of German and Italian POWs, and later he organised Allied co-operation with the *Resistenza* in Italy. Henderson regarded himself, and his generation, as having grown for war (*AM*, p. 319). His poem 'Ballad of the Twelve Stations of My Youth' is a testament to this feeling, as the final 'station' records his climbing the cobbled streets 'with other conscripts . . . From now, my boyhood's done' (*CPS*, p. 24).

Following his demobilisation, Henderson published his *Elegies*. Conceived in the arena of war, the poem-series was only completed on his return to the UK. It was awarded the Somerset Maugham award in 1949 and was received with considerable plaudits. A year previously Henderson had also published the *Ballads* under the auspices of a private members' club – 'The Lili Marleen Club of Glasgow'. Among these songs were some of Henderson's own works, alongside American, Italian, German and French-Tunisian soldiers' songs he had collected from servicemen on both sides of the conflict. He produced other poems and songs during this period, some of which found publication in periodicals during and after the War. Though these will also be addressed, the twin volumes of the *Elegies* and the *Ballads* constitute a concise and appreciable demonstration of Henderson's cultural politics, rendered in different aesthetic forms. These works, their shared aspects and defining differences, offer an illuminating framework for the analysis of this formative period for Henderson's poetic style.

Elegies for the Dead and the Living

Henderson's experiences of war, his sensitivity towards its complex causes and its uncomplicated human cost, and his awareness of the historical (and trans-historical) enormity of these events and their fundamental causes, found expression both in the 'art-poetry' of the *Elegies*, and the 'folk art' of the *Ballads*. Though these projects share some qualities in this respect, they rely on very different forms of expression. As reviewers at the time and critics and literary historians since have recognised, Henderson's poem-cycle shows a modernist sensibility in its metaphysical explorations and its free verse. In terms of form, the poems have been compared to those of Eliot and Pound.[9] Naturally, the *Elegies* have also been analysed as 'war poetry' and, more often, as '*Scottish* war poetry'.[10] However, it is not the aim of this chapter to consider Henderson's poems in relation to the debated canon of 'war poetry' – though he did acknowledge Wilfred Owen's influence (*AM*, p. 450) – rather, to trace those elements that seem to precipitate his later work.

Commentators have often noted the documentary force of the *Elegies* – as a descriptive recording of a soldier's experiences of the desert and of the warfare it hosted.[11] The persistent sense of place and the over-bearing atmosphere of Henderson's elegies invoke a tone of verisimilitude. Lorne Maclaine Campbell V.C., who served as a Lieutenant Colonel in North Africa, wrote to Henderson praising his work for giving 'a voice to all the, for me, quite inarticulate feelings one had in the desert' (*EDC*, p. 68). In his introduction to the 1977 edition, Sorley MacLean wrote: 'what I remembered of it [the desert war] in 1949, when I first read the Elegies, and what I still remember of it, responds sharply to the impact of the physical and psycho-physical "feel" of it in the poems' (*EDC*, p. 12). The setting inhabited by individual soldiers, embedded in the vast desert landscape; the intimated movement of jeeps across its surface; the dulled impact of shells in the distance; and the community of soldierly life, are all repeatedly revisited in the *Elegies*. In his essay 'Germany in Defeat' (1948), Henderson explained that in the North African desert it had occurred to him that the Surrealist painters of the 1930s were 'merely prophetic':

> The debris of a desert battle-field, every conceivable object in creation thrown out of the world's lumber room on to a 'nostalgic landscape' of Paul Nash; the skeletal silhouette of a crashed Stuka leading the eye away into an infinity of sterile desolation; the earliest littoral life, and wrecked upon it some grotesque memento of human mortality – all these one had seen before. (*AM*, p. 365)

The theatre of desert war, then, already belonged to the artistic imagination before the soldiers arrived. It was a site for the collision and detritus of symbols and histories, and Henderson would transpose several landscapes over it, imbuing all with a kind of collective and transcendent *memento mori*. He concludes his preface by recalling the comments of a friend on the central ideas of the proposed poem-series. He remarked that 'surely, having been so much in the midst of things, you must find it very difficult to be impartial'. With hindsight, Henderson surmises that, as he gradually understands how people form their opinions, it seems 'next to impossible' to achieve this impartiality, *unless* one has been 'in the midst of things' (*EDC*, p. 16). This feeling, of a poetic voice that has been fully submerged in the experiences it depicts, being 'in the midst of things', is one that endures even through the more abstracted and less situational passages of the *Elegies*.

Beyond the physical setting, Campbell and MacLean suggested a deeper and more enduring consciousness in Henderson's rendering of the desert war that corresponded poignantly with their own experiences. Something of this 'feeling' is explained in the preface to the *Elegies*: '. . . it was the remark of a captured German officer which first suggested to me the theme of these poems. He had said: "Africa changes everything. In reality we are allies, and the desert is our common enemy"'. Henderson explains how this comment struck him:

> In the early stages of the desert war they [the opposing troops] were to a large extent forced to live off each other. Motor transport, equipment of all kinds and even armoured fighting vehicles changed hands frequently. The result was a curious 'doppelgaenger' effect, and it is this, enhanced by the deceptive distances and uncertain directions of the North African wasteland, which I have tried to capture in some of the poems. (*EDC*, p. 16)

The *Elegies* were written between 1942 and 1947 in North Africa, Italy and Scotland. The 'doppelgaenger [sic] effect', an 'effect of mirage and looking-glass illusion' as Henderson also described it, was, in the years following the events the poems describe, to expand its significance and gain a metaphorical reach that would be central to Henderson's poem-cycle:

> the memory of this odd effect . . . persisted, and gradually became for me a symbol of our human civil war, in which the roles seem constantly to change and the objectives to shift and vary. It suggested too a complete reversal of the alignments and alliances which we had come to accept as inevitable. The conflict seemed rather to be between 'the dead, the innocent' – that eternally wronged proletariat of levelling death in which all the fallen are comrades – and ourselves, the living, who cannot hope to expiate our survival but by 'spanning history's apollyon chasm'. (Ibid.)

In a later interview Henderson explained his reference to 'Apollyon', the beast with flames in his belly, who faces Christian in *The Pilgrim's Progress*, as a symbol of that which must be overcome in reconciling the survivors with the dead – 'facing up to the problems they would have faced had they been alive'.[12] This relationship, between the living and the dead, and the compulsion to try to reconcile this 'conflict' with history itself, can be traced throughout the poem-series. As Henderson's explanation suggests, the poetry came out of the landscape: the sensory experience of warfare was taken home and mulled over, intellectualised and imbued with an expansive metaphorical significance. While opposing armies faced one another across the desert, the human on either side was a reflection of itself, united in its struggle with an inhuman landscape. Giles Romilly recognised this marriage of setting and symbol: 'the desert was like the stain of dye with which a scientist colours a piece of matter before looking at it under a microscope. It allowed detail to stand out and take on symbolic value' (*EDC*, pp. 62–3).

The *Elegies* inhabit the desert from multiple perspectives. Henderson, or at least, the constructed voice of the 'poet', is apparent throughout, making comment on the task of the poem-series itself, both as a record of the events and an attempt to explain their significance for the individual and the collective. The prologue initiates this reflexive stance, proclaiming the poet's motivation: 'this, my rash / Ambitious wish in verse to write / A true and valued testament' (*EDC*, p. 17). The first elegy, 'End of a Campaign', then introduces the reader to the 'brutish desert' – a 'landscape of half-wit / stunted ill-will' – and, after musing on the body of the dead, on their lives and their deaths, finishes by reflecting on the task of the elegist:

> . . . and seeing that all
> have gone down like curs into anonymous silence,
> I will bear witness for I knew the others.
> Seeing that littoral and interior are alike indifferent
> and the birds are drawn again to our welcoming north
> why should I not sing *them*, the dead, the innocent?
> (*EDC*, p. 22)

This allegiance with the dead and the compulsion of the survivor to 'sing *them*' in the face of indifference, is critical to the poet's attempt to circumvent the popular reflex: to herald the sacrifice of the dead. A sombre, qualified glorification of sacrifice and its contingent martyrdom might be expected from a series of elegies for the war-dead. However, Henderson rejects the implied premise of this 'sacrifice', refusing to accept that these deaths are in any way inevitable and therefore justifiable, even in the fight against Fascism. It is in relation to this aspect that his war poetry has been compared to that of Sorley MacLean.[13]

Throughout the period in which Henderson was writing, he became a keen reader of MacLean's poetry, carrying a copy of *17 Poems For 6d* (1940), a collection in Scots, English and Gaelic, by MacLean and Robert Garioch, with him through the War. He was among the first to recognise the importance of MacLean's work and to introduce it to a broader readership (*TAN*, p. 302). In an article for the *Daily Worker* in 1949, he described MacLean's as 'some of the finest Marxist poetry in modern European literature', noting that for MacLean, and the generation of Scottish poets to which he belonged, MacDiarmid's *Hymns to Lenin* and the Spanish Civil War represented two important 'turning-points' in the formation of their political worldview and the forms their cultural expression would take (*AM* pp. 444–5). These observations pull Henderson and MacLean into alignment and encourage a comparison of their impressions of war and their intellectual responses to it.

'Part Two' of Henderson's elegy series is prefaced with verses selected from MacLean's poem *Glac a' Bhàis* (*Death Valley*):

> Sitting dead in 'Death Valley'
> below the Ruweisat Ridge,
> a boy with his forelock down about his cheek
> and his face slate-grey.
> I thought of the right and joy
> he had from his Fuehrer,
> of falling in the field of slaughter
> to rise no more . . .
> Whatever his desire or mishap,
> his innocence or malignance,
> he showed no pleasure in his death
> below the Ruweisat Ridge.
> (*EDC*, p. 35)[14]

The positioning of these stanzas demands a comparison with the preface to 'Part One' of the *Elegies*, which comes from Goethe:

> The gods, the unending, give all things
> without stint to their beloved:
> all pleasures, the unending,
> and all pains, the unending, without stint.
> (*EDC*, p. 19)[15]

This statement pre-empts the distressing but nevertheless humane account of the desert war that is to follow. The enduring and abstracted condition of humankind – as the object of the gods' love and, consequently, subject to 'all' pleasures and pains – functions as a qualifier for the desert war. Indeed, this premise gets dangerously close to excusing mass death and suffering; proposing that the concentration of 'pain' has its counterpart 'pleasure' elsewhere, out of sight. This is not to say that Goethe's lines bear no relation to the minutiae of life detailed in some of the poems; he repeats: *all* things – pleasures and pains – are proffered. The lines from MacLean, however, offer an elaboration of this state of being, giving an unflinching account of the real implications of war, and the vast inhuman space between the language of the structures that orchestrate the conflict ('the joy and the right'), and the human tragedy of dead soldiers. MacLean addresses a singular consequence of Goethe's truth. The relationship between these two passages becomes more striking when Henderson's explanatory note is taken into account: 'Goethe's quatrain was frequently included in small anthologies "for the Front" carried by German soldiers in the field – and indeed its thought lies very near the mood of many of them'. In this sense Goethe's words were an interpretative framework for the soldiers, one that contextualised their wartime hardships with a transcendental premise, and encouraged acceptance and stoicism, or at least a recognition of the limits of individual agency. Henderson sets this alongside the 'sceptical ironic spirit' of MacLean (*EDC*, p. 58). Together these excerpts offer a fragment of dialogue between two economies of scale that can be brought to bear on conflict and sacrifice. He reminds us that any grand vision of our human condition must accommodate the most extreme pleasures and pains, whilst insisting that we ought not to lift war out of its own reality when we seek to understand it. Neither the actuality of the 'dead' in Cyrenaica nor the seeming inevitability of war and of death is allowed to take precedence in these poems: both realities must be reconciled.

Citing a letter in which the poet describes the scene that inspired the poem, Joy Hendry offers some context for the compassionate eye MacLean casts on the boy below the Ruweisat Ridge: 'seeing his inglorious death made him ashamed of his "many foolish generalisations" about the need to wipe out fascists, and he realised that the ordinary soldier is not "any kind of an 'ist' at all"'.[16] Henderson viewed the War from a similarly humanistic stance. The inclusion of MacLean's lines indicates that one temporal site for the 'unending' complex of pleasures and pains that Goethe's gods have given to humankind is that of war. It is a site clearly imbalanced by its proclivity for pain. Henderson's final five elegies (which are prefaced by MacLean's verse) illustrate the difficulties implicit in engaging with the dead – those casualties of 'our human civil war' – their reality, and their relationship with 'us', the living. In this sense, Henderson tests the limits of Goethe's quatrain. These lines on the gifts of the gods can be approached as an exordium for the experience of warfare, as well as for these particular elegies for the dead and, as such, they refer to an incontrovertible condition of human life. Though Goethe's statement might not satisfy our need for an explanation for death, pain and suffering, it does describe the relentlessness of our capacity for 'all things', including those most cherished *and* those most feared. In Henderson's hands both Goethe and MacLean address humanity's unceasing propensity for wretchedness, though from different vantage points: one, in terms of the celestial 'gift' of human life and, the other, from the only certainty that can be read on the face of a dead serviceman.

In the sixth elegy, 'Acroma', Henderson writes of the various, and sometimes conflicting, perspectives of the War:

On one point however there is unanimity: their sacrifice
though hard and heroic was on the whole 'necessary'.
I too have acquiesced
in this evasion: that the unlucky
or the destined must inevitably fall

> . . .
> Yet how can I shame them, saying that they
> have died for us: that it was expedient
> a generation should die for the people?
> (*EDC*, p. 37)

Henderson's acknowledgment of the 'necessary' sacrifice was perhaps a response to Auden's 'Spain': 'To-day the deliberate increase in the chances of death, / The conscious acceptance of guilt in the *necessary murder*' (emphasis added).[17] Orwell famously dismissed Auden's phrase as evidence of the poet's 'amoralism' and 'warmongering', assuring his readers it was indicative of the position of many poets in the 1930s: 'so much of left-wing thought is a kind of playing with fire by people who don't even know that fire is hot'.[18]

The fraught relationship between the living and the dead resurfaces, and Henderson's poetic voice goes on to wonder how he might acknowledge the dead: 'what requiem can I sing in the ears of the living? // No blah about their sacrifice . . .' The final stanza reads:

> So the words that I have looked for, and must go on looking for,
> are words of whole love, which can slowly gain the power
> to reconcile and heal. Other words would be pointless. (*EDC*, p. 38)

The search for these words is the task of the *Elegies*. The seventh elegy, 'Seven Good Germans', which is perhaps the closest in tone to MacLean's, sketches out the lives and deaths of seven Germans, who now 'bide under their standing crosses'. Their characters reflect the variety of attitudes and circumstances that make up the body of the 'enemy', exploding any homogenising conception of 'the fascists'. They include: a man who had unshakeable 'faith in the Endsieg'; one who only wanted to return to his sweetheart; a Pole (or 'Volksdeutscher') who 'talked of the dirty Polacken'; and a legionnaire with 'one more chance to redeem his lost honour' (*EDC*, pp. 39–41). These sketches are gathered under the gaze of the soldier-poet and they establish a climate of empathy, set 'in the midst of things', recognising the arbitrariness of that which distinguishes the speaker from the 'enemy'. The poem finally unites the seven soldiers in their deaths, rather than in their living values, their loyalties, or their uniforms.

The ninth elegy, 'Fort Capuzzo', considers a soldier looking at the grave of one of the enemy. The poetic voice states that this episode helped him to understand the meaning of the 'hard word "pietas"' (one of the Roman virtues, usually translated as 'duty' or 'devotion'). A parenthetic aside states that it is a word unfamiliar to the newsreel commentator, the pimp, the informer and the traitor. Henderson's note on the elegy explains that the 'mike-side [sic] manner . . . ignoble gibes at the expense of enemy front-line soldiers' of some radio commentators filled him, and others, with 'shame and fury' (*EDC*, p. 60). The thoughts of the soldier looking on the grave are recorded:

> . . . Yes, the only good Jerry,
> as they say, is your sort, chum.
> Cheerio, you poor bastard.
> Don't be late on parade when the Lord calls 'Close Order'.
> Keep waiting for the angels. Keep listening for Reveille.
> (*EDC*, p. 47)

The 'good Germans' of the seventh elegy reappear. The language of the 'good Jerry as a *dead* Jerry' is appropriated by the soldier's sympathetic voice ('you poor bastard'), which is then quickly elevated to the celestial, to a heaven that awaits both Allied and Axis casualties. The commonality of the living troops on both sides is not only based on the landscape they inhabit – the desert, their common enemy – but also on the ultimate unifier of the living: 'the proletariat of levelling death', which faces them all and demands atonement (*EDC*, p. 25). The collective dead are repeatedly described in these terms, as Henderson reminds us that it is not only nationality that dissolves in death but also class. Through his subscription to a broadly Marxian worldview, the collective dead become the revolutionary force of human history. Our mortality makes us equals and only in death can this truth be consummated.

The relationship between the living and the dead is, in turn, the basis of the relationship between humanity and history. It is to the dead that we, the living, are held accountable. In the final elegy, Henderson's poetic voice considers his 'duty', in that 'deadland', as 'Remembrancer', to sing for those (the dead) who 'amnestied / escaped from the tumult':

> We fly from their scorn, but they close all the passes:
> their sleep's our unrest, we lie bound in their inferno –
> this alliance must be vaunted and affirmed, lest they condemn us!
> . . .
> . . . Either build for the living
> love, patience and power to absolve the tormented,
> or else choke in the folds of their black-edged vendetta!

These lines lead to the final proposition: that we take to the living, the 'blood, fire and red flambeaux of death's proletariat [. . .] At last, spanning this history's apollyon chasm, proclaim them reconciled' (*EDC*, p. 51). The terms of this reconciliation between the living and the dead are not clear. The living are implicated in the fact of the dead, and one must 'build for the living' if we are to sustain 'our human house', which incorporates the dead, the living and the not yet born. These closing lines of the final elegy gather metrical momentum and leave a carefully prepared space for that reconciliation, though it is never expressly achieved. It seems that it is only possible to describe a *movement towards* this final syncretism between the living and the dead. In this sense it can be understood as a comment on the limitations of poetic examination.

This construction is lifted out of the modern desert war and given a transhistorical setting in the final poem of the series, 'Heroic Song for the Runners of Cyrene'. It is based on the legend, recorded by Sallust, of the Philaeni brothers of Carthage, who ran out from their city towards the runners of Cyrene, to determine the outer limits of their city colonies without going to war. At the point of meeting, the competitors were to be buried alive, thereby marking the boundary.[19] Henderson states that, for him, Cyrene is a symbol of 'civilised humanity, of our "human house"' (*EDC*, p. 60n). The eponymous runners, who will 'reclaim the dead land / for their city of Cyrene', have 'history the doppelgaenger / running to meet them' (*EDC*, pp. 54–5). The 'doppelgaenger' effect that Henderson felt so keenly in the mid-twentieth century is given an ancient precedent. The song for the runners then gathers pace: 'the goal is in sight. Simultaneous the onrush, / the clash close at hand, o incarnate dialectic!' On impact, the runners and their counterparts finally fall, 'locking like lovers / . . . / down the thunderous cataract of day' (*EDC*, pp. 56–7). This 'dialectic' is the history of humanity: human civilisation must grapple with the common structures of its past, with its origins, if it is to be preserved. As Henderson's series culminates with this point, the survivor's guilt that is evoked in earlier verses seems to have been absorbed and superseded by this larger process. Nevertheless, the 'dialectic' is made *incarnate* through the bodies of the historical runners. The grand narrative of civilisation cannot be extricated from its human cost; the bodies of the contemporary war-dead are, like the runners, physical incarnations of the dialectic.

The apparent 'flavour of dialectical materialism' in the *Elegies* attracted criticism from some reviewers. However, MacDiarmid celebrated this aspect, insisting that Henderson's were Marxist poems, and the result not only of 'intense experience' but an underlying 'theory of social causation' that afforded great insights and a distinctively *modern* mode of expression.[20] More recently, Angus Calder commented that the eighth elegy, 'Karnak', comes close to 'dissolving into a view of history as cyclical rather than progressively dialectical', in its reference to historical conquests in Egypt.[21] In this sense, Henderson's poetry might be conceived as a study of mythopoeia rather than of history. Calder goes on to identify an irreconcilable contradiction between Henderson's compassion for the Germans and his belief – and the position of an assumed Marxist orthodoxy – that Fascism ought to be fought 'ferociously'. These criticisms are, however, successfully negotiated within the *Elegies*. The need of the living to 'expiate' themselves in the face of the 'proletariat of death', and the challenge for humanity to reconcile itself with its history, sets Henderson's work at a level of engagement that can absorb both the need to defeat Fascism and the need to resist dehumanising enemy soldiers. The poetic voice can promote a model of history as dialectical, and can be *at least* hopeful of progress, without making unfounded predictions or glossing over the common features of past and present conflicts.

Henderson draws from Denis Saurat's 'Death and the Dreamer' for his preface to 'Heroic Song for the Runners of Cyrene':

> Without suffering and death one learns nothing.
> We should not know the difference between the visions
> of the intellect and the facts.
> Only those ideas are acceptable that hold through
> suffering and death . . .
> Life is that which leaps.
> (*EDC*, p. 53)

If we return to the task Henderson set for his elegies – reconciling the living with the dead and humanity with the history of civilisation – Saurat's lines provide the final 'song' with an important proposition. The runners' symbolic embrace is an enactment of the fact that 'life is that which leaps': resolve is only possible through such commitment. Death, suffering and pain are antitheses to the theses of life and pleasure, as in Goethe's lines. The explorations that the bulk of the elegies are given over to suggest, as Calder noted, that a solution to the dilemma does not seem possible; rather, in the 'hazy unconvincingness' of the rhetoric there is only an 'impasse'.[22] The grand reconciliation that the *Elegies* seek is perhaps beyond the remit of poetry: it is a task continually deferred to the end of history. Henderson's poems reaffirm the futility of the 'elegy' as a lamentation that can only mourn or regret, where a conclusive reconciliation between the elegist and the dead is what is required. He is sensitive to the limits of poetry as an instructive or explanatory force, openly acknowledging what cannot be resolved by the poet, or at least, what cannot be fully expressed or understood. In this, the attitude of the *Elegies* is similar to that expressed in Romain Rolland's aphorism 'pessimism of the intellect, optimism of the will', a favourite phrase of Antonio Gramsci's, repeated in both his *Prison Letters* and his *Prison Notebooks*, and acknowledged by Henderson in his work on the Italian Marxist.[23] In the wake of these unknowns, there is only an inexplicit and inexpressible human resolve to continue, to persevere.

Henderson's manifesto, 'Freedom Becomes People', designates the *Elegies* as poetry of 'endurance' and 'passive suffering', as opposed to the 'resolve', 'transformation' and 'insurrection' that are the aims of his later work. However, the abstracted narrative movement of the elegies, setting out the dialectic of the dead and the living, that between humanity and history, and the compulsion to traverse these 'apollyon chasms', are better understood as an exploratory gesture towards this forward-looking 'resolve'. In the *Elegies*, these two poetic phases, first of endurance and then of insurrection, are mutually dependent, and together they form a coherent progression. As the poem-series wrestles with life, death and history, and ends with an inexpressible impulse to span the metaphorical chasm and proclaim a great reconciliation, Henderson's new poetic project is to build from this point, towards a reconciliation of the artist with society, of poetry with people. The elegist seeks to overcome a similar dilemma, to 'build our cairn', to find words of 'whole love, which can slowly gain the power / to reconcile and heal' (*EDC*, pp. 51, 28, 38).

'War Poetry' and *Our Time*

In his introductory reader, *War Poetry* (1995), Simon Featherstone presents Henderson's work as an example of the alternative streams of the genre that challenge and expand our understanding of it, beyond the narrow constructions that tend to dominate. By taking broader literary traditions, cultural political beliefs and gender politics into consideration, Featherstone aims to revise the canon and escape from what David Jones termed the 'parenthesis' of war as a limiting, or exceptional, state that separates those within it from any other frame of reference. In his *Elegies* Henderson draws directly from the canon, but also embodies a peripheral Scottish Highland culture that challenges the perceived 'Englishness' of war poetry.[24] For Featherstone, Henderson's Scottish cultural and historical references set him, like Sorley MacLean, apart from the disillusionment suffered by writers like Orwell and Spender, offering a view of the War as 'the continuation of a tradition of heroic political struggle that found its expression in the oppositional language and traditions of Scottish nationalism and in the old alliance with European, rather than English, cultures'.[25] Henderson's European credentials are not only evident in the language and content of the *Elegies* but in the inspiration he drew from writers like Hölderlin, Goethe, Rilke, Dante and Cavafy, who are all either mentioned or cited in the poem-series.

While Henderson assumes this role in Featherstone's argument very comfortably, the national element of his war writing can be overstated. Despite Henderson's admiration for the achievements of the Scottish Literary Renaissance, his allusions to Scots language, Scottish landscapes and historical events need not be read as declarations on national distinctiveness, especially when they are transposed onto the desert landscape of the War through the homesickness and cultural memory of the soldier-poet. In the 'Interlude', for example, the historical voice of Kirkpatrick, by Robert the Bruce's side at the stabbing of the Red Comyn, sounds in the voice of the war poet:

> We'll mak siccar!
> . . . against the worked out systems of sick perversion
> mak siccar

> against the executioner
> against the tyrannous myth and the real terror
> *mak siccar*
> (*EDC*, p. 33)

As this example demonstrates, references to Scottish history are not necessarily devised in the service of a resurgent nationalism. The defiant intention to 'mak siccar' is taken out of the narrative of Bruce's accession to power and universalised through the context of the North African campaign, in opposition to those conceptual structures that induce such 'human civil war'. Similarly, in the first elegy of the collection, the poet, in his efforts to 'bear witness' to the war, is mindful of 'the great word of Glencoe's / son, that we should not disfigure ourselves / with villainy of hatred' (*EDC*, p. 22). This is in reference to the reputed comments of a 'son of old Glencoe' among the Jacobites who occupied Edinburgh in 1745, and insisted on guarding the house of the Master of Stair from looters – the house of those said to have orchestrated the massacre. Henderson regarded this a 'heroic, magnanimous statement' that had relevance for the contemporary global conflict.[26] As its title suggests, the fifth elegy, 'Highland Jebel', fuses the language and landscapes of the highlands of Scotland and the mountains of North Africa by evoking the 'burning byres' of the Clearances in the barren, burning desert (*EDC*, pp. 29–30). The *Elegies* also explore the ancient civilisations of Egypt and Libya, alongside Scotland's more recent pasts. In this respect the collection explores the kind of 'combined landscapes' that Henderson accredited to his song 'The 51st Highland Division's Farewell to Sicily', where, in the 'shebeens and bothies', 'kind signorinas were cheerie' (*CPS*, p. 84).

Featherstone also writes of Henderson's *Ballads of World War II* as an example of engagement with 'popular culture' that again challenges the typically accepted forms of war poetry.[27] In his foreword Henderson explains that the balladry of World War II grew up under the shadow of – and often in virtual conflict with – the official or commercial radio of the combatant nations.

> The state radio in time of war does not encourage dissidence from the straight patriotic line. It regards most expressions of the human reaction to soldiering as a drag on the national war effort . . .
> For the Army balladeer comes of a rebellious house. His characteristic tone is one of cynicism. (*BW*, p. iii)

For Featherstone, the project of the *Ballads* signifies an argument for the political importance of soldiers' songs as subversions of official discourses of war. Henderson is not alone in promoting this kind of material. Indeed, as Featherstone also notes, Edgell Rickword, a poet of the First World War who later edited the journal *Our Time*, proposed that the War offered the opportunity to foster a truly radical popular culture. Rickword asserted that the material pressures of the War could help to 'restore the balance between the written and the spoken word'. He supported his claims with the example of the Spanish Civil War, in which 'thousands of . . . ballads were composed by amateur poets and circulated in the village or the regiment'.[28] Similarly, Henderson retrospectively explained the source of the political and 'humanistic' character of Scottish folk revivalism, and the development of his own ideas of collective cultural expression during the War, as going back to a 'conscious anti-fascist pattern' that arose in the period of the Spanish Civil War.[29] Rickword and Henderson's approach to popular culture is conceived as an organic corrective to the obfuscations of fascist propaganda and its claims on collective identity. It is, therefore, an ideologically defined position, as opposed to an entirely practical response to the military threat of fascist imperialism.

Further parallels between the development of Henderson's cultural politics in response to the War and those promoted by contributors to *Our Time* are plentiful, and help to put Henderson's work in context as part of a larger movement among many on the Left to address the experience of war through the study of popular culture. *Our Time* was a socialist magazine that ran between 1941 and 1949. It had originated as a pamphlet series titled *Poetry and the People* (1938–41) and had connections with Victor Gollancz's Left Book Club. While it was the later incarnation that sought to promote radical popular culture, moving away from its predecessor's focus on popular political poetry, the original title is a construction similar to Henderson's modification of Heine, 'Poetry becomes People'. In an early editorial in *Our Time*, Alfred Sharp set out the magazine's general objectives in the context of the War:

> *Our Time* does not aim at being merely so many pages of pleasant reading. It aims at becoming the conscious voice of all efforts to build a national people's culture, which at this moment will be a vivifying force in the effort to victory, and which will later become the rallying point for rebuilding peace.[30]

Our Time presented itself as part of a campaign to open up a new cultural front in the war, by driving for an organic and democratic movement that could give expression to the lives of 'the people' whilst contributing to the ideological conflict with Fascism.

Henderson's own contributions to *Our Time* began with a collection of three translations of the Sudeten poet, Louis Fürnberg. One of these poems, 'Requiem for the Men the Nazis Murdered', is awash with images of blood, and the crops and harvests of death. The dead condemn the living and threaten to rise again, to cut down 'the sowers who in the furrow / once sowed the bloody seed'. Though the poem seemingly offers up an unambiguous reading which sees these threats levelled at the Nazis, their sympathisers, and those who failed to resist them, it can also be understood as a more enduring and abstracted conflict, as in Henderson's *Elegies*, between the dead and the living: humanity and the casualties of its history. This metaphorical extension of the agricultural calendar lends the poem a sense of tragedy and farce, of the cycles of human history, predictable as the seasons. Another translation of Fürnberg, 'You, my poems, are my weapons', also merits comparison with Henderson's responses to the War and to his cultural politics more generally. Addressed to the writer's own poems, this piece dismisses 'those that call themselves pure poets / [as they] fumble through life solitary and blind', and reveres that poetry which can be wielded as a 'gun ready for action', 'to use against those we know of'. In calling for an engaged and active poetry that is not isolated but that could be 'seized like rifles' by the people, Fürnberg promotes a poetry that can *become people*. This is expressed in the language of violent rebellion; nevertheless, it appoints poetry a place in the vanguard, in facing the conflict brought forth by the others, those 'gangsters [that] are looting and burning'.[31]

Several of Henderson's songs, poems and translations appeared first in *Our Time*, and in 1949 he guest-edited a special Scottish number, for which he wrote a survey of contemporary Scottish writing, alongside articles by MacDiarmid, Goodsir Smith, MacLean and George Campbell Hay.[32] It is difficult to establish the extent to which Henderson was influenced by those *Our Time* writers who, as Featherstone suggests, promoted very similar viewpoints to his own. However, given Henderson's relatively frequent work for the magazine after 1943, it seems safe to assume that he was at least aware of its intellectual thrust and its political leanings.

Many early contributors to *Our Time* advocated an engagement with popular culture, and with song in particular. Their interpretations of song culture and their understanding of its political potential are often remarkably similar to those principles that Henderson later set out in the *Ballads*. In the inaugural edition of *Our Time*, Montague Slater wrote of the commercialists, the 'big men of Tin-pan Alley', who had the intelligence to 'keep an ear open for the true folk songs as they sprout in and around the services'. He considered one army song in particular, 'Bless 'em All', which was bowdlerised in the process of commercialisation, with 'bless' replacing the original 'fuck':

Bless 'em all, bless 'em all,
The long and the short and the tall,
Bless all the sergeants and double-u O ones [W.O.1's]
Bless all the corporals and their blinkin' sons,
'Cos we're saying good-bye to them all,
As back to their billets they crawl,
You'll get no promotion this side of the ocean,
So cheer up, my lads, BLESS 'EM ALL.[33]

Slater heralds the piece as a 'modern folk song' and, even in its censored adaptation, as a 'tight-lipped, ironical joke'.[34] In this respect, the song reflects the 'tone of cynicism' that Henderson accredits to the Army balladeer (*BW*, p. i), and even something of the 'sceptical ironic spirit' he admires in MacLean's 'Death Valley' (*EDC*, p. 58).

A. L. Lloyd, who later became one of the most influential folklorists of the revival in England, also contributed to *Our Time* throughout the War. In articles such as 'Songs of Musso's Army' (May 1943), 'The Songs of Tito's Partisans' (April 1944) and 'The Guerrilla Songs of Greece' (December 1944), Lloyd explored the sociological and political insights that could be afforded by the timely analyses of soldiers' folksongs, and set a precedent that Henderson began to work towards with his *Ballads*. Lloyd describes the folksongs popular in the Italian army as those of complaint of the soldierly life, of a tragic and melancholy tone; or else songs celebrating an imagined end to the War, anticipating the return home. While the character of these songs is to be expected in the 'Anglo-Saxon' model, Lloyd suggests that it is at odds with the fascist spirit of Italian militarism as propagated by Mussolini. He concludes addressing the dictator directly:

> Serious, Signor Mussolini? Ethical? Religious? [some of the qualities that *Il Duce* ascribed to fascism] You may protest that these songs in no way reflect the world-outlook of fascism. And without a shadow of a doubt you are right. But somehow, Signor Mussolini, these songs seem to tie up closer to the history of our times, seem to explain better the Italy of to-day, than do all the high-sounding definitions of principle that you so glibly wrote in chapter F of the Enciclopedia Italiana, and which, so you solemnly swore, represented the true national feeling of the new, liberated, glorious, martial Italy.[35]

Lloyd uses popular folk material to challenge the ideological authority of the Italian government that would embroil its people in war. In this respect, the article describes the subversive nature of soldiers' songs, which Featherstone found in Henderson's *Ballads*, and which afforded him an important role in exploding the canon.

The Army Balladeer and his 'Rebellious House'

Though Henderson did not set out his findings in the kind of direct propagandist terms that Lloyd used, the act of folksong collection that he undertook with Allied troops, partisan fighters and enemy POWs alike, and the fact that the resultant materials are undifferentiated in the published collection, suggests that Henderson was conscious of the political potency of this endeavour. Indeed, Henderson published the ballads under the auspices of the fictitious 'Lili Marleen Club of Glasgow' whereby the transaction involved in buying a copy was technically recast as the paying of a subscription to join the club, followed by the receipt of a complimentary collection of wartime ballads. This evasive strategy of publication was said to have been inspired by Goodsir Smith's Auk Society and was taken up principally because many of the songs were bawdy, and Henderson, as he expressed in his introduction, refused to 'insult [the] ballads by bowdlerising them'. Nevertheless, Henderson's recognition that the ballads' publication risked police intervention suggests that their subversive power was not down to ribaldry alone.[36] Though it seems to have been this aspect that Henderson thought risked censorship, the collection does more than potentially offend the sensibilities of the day: it challenges popular, officially sanctioned conceptions of the war-effort and the soldier's place within them; offering instead, the unexpurgated song-voice of the combatants. If approached individually, the songs might not display a radical point of view, or demonstrate an active political agenda but, when collected and published together under the emphatic and seemingly comprehensive title *Ballads of World War II*, and released through this 'Lili Marleen Club' device, they assume a more subversive and authoritative voice.

The most extreme example of this bawdiness is one of the ballads Henderson himself wrote, though it remains anonymous in its published form. 'The Ballad of King Faruk [sic] and Queen Farida' (*BW*, pp. 19–22), to the tune of Egypt's national anthem, is a brutal attack on the corrupt character of King Farouk and the British Colonial administration that supported his rule. Egypt was officially neutral for most of the War, though it was widely understood that the King held Axis sympathies. The song condemns the King, and his subjects for their loyalty, and the resentment of the Allied troops is invested in every scatological and sexually explicit phrase, not least in the repeatedly adapted line: 'O you can't fuck Farida, if you don't pay Faruk [sic]'. Neat writes, 'wherever loyal Egyptian citizens rose to salute their monarch, well-oiled Allied soldiers were likely to bellow out Hamish's "alternative anthem", as a magnificent, revolutionary bacchanal!'[37]

The precise setting of the ballads, and their relationship with the environments in which they were conceived and sung, helps to explain the appeal that they held for the soldiers. Henderson's notes in the *Ballads* provide these contexts. With 'The Ballad of King Faruk [sic] and Queen Farida' and other songs, Henderson supplies information on which regiments and divisions carried the songs and were thought to be their sources; he details the events that they depicted and the tunes to which they were sung. Though portrayed entirely differently, the manoeuvres and movements of the soldiers at war are as central to the *Ballads* as they are to the *Elegies*. 'Canaglia Pezzente' ('The Penniless Canaille'), a Tuscan partisan song with the refrain 'long live the Soviets! Long live Lenin and Stalin!' is, for example, preceded by a note which associates the song with 'the famous Garibaldini Division of the Arno, whose already legendary General "Potente" was killed in action against the 4th German Paratroop

Division in Florence (August, 1944)' (*BW*, pp. 37–8). 'The Ballad of Wadi Maktilla' is characterised as a description of the 'somewhat abortive raid by the 2nd Camerons on an *Iti* outpost about 12 miles East of Sidi Barrani – 1940' (emphasis added) (*BW*, pp. 7–8).[38] In this instance Henderson even reproduces the language of the 'squaddies' with the pejorative for the Italians – '*Iti*'.

Henderson's *Ballads* presents the 'rebellious house' of the Army balladeer common to Allied and Axis forces. The result is similar to that of the 'proletariat of levelling death' in the *Elegies*, that is, a recognition of the validity of the voices and experiences of soldiers on both sides of the conflict, through their ultimate unity as *living*, mobilised troops. In this case however, they are united by their cynicism, their common frustrations with the absurdities of the War and their roles in it, and by their tender thoughts of home and their imagined return. In his introduction, Henderson notes that 'Shakespeare, who ran God close in the matter of creation, knew him [the Army balladeer] well and called him Thersites'. In *Troilus and Cressida*, Thersites, who first appeared in Homer's *Iliad*, is worked up into a major character, and though he plays the fool, he speaks truth to power. In Henderson's understanding Thersites represents an apparent archetype for the soldier's sardonic sense of humour. He revisited this image in a later retrospective article, in which he recalls his secret nickname, 'Thersites', for the Private who was his driver in North Africa and who was a source of endless bawdy folklore (*AM*, p. 312).

A German song included in the *Ballads*, 'Kennst de den Avanti Schritt?' ('Do you know the *Avanti* Step?'), is a good example of the kind of material Henderson associates with his 'Army balladeer'. He notes that 'from the desert days onwards the Italian word *Avanti* (Forwards) became for the Germans a synonym for retreat. To "do an Avanti" meant to beat it good and proper'. The song includes the lines (in Henderson's translation): 'Do you know what the Avanti step is? / One step forward and ten back . . . / Adolf can't hold them any longer . . . / What are Adolf's new weapons? The young laddies and the old apes' (*BW*, pp. 39–40). This sardonic tone has its equivalents among the songs of the British regiments. For instance, in Henderson's own 'Ballad of the Big Nobs' (*BW*, pp. 11–12) (which is unaccredited in the *Ballads*) various political and military leaders are evaluated according to their use to the 'Eighth Ar-mee':

> There's Ritchie, there's Ritchie
> And his arse is feeling itchie
> For he wasn't much fuckin' use
> to the Eighth Ar-mee.[39]

The military failures of the Allies are also mocked, as in 'Kennst de den Avanti Schritt?', in a limerick-type piece written by Henderson, 'The Fall of Tobruk': 'Tommy thinks he holds Tobruk. / Along the road comes Rommel. / Inside two shakes Tobruk is took / And Tommy's on the bummel [journey / trek / hike]' (*BW*, p. 28).

'Lili Marlene' is the most enduring symbol of the common folk voice of soldiers on both sides in the Second World War. As Henderson notes in his introduction to the *Ballads*, this song 'sprouted variants and parodies galore in the authentic ballad manner', and the variants of this particular song lie at the heart of the project. Originally written by Hans Leip of Hamburg in 1923, 'Lili Marlene' was popularised among German, British, Italian and French troops alike after its frequent broadcasts, firstly on the German Belgrade Radio Station and, later, further afield.[40] In *Alamein and the Desert War* (1967), Derek Jewell writes, 'it became a song for marching to, a song for sitting down to – the property of virtually every nation engaged in the war'.[41] Henderson includes the original version in his collection, which presents the voice of a homesick soldier, doomed to die, pining for his lover and hoping to meet her again by the lamp post outside the barracks. He also reproduces a fairly faithful Italian version of the original before moving on to parodies (*BW*, pp. 31–6). The most popular English song to this melody was 'Ballad of the D-Day Dodgers', which has become closely associated with Henderson. Neat explains: 'it is a genuine soldier's ballad – a collective creation – given form and artistic force by the hand of a master [Henderson]'.[42] The song addresses the rumour current in the Eighth Army at the time that Lady Astor had referred to those fighting in Italy as 'D-Day Dodgers'. The lyrics of the first six verses detail the apparently glamorous lifestyle of the soldiers serving in Italy: 'We didn't go to fight there – we went there for the ride. / Anzio and Sangro were just names, / We only went to look for dames' (*BW*, pp. 9–10). This lavish satire leads to the penultimate stanza in which Lady Astor's mouth is described as 'too bleeding wide', before the pathos of the final lines:

> Look around the mountains, in the mud and rain –
> You'll find the scattered crosses – (there's some which have no name).
> Heartbreak and toil and suffering gone,
> The boys beneath them slumber on.
> Those are the D-Day Dodgers who'll stay in Italy.[43]

Fragments from two German parodies of 'Lili Marlene' are also set out in the *Ballads*. Henderson translates lines from one of these: 'To the West of Moscow, before the great gates there stands the German Army and it can't advance a yard. So everyone can see how Adolf Hitler comes to grief, as Napoleon did before him [repeat; 'as Napoleon did before him']' (*BW*, pp. 34–5). 'Lili Marlene' also supplied Henderson with the name for his imagined club, under which the collection was published. As a title it embraces the soldier's song as a form of collective self-expression transcending the distorted dividing lines of war. In this context, it is no surprise that the song also punctuates the closing lines of Henderson's seventh elegy: 'seven poor bastards / dead in African deadland . . . *wie einst Lili* / dead in African deadland / *einst Lili Marlene*' (*EDC*, p. 41).

Although Henderson described the *Ballads* as a collection of the anonymous and collective work of the Army Balladeer, on closer inspection it is clear that he was the primary balladeer he had in mind. Of the twenty-three songs included in the volume, eleven are Henderson's own. 'The D-Day Dodgers' was only 'given form' by Henderson, as Neat has explained. However, it is difficult to determine whether or not some of the other pieces belong to the anonymous collective of the various armed forces, given that many are unambiguously accredited to Henderson in the *Collected Poems and Songs*, in the first volume of Neat's biography and elsewhere by Henderson himself. This leaves only five English language songs in the *Ballads* that were almost certainly not written by Henderson.[44] The eponymous *Ballads of World War II* can therefore be seen as a collection largely of his own work and, as such, it must be regarded as subject to his own political and cultural outlook and associated with the war that he personally experienced (in the North African and Italian campaigns). In his efforts to give an impression of the many voices of soldiers' song, collected and compiled by 'Seamus Mor MacEanruig' (Henderson's Gaelic moniker), Henderson offers up his own ideal of the collective transnational folk culture of the War. The cover concedes at least this much, as it reads: 'Hamish Henderson's Ballads of World War II Collected for the Lili Marleen Club of Glasgow', though it is intentionally ambiguous with regard to Henderson's position, as the author, collector, editor, or simply as the individual whose particular experience of war this collection represents. It is not my aim to consider how this might undermine Henderson's work, but rather to explore the characteristics of the collective voice he sought to promote. The question of authenticity plagues critical discourse in folk-song and folk poetry. Nevertheless, Henderson demonstrates an awareness of this interface between the individual agent (the poet, songwriter or complier) and the anonymous masses who might be imagined as the foundation for a collection titled *Ballads of World War II*.

Henderson's official role as the collector of these ballads, and his undisclosed, or at least, ambiguous role as the author, can perhaps be understood with recourse to his later thoughts on the 'folk process':

> When one speaks of anonyms, of course, one must bear in mind that at many stages of the folk process individual minds – and sometimes, quite clearly, powerful ingenious minds – have set their seal on new variants. Sometimes a craftsman-poet, endowed with 'a nice judicious ear' (to quote Burns) and immersed in the musical and linguistic traditions handed down to him, must have composed song-poems in the time-honoured prescriptive idiom which were already halfway towards becoming folk-songs.
> (*AM*, p. 73)

Henderson 'set his seal' on the ballads of the War, forming 'song-poems' out of those already becoming 'folk-songs' out among the soldiers. The degree of original composition is therefore unknowable and, in some sense, irrelevant. It should be noted that Henderson chose not to accredit any of the materials in the *Ballads*, and that while he used this omission to include much of his own work, the songs as a whole are only attributed to a military regiment, or else a particular arena of war; the notion of an individual author is very explicitly eschewed.

The implied communality of the *Ballads* is similar in its function to one of Henderson's earlier creative projects: 'Songs of Sabotage and Sedition' (1939). This unpublished booklet contained songs that 'were created with the specific aim of undermining the Chamberlain government . . . made to be circulated "underground" . . . proof of the widespread anti-establishment undercurrents flowing through Britain throughout the Phoney War period'.[45] Though the *Ballads* share something of this 'underground' rebelliousness, the political agenda of the collection is less auspicious. Henderson does include some of his own politically engaged songs, perhaps to give the impression that his views were shared more widely among the troops with whom he was stationed. In 'Ballad of the Taxi Driver's Cap', for example, Henderson portrays the Allied soldier's admiration for Stalin in a playful and perhaps sardonic tone:

> O Hitler's a non-smoker
> and Churchill smokes cigars
> and they're both as keen as mustard
> on imperialistic wars.
> But your uncle Joe's a worker
> And a very decent chap
> *because he smokes a pipe and wears*
> *a taxi-driver's cap.*
> (*BW*, pp. 13–14)

Another of Henderson's songs, 'The Blubbing Buchmanite', also considers Moscow's call for 'Workers of the world [to] unite!' from the perspective of the Scottish squaddies. Tam, a socialist from Greenock, and Micah Grant, a Buchmanite (a supporter of Frank Buchman's evangelical movement) from Shotts, engage in a kind of casual flyting in verse. The arguments for a world view couched in terms of class war are rehearsed and the delusive force of Grant's spiritual beliefs are attacked by Tam for their suppression of revolutionary class consciousness:

> It's canting cunts like you who sap
> The worker's spirit. Shit your trap!
> A revolution in the soul

Will leave the bosses' profits whole.
A revolution in the heart
Won't help the worker's cause a fart.
(*BW*, pp. 23–4)

The *Ballads*, as a collection of soldiers' songs drawing from across the Allied-Axis divide, and as a vehicle for the dissemination of Henderson's own song-poems and therefore his own cultural political prerogatives, are, like the *Elegies*, a demonstration of the poet's commitment to 'sing' for soldiers of the Second World War. Where the *Elegies* seek to 'sing *them*, the dead, the innocent', by inhabiting the environment of the living soldier and exploring his relationship with death and history, those forces that surround him, the *Ballads* inhabit the collective song voice of those at war, the 'rebellious house' of the Army balladeer that can be built on any battlefield, in any language (*EDC*, p. 22).

Elegies and Ballads *Becoming People*

John Mitchell conceived of Henderson's revival as a cultural front in the *class war*. Pointing to the leftist credentials of the leaders of the folk revivalist movements, figures like Henderson and Lloyd, he asserts that 'never before had "the arts" in Britain been forcibly modified from below in this strategic way'.[46] Mitchell celebrates the contributions of individual organisers like Henderson but he also emphasises popular investment in folk-song. The strategic vision and its popular endorsement are conflated. To illustrate the genesis of these revivalist strategies in Henderson's creative work, Mitchell constructs an opposition between the art-poetry of his *Elegies* and his modern folk poetry, which he describes as '[combining] a closeness to and fruitful exploitation of folk, traditional and popular material with a *rich development of ideas and emotional implications*'. The greatest examples of Henderson's revivalist art are, for Mitchell, 'The 51st Highland Division's Farewell to Sicily' and 'The Freedom Come-All-Ye', because of their folk-based forms, and their delicate 'balance of intellect and emotion'.[47] In contrast, though he recognises the progressive 'forward movement' of the *Elegies* in their urge towards 'wholeness', Mitchell criticises the dialectics of the poem-series as having become too abstract, thereby leading to a 'false objectivity which is unnatural to [Henderson] and the opposite of what we find in his songs':

> There is a certain fatalism, a separation of history and agent. In freeing himself from all petty antagonisms and cant in the face of levelling death the poet retires to such rarefied philosophical heights that the historical struggle is too often gutted of its flesh and blood – the concrete moral, class issues of the epoch: barbarism versus humanism, fascism versus the people.[48]

Mitchell believes that the poems risk simplifying the ideological and historical conflicts of the War and dismissing them as 'petty antagonisms'. However, this view is based on a rejection of the Henderson's nuance on death and history. Mitchell does not, for example, recognise that the poems encourage us to appreciate that repulsion towards fascism as an ideology and, the refusal to see the enemy as unambiguous manifestations of this ideology, can easily coexist. As with Calder, Mitchell sees the two positions as forming a disabling contradiction, weakening the political resolve of the series. Despite the fact that among many early twentieth-century poets, contradiction and paradox are often liberating rather than constraining phenomena, this criticism furthermore relies on an assumption about the political position that Henderson ought to promote, that is, a straightforward moral dimension untouched by philosophical ambiguities.

Nevertheless, this perceived 'false objectivity' and its definitive opposition to the supposed values of Henderson's songs gives a misleading impression of his creative responses to the War. This constructed division between his poetry and his song suits Mitchell's purposes as he tries to conceive of a consistent 'moral standpoint as we know it from his . . . work'.[49] The assumption that Henderson's songs are a more accurate embodiment of his 'moral standpoint' than the poems, is, however, problematic, and it conspires to detach the dilemmas and grand dialectics of the *Elegies* from the common song of the soldiers on the basis of a different level of philosophical engagement. The other assumption at work is that there is in fact *less* philosophy in popular poetry or song. The comparison falls down when Mitchell asks that Henderson's songs and poems present a consistent cultural-political vision whilst also claiming that the two forms are unequal in their capacity for philosophical thought. By exploring those elements that are shared and developed in and between Henderson's *Elegies* and his *Ballads*, I argue that the difference between these materials is principally one of form and technique, rather than of morality or of political philosophy, as Mitchell might have it.

Douglas Young's critique focused on this very problem. It was clear to him that Henderson had 'nothing to learn' in terms of 'verse-making', given the quality of his folk-song, but he regretted that Henderson wrote the *Elegies* from a journalistic pose, in keeping with 'a certain fashion of decadent English bourgeois writing pretending to be poetry'. He goes so far as to claim that the *Elegies* do not constitute poetry at all and will therefore not 'outlive the transitional period [they] sprang from'. In Young's analysis, it is not that there is an imbalance between the capacity of folk-song and 'lineated prose' (as he might have it) for philosophical thought; it is that Henderson's work cannot endure because it fails to become poetry. Though Young admires much of the sentiment behind the series, it is clearly the free verse form that he disapproves of most passionately (letter dated 30 January 1949).[50]

The thesis of 'Freedom Becomes People', which was discussed at the beginning of this chapter, offers a framework for the unifying aspects of Henderson's war poetry and soldiers' songs. Both the *Elegies* and the *Ballads* can be seen as chapters in Henderson's movement towards the position he takes in this document of 1968, proposing the creation of a 'genuine people's culture'. Despite Henderson's own admission that the *Elegies* conveyed a poetry of 'endurance' and 'passive suffering', the final constructions of the series can be understood as a movement towards the kind of life-affirming 'resolve' and 'transformation' that Henderson later sought in 'Freedom Becomes People'. The *Ballads* offer an explicit example of what Henderson later articulated as a need to 'go to school with the folksinger' and to celebrate and promote 'voracious popular culture, its secrecy, its turbulence, its victorious gaiety, and . . . its unbeatable lust for life'.[51] However, it is in their insurrectionary qualities that both volumes contribute most forcefully to Henderson's developing cultural politics.

As Neat has discussed, Henderson did not feel that he could work with the models of poetry that seemed to be in vogue throughout the War. He had particular issues with the Cairo intelligentsia:

> They expect poets to be Audenry or Spenderish . . . When I gave them poetry that was neither Audenry or Spenderish but coarse, sensual, numinous and song-like, acknowledging as influences Lorca, Heine, Clare, Dunbar and Burns and drawing much vigour from my association with Scots and Irish working class people, they squealed and scooted.
> (note written on the back of a copy of *Orientations* literary magazine, No. 3. May 1942)[52]

As Featherstone's study of the canon of 'war poetry' also suggests, the character of Henderson's desired war poetry was at odds with those who had drawn their inspiration from the 'Auden Group' (or the 'Thirties Group') and who, despite celebrating the innovations of their verse, contributed to what was to become the poetic orthodoxy of the post-war period. The difficulties we encounter when trying to place Henderson in this context come as a result of his rejection of the consensus around what constituted poetic *progress*.

Henderson's war poems and soldiers' songs have often been published in collections produced by the Salamander Oasis Trust, which was established after the War to collect and edit the poetry that had emerged from the various conflicts.[53] The Trust was named after two early series of anthologies of soldiers' verse titled *Oasis: The Middle East Anthology of Poetry from the Forces* (1943) and *Salamander: A Miscellany of Poetry* (1947). Henderson was one of the contributors to the original *Oasis* collection, and he consciously aligned himself with publications like *Oasis*, *Salamander*, *Citadel* and *Orientations*, as opposed to magazines like *Personal Landscape*, which was generally associated with the 'Cairo poets' (including Robin Fedden, Lawrence Durrell,

Terence Tiller and Bernard Spencer) and was widely regarded by the men in uniform as 'highbrow or mandarin' (*AM*, pp. 311–2). The *Oasis* approach, as described by Victor Selwyn (founder of the Trust), appealed to Henderson: 'our concern has been . . . to seek the writings of those who *became* poets as a result of going to war' (*AM*, p. 319). Henderson's vision for a popular poetry, still being formulated in the years immediately following the War, could be reconciled more readily with an open and inclusive policy such as Selwyn's, than with those who sought out the 'Spenderish' line.

The insurrectionary and rebellious nature of the *Ballads* is clear but that of the *Elegies* can be extended a little further. In the first, the regrets of the dead are said to have 'nothing to do with / race and leader, realm indivisible, / laboured Augustan speeches or vague imperial heritage. / (They saw through that guff before the axe fell.)' (*EDC*, p. 21). This gives an indication of the position from which these elegies embark on their troubled task of remembrance, immediately disregarding the propagandist language of officialdom and replacing it with a more conceptual consideration of death and the need for the living to reconcile with it. The *Elegies* rebel even against the conventions of the 'elegy' as an expression of redemptive grief. David Kennedy, in his study of the elegy, asserts that 'writing an elegy risks placing the elegist at the disposal of competing and dubiously truthful discourses'. These discourses arise and are immediately discounted in Henderson's series: 'no blah about their sacrifice' (*EDC*, p. 38). In Henderson, Kennedy discerns 'a refusal to submit to the ultimate end of the genre: detachment from the dead'.[54] This refusal is manifest in lines like those of the ninth elegy: '[the dead] their sleep's our unrest, we lie bound in their inferno – / this alliance must be vaunted and affirmed, lest they condemn us!' (*EDC*, p. 51). These aspects of the *Elegies*: their resistance to unproblematic accounts of war, death, and the function of the 'elegy', all precipitate the fraught task the poem-series sets itself: to search for 'words . . . of whole love' (*EDC*, p. 38) and thereby reconcile humanity with history. To emerge from the other side of this process would be to achieve the 'detachment from the dead' that Kennedy writes of but it would also be to betray the dead and fail to expiate the living.

The songs from the *Ballads* that have been discussed in this chapter have predominantly been those that, in their bawdiness or their political rhetoric, are difficult to reconcile with the aims of 'Freedom Becomes People', to represent a 'moment of resolve, transformation and insurrection'. However, their role is, like that of the *Elegies*, a contributory one. These volumes of war poetry and soldiers' songs can be regarded as an exploration of the ground upon which Henderson's later cultural politics were to be built. Indeed, the criteria of a 'poetry that becomes people' by learning from the folksinger while retaining a poetic ambiguity of emotion and intellect, is met by many of Henderson's own songs and poems. 'The 51st Highland Division's Farewell to Sicily', for example, fuses the landscapes of the Highlands and Sicily, and evokes the melancholic farewell of the departing soldiers, whilst also bringing to mind the ballads of the Highland Clearances, another sub-genre of farewell songs:

> Fare weel, ye banks o' Sicily
> (Fare ye weel, ye sheiling an' ha');
> We'll a' mind shebeens and bothies
> Whaur Jock made a date wi' his dearie.
> Then tune the pipes and drub the tenor drum
> (Leave your kit this side o' the wa').
> Then tune your pipes and drub the tenor drum
> A' the bricht chalmers are eerie.
> (*CPS*, pp. 84–5)

This combination of historical and geographical spaces, and movements of people, helps the song to transcend its apparent subject matter and approach a more enduring portrayal of human responses to departure, exile and transition.[55]

One of the central images of the *Elegies* is the 'apollyon chasm'. In this context it can be understood as that disjuncture between the living and the dead, and between humanity and history, that is explored throughout the poem-series. However, the image recurs in Henderson's later writings with a different function. During the 'Folksong Flyting' of 1964 Henderson drew MacDiarmid's attention to the lines of his 'Second Hymn to Lenin', which begin: '*Are my poems spoken in the factories and fields, / In the streets o' the toon?*'[56] For Henderson, the passage is 'an eloquent, and even poignant statement of the artist's awareness of his isolation in modern society, and of his duty to look outwards, and to attempt to communicate across the apollyon chasms' (*TAN*, p. 124). The image is thus extended to incorporate that rift between art and the people, a separation that the committed poet must endeavour to overcome. This provides another connection between the early war-related poems and Henderson's cultural politics as formulated throughout the period of the folk revival. Naomi Mitchison made an inadvertent prediction about the role of the *Elegies* in the formulation of Henderson's cultural politics when she gave her review the subtitle, 'A Bard Who Picks Up the Song of the Future'.[57]

Henderson was born exactly a year after the armistice of the First World War and he was nineteen when the second war was declared. His early adult years were therefore indelibly marked by this period of global conflict. This chapter began by proposing that the War had an enduring influence on Henderson's literary work, and on his ideals and cultural politics. Henderson frequently acknowledged the breadth and depth of this influence in his later years. In the sleeve notes for a recorded collection of his songs and poems, *Pipes, Goatskins & Bones* (1992), he wrote:

> the songs and poems . . . represent a sort of fusion of two of my greatest loves: the anonymous song poetry of Scotland, which I was lucky enough to hear quite a lot of from my mother when I was a child, and the comradely solidarity of the anti-Fascist struggle which dominated much of my early manhood. I soon found the music of the one love merging with the music of the other. (*AM*, p. 454)

In describing his work as a 'fusion' of these loves, Henderson infers an essential confluence between the communally experienced, ideological and physical conflict with Fascism and the power of expression of the anonymous voice of folk culture. The *Elegies* and the *Ballads* constitute early experiments with these ideas, the former exploring the implications of this violent struggle and the latter setting down an 'anonymous song poetry' sprung from the experiences of War.

Rickword, in another early article for *Our Time* (April 1941), wrote:

> The true poets of this war have a vast potential audience, and the fact that they are bound up with the masses themselves will determine the significance of the war literature to come . . . emotions will not expand themselves in anger and pity, but . . . [will] forge instruments to free men's minds from false hatreds and bring out their underlying confidence in their own ability to make the rebel songs come true.[58]

This passage sets out the programme for Henderson's *Elegies* and *Ballads*, which were to be written throughout the following seven years. Again, Henderson's work represents an attempt to fulfil the aims of those on the Left who saw the War as an opportunity for a 'genuine people's culture'. E. P. Thompson was perhaps the most perceptive reviewer of the *Elegies*. He recognised Henderson's desire 'to speak directly, out of his experiences, to his fellow men', but qualified this with a warning against donning an 'impersonal dialectic' in the interests of appealing to those 'circumscribed by the coteries and sophisticated reviews'.[59] In a personal letter to Henderson, and after another similar warning, Thompson writes:

> They [the 'culture boys'] would kill your writing, because you, more than any other poet I know, are an instrument through which thousands of others can become articulate. And you must not forget that your songs and ballads are not trivialities – they are quite as important as the Elegies.
> (letter dated 10 Feb. 1949) (*TAN*, pp. 28–9)

Thompson's comments are an early recognition of how Henderson's creative works were conceived, articulated in a way that connects them directly to the cultural political principles that Henderson was to set out for his literary work almost twenty years later, in his 'Freedom Becomes People' thesis. The idea of a poet being an 'instrument through which thousands of others can *become articulate*' (emphasis added), is closely related to the proposal for a poetry that *becomes people*, and it necessitates something of the lessons of the folksinger, who, unlike the literary poet, offers up a framework for self-expression that can be absorbed and reproduced with ease. In the years following his demobilisation, Henderson translated Antonio Gramsci's *Lettere dal Carcere* ('Prison Letters'), began song collecting in earnest back in Scotland and found employment as a folklorist in the University of Edinburgh's School of Scottish Studies. He contributed intermittently to many cultural, political and literary debates through various articles and opinion column letters, and he tirelessly promoted Scottish folk culture, negotiating with, and defending against the revival's critics along the way. Throughout all of this, Henderson developed his ideas of folk culture and literature and of the cultural politics that were their foundation. Nevertheless, his original creative responses to the War signal Henderson's first sustained efforts to create culturally and politically engaged art, and these lyrical experiments were to reverberate on some level in all of his subsequent artistic and critical work.

Notes

1. Henderson, 'Freedom Becomes People', p. 1.
2. Gifford, 'Literature and World War Two', pp. 94–5.
3. Neat, *Making of the Poet*, p. 236.
4. See Concise Scots Dictionary (2005), s.v. 'breenge': 'rush forward recklessly or carelessly; plunge; make a violent effort'.
5. 'Freedom Becomes People', p. 1.
6. Ibid. p. 1.
7. *Elegies for the Dead in Cyrenaica* (1948) and *The Ballads of World War II* (1947) will be referred to as the *Elegies* and the *Ballads* respectively.
8. For Henderson's early University career, his work for the Quakers and his wartime experiences, see Neat, *Making of the Poet*, pp. 35–176; and Nicholson, *Poem, Purpose and Place*, pp. 134–5.
9. See Calder, 'Scottish Poets in the Desert', p. 69; Morgan, 'The Sea, the Desert, the City', p. 36; Glen, 'Hamish Henderson: Poetry Becomes People', p. 63; and Craig, 'A National Literature? Recent Scottish Writing', p. 162.
10. See Featherstone, *War Poetry*, pp. 85–7; Watson, 'Death's Proletariat', pp. 315–39; Gifford, 'Literature in World War Two', pp. 93–100; and Mackay, 'Townland, Desert, Cave', pp. 91–3. For early reviews of the *Elegies* and Henderson's reputation as a 'war poet' more generally, see Neat, *Making of the Poet*, pp. 355–61.
11. Morgan, 'The Sea, the Desert, the City', pp. 36–9; Nicholson, *Poem, Purpose and Place*, p. 139; Thwaite, 'The Barbarous Arena', p. 1077; Watson, 'Death's Proletariat', p. 322.
12. Nicholson, *Poem, Purpose and Place*, p. 151.

13. Watson, 'Death's Proletariat', pp. 325–8; Calder, 'Scottish Poets in the Desert', pp. 69–70; Hendry, 'Sorley MacLean', pp. 29–30.
14. Maclean, *From Wood to Ridge*, pp. 211–13.
15. The original quatrain was never published by Goethe, it appears in a letter to Countess Stollberg dated 1777: 'Alles geben die Götter, die unendlichen, / Ihren Lieblingen ganz, / Alle Freuden, die unendlichen, / Alle Schmerzen, die unendlichen, ganz.'
16. Hendry, 'Sorley MacLean', p. 29.
17. Auden, *Selected Poems*, p. 57.
18. Orwell, 'Inside the Whale', pp. 36–7.
19. *Dictionary of Greek and Roman Biography and Mythology*.
20. MacDiarmid, 'Editorial', *National Weekly* (1:30, 9 April 1949, p. 5).
21. Calder, 'Scottish Poets in the Desert', p. 71.
22. Ibid., p. 71.
23. Neat, *Making of the Poet*, p. 244.
24. Featherstone, *War Poetry*, p. 48.
25. Ibid., p. 86.
26. Nicholson, *Poem, Purpose and Place*, p. 141.
27. Featherstone, *War Poetry*, pp. 47–8.
28. Featherstone, *War Poetry*, p. 46.
29. Henderson, 'Resurgimento!', p. 13.
30. Sharp, Editorial, *Our Time* 2:7, Nov. 1942, p. 3.
31. Fürnberg, *Our Time* 4:3, Oct. 1944, p. 8.
32. After Henderson's death Arnold Rattenbury claimed that in fact he had edited the 'much-noted' Scottish issue of *Our Time*, though Henderson's influence is, nevertheless, clear ('Flytings', p. 27).
33. 'W.O.1' is a class one Warrant Officer.
34. Slater, 'Bless 'em All: A Piece About Army Songs', pp. 23–5.
35. Lloyd, 'Songs of Musso's Army', pp. 18–21.
36. Neat, *Making of the Poet*, p. 203.
37. Ibid., p. 95.
38. See 'Puir Bluidy Swaddies are Weary' (*AM*, pp. 327–38).
39. This stanza is in reference to Major-General Neil Ritchie, who was promoted to head of the Allied North African Command in 1941, and who failed to halt Rommel's advances. In other verses the song addresses other Generals and even Stalin and Churchill.
40. See Hieble, 'Lili Marlene – A Study of a Modern Song'; and Leibovitz and Miller, *Lili Marlene: The Soldiers' Song of World War II*.
41. Jewell, *Alamein and the Desert War*, p. 149.
42. Neat, *Making of the Poet*, p. 152.
43. Neat credits Henderson with this final verse (*Making of the Poet*, p. 153).
44. Roderick Watson only recognises three of the songs in the collection as Henderson's ('Death's Proletariat', p. 317).

45. Neat, *Making of the Poet*, p. 46.
46. Mitchell, 'Hamish Henderson and the Scottish Folk-song Revival', p. 200.
47. Ibid., pp. 204, 206–13.
48. Mitchell goes on to acknowledge the 'Interlude' as the point at which Henderson's 'actual sympathies' are exposed (pp. 202–3).
49. Ibid., p. 203.
50. Letter, Douglas Young to Henderson (NLS Archives, Acc. 10788).
51. Henderson, 'Freedom Becomes People', p. 1.
52. Neat, *Making of the Poet*, pp. 78–9.
53. See *Return to Oasis* (1980); *From Oasis to Italy* (1983); *Poems of the Second World War* (1985); and *The Voice of War* (1996).
54. Kennedy, *Elegy*, p. 74.
55. See 'Ballad of the Simeto', 'The Ballad o Corbara' and 'Anzio April' for further examples (*CPS*, pp. 78–83, 86–92, 109–10).
56. MacDiarmid, *Complete Poems*, pp. 321–8.
57. Mitchison, 'Wild Poets Chasing Stars'.
58. Rickword, 'Poetry and Two Wars', p. 6.
59. Thompson, 'A New Poet', p. 158.

CHAPTER

3

GRAMSCI'S FOLKLORE

That heroic genius, Antonio Gramsci,
Studying comparative linguistics in prison.
For, as he said in his Lettere dal Carcere,
'Nothing less! What could be more
Disinterested and für ewig*?*
(Hugh MacDiarmid, 'In Memoriam James Joyce')[1]

Gramsci, friend and antagonist of Croce, was a polymath who, ranging as widely as MacDiarmid (and digging far deeper), was always ready to learn from, and appreciate, popular culture ... What binds [his] *various subjects together, he says, is 'the creative spirit of the people in its diverse phases'.*
(Henderson, extract from a letter to *The Scotsman* during 'The Folksong Flyting', 12 April 1964) (*TAN*, p. 131)

Henderson repels MacDiarmid's attacks on the then flourishing Scottish folk revival. Evoking the poet's reference to Antonio Gramsci in his recent work and, by asserting that the celebrated Italian Communist possessed values at odds with those projected by MacDiarmid in the on-going debates, Henderson used his understanding of the political philosopher to promote his own agenda and discredit his opponent's. The flytings are a condensed account of Henderson's cultural politics, concentrated and sharpened in the pattern of accusation and rebuttal. Yet, Gramsci comes to represent the contested ground. After MacDiarmid himself, the Sardinian thinker is perhaps the figure most frequently invoked throughout Henderson's disparate writings.

Henderson first discovered Gramsci in Northern Italy in 1944, whilst serving as an Officer in the Intelligence Corps. The Communist partisans of the Italian *Resistenza* introduced Henderson to a hero, martyr, journalist, agitator, co-founder and former Secretary General of the Italian Communist Party (PCI). They told Henderson of the hardships of Gramsci's life, his incarceration in Mussolini's prisons, his ill health and his consequent death at only forty-six. They also made the young officer aware of the growing reputation, which had already taken root on a local level, of Gramsci as *un grande pensatore*, that is, 'a great thinker' (*AM*, pp. 339–44). Following the success of his *Elegies for the Dead in Cyrenaica* (1948) Henderson spent the period 1948–51 translating Gramsci's *Lettere dal Carcere* ('The Prison Letters'). The enduring influence of this period of intense scholarly activity is apparent throughout Henderson's later work as a complex of explicit references to, and implicit invocations of, Gramsci's life and thought.

Since his death Gramsci has informed almost every discipline in the Social Sciences and Humanities: from postcolonial studies to political philosophy, linguistics to cultural studies.[2] His concept of cultural hegemony in particular, is widely used to describe the myriad ways in which dominant ideologies are cultivated, enforced and maintained. The success of this theory lies in the space it makes for the complexities of coercion and consent, and for the role of 'culture' in the exercise of power. Henderson's relationship with Gramsci began long before the philosopher's work had extended its influence so deeply and broadly and, perhaps, as a consequence, his conception of the Sardinian thinker is not easily reconciled with these other streams of Gramscianism.

In the thirty years following Henderson's initial translation, Gramsci became an important influence among thinkers associated with the British New Left. Excerpts of Henderson's translations of the letters were first published in E. P. Thompson and John Saville's *New Reasoner* in 1959 but this did not mark the beginning of the assimilation of Gramsci among British socialist thinkers. Due to a long delay in publication, Henderson's translation did very little to extend Gramsci's influence in this period. Some of the Sardinian philosopher's ideas were indirectly promoted in Henderson's writings and in his folk revivalism but his influence often went unacknowledged. Henderson wrote principally about folklore and, as such, his articles were not an obvious foundation for those looking to construct an alternative theoretical framework for the Left. After the events of 1956 – Khrushchev's speech and the Polish and Hungarian crises – the old Marxist orthodoxies were rejected by the British Left and the search was on for unsullied Marxist texts. Nevertheless, even Louis Marks' early translation of selections from the prison notebooks, *The Modern Prince and Other Writings* (1957), which had been refused publication prior to the fallout of 1956, failed to make an impact in this climate.[3] Tom Nairn was one of the first to apply Gramsci's thought to an analysis of Britain and its social and political history.[4] Throughout the 1960s Nairn and Perry Anderson produced a series of articles now known as their 'thesis', in which anomalies in the history of the British state and the labour movement are described and explained. Their analyses drew from Gramsci's conception of national history, and from his proposals for a developed Marxism more attuned to cultural and ideological factors than the reductive conception of 'base' and 'superstructure' that had formerly prevailed.[5]

David Forgacs notes that the New Left in Britain, and particularly E. P. Thompson and Raymond Williams, had prepared the ground for the assimilation of Gramsci's political philosophy by promoting a form of 'Marxist humanism' and prioritising an analysis of 'culture and community'.[6] By the 1970s these thinkers, and other cultural Marxists of the period, made an overt turn to Gramsci in formulating their ideas. Williams, Thompson, Eric Hobsbawm and later, Stuart Hall, adopted the concept of 'cultural hegemony', the distinction between 'coercion' and 'consent', and the shift in focus from the state to civil society that is implicit in these ideas, as a framework within which the cultural might be understood as political.[7] They sought to centralise the study of popular culture as a forum for analysing the 'real' political landscape. In this sense, the vast complex of cultural channels that sustain a hegemonic consensus could be understood in all of its latent and 'consensual', and explicit and 'coercive', forms. In his introduction to the *Prison Letters* Henderson praised Open University teaching materials for their emphasis on Gramsci's ideas of popular culture, in particular, a booklet based on the work of Stuart Hall and Tony Bennett. He also commends *Marxism Today* (1977–91) as a publication that applied 'Gramscian methods of political and cultural analysis to the concrete situation in Thatcher's Britain' (*PL*, p. 11).[8] Henderson admired these approaches to Gramsci because they acknowledged the importance of the study of 'popular culture', which was readily extended to 'folk culture' in his own work.

In *Gramsci: Here and Now* (1987), a televised panel discussion on Gramsci's relevance in contemporary Britain, Henderson was asked what it was, 'as a Briton', that appealed to him about Gramsci.[9] He replied that, '*as a Scot*', Gramsci's relationship with his native Sardinia was of great interest. He then discussed, as he does in his introductory essay to the *Letters*, the parallels between Gramsci's comments on the distinctiveness of Sardinian culture and society within Italy, and the case of Scotland within Britain. He cited the rejection of Thatcherism north of the border as an example of Scotland's cultural and political distinctiveness. Neil Davidson acknowledges Henderson as the 'first direct link' between Gramsci and Scotland.[10] Henderson and Nairn's work on Gramsci preceded an upsurge of Scottish interest that was pursued, for example, in Bill Findlay, Raymond J. Ross and John Burns' magazine *Cencrastus*. Writing for *Scottish International* in 1972, Ray Burnett addressed the relationship between the Scottish Left and the national framework, and sought, like many Scottish writers of the earlier part of the century, to reconcile socialist internationalism with Scottish nationalism.[11] In particular Burnett called for a more nuanced understanding of the national situation, which, he argued, could be achieved by 'deflecting' the truths of Gramsci's theoretical constructions 'through a Scottish prism'.[12] Angus Calder wrote of the problematic distinction between 'workers' culture' and 'popular culture' in its Scottish context, and again Gramsci's principles are part of the proposed solution for the fraught terminology of a national framework for cultural or political analysis.[13] In his introduction to *The Red Paper on Scotland* (1975), Gordon Brown wrote of Gramsci's relevance as a thinker who recognised that 'the transition to socialism must be made by the majority of people themselves and a socialist society must be created within the womb of existing society and prefigured in the movements for democracy at the grass roots'.[14] Davidson extends his study of the 'Scottish Gramscians' to Christopher Harvie and James D. Young.[15] While each of these apparent Gramscians interprets him differently, Davidson's survey demonstrates that, on the whole, Gramsci's reception in Scotland has been closely related to the task of reconciling the national framework with a socialist perspective. This has been attempted through analyses of Scotland's socio-political history, through diagnoses for the problems of the Scottish Left, and through proposed strategies for leftist thinkers that might renegotiate with the national paradigm and with *popular* nationalist sentiment.

Except through this 'Scottish prism', Henderson rarely appears even in the marginalia of critical material on Gramsci. In works on Henderson on the other hand, Gramsci is given due recognition as an enormous influence in the development of his thought. This relationship, however, has not yet been examined in any depth.[16] Redressing this critical shortfall, this chapter will firstly account for Henderson's early recognition of Gramsci's worth, both as a political martyr and folk hero, and as a theorist whose work reveals underlying political and cultural structures. Following an examination of the letters, I will propose that Gramsci's more consciously 'cultural' writings provided a basis for Henderson's cultural politics and, subsequently, the project of folk revivalism. The extent to which Henderson assumed a political theoretical framework based on Gramsci's work will then be explored in relation to the seemingly irresolvable contradictions that he also inherited, and that are put into sharp relief when we transpose Gramsci's philosophical principles onto Henderson's cultural-political agenda. In his later writings on the folk revival Henderson referred to the Edinburgh People's Festival (1951–4) as an instance of 'Gramsci in action'.[17] This idea will be explored, both in relation to the Festival, and to Henderson's vision for the modern Scottish folk revival more generally. Henderson's responses to Gramsci not only predate the bulk of critical opinion but also function at a remove from it. While it is possible to trace Gramsci's influence in his work, his writings are not presented as a conscious reassessment of the philosopher's theses. Instead, Henderson seems to have absorbed Gramsci's thought and implemented it through innumerable channels.[18]

The Disciple and his Prophet

The *Prison Notebooks*, on which Gramsci's reputation is now largely built, has been aptly described as an 'open text' as it lends itself to countless interpretations.[19] This 'openness' is partly due to the circumstances in which the notebooks were produced. They were written in prison and not intended for publication, at least, not in the form in which they survived. Gramsci conceived of his work as a holistic, though not necessarily systematic, project to develop and refine his politics through cultural and philosophical modes, as opposed to the political journalism that typified his pre-prison writings (*PL*, pp. 44–6). In a letter to Tatiana Schucht, his sister-in-law, Gramsci wrote of the publishing offers he had refused: 'they [his journalistic writings] were ephemeral things, written for a particular day, and in my view they had no business to go on living after that day was over' (*PL*, pp. 159–62). In the same letter he expounds on his study of Italian intellectuals, and on his critical extension of the concept of the 'intellectual' to a trans-historical force present across all forms of human society. His notebooks ought to be seen in this light: even where Gramsci deals in specifics, his theoretical constructions are devised with posterity and universality in mind. We might understand Gramsci's oft-quoted aspiration to be 'disinterested and *für ewig* [for ever]', in this light (*PL*, p. 45).

In the original notebooks, explanatory notes are poorly distinguished from the body of the text, titles are almost wholly absent and, perhaps most significantly, the argumentative thread that is ordinarily so central to serious study and, particularly to Marxist theses, is missing. The fear of censorship inspired Gramsci to adopt coded terminology, which compounds the text's obliqueness. He frequently mentions 'the philosophy of praxis', which is usually interpreted simply as 'Marxism' or 'historical materialism', though this substituted phrase might also reveal something of his understanding of this political philosophy, as a worldview *and* as a method of inquiry.[20] Gramsci's work has been collated, edited and reorganised for print, by generations of scholars but, arguably, this process began even before his death, as Tatiana numbered and catalogued the notebooks and smuggled them out of prison, and out of Italy (*PL*, p. 8). The largest proportion of Henderson's direct study of Gramsci, the translation of the letters, was undertaken when only a small portion of the works had been published, and that only in Italian. Henderson first approached Gramsci with little more than his own prerogatives and the admiration of the partisans to inform his reading.

Joseph Femia refers to the 'battle of citations' that occurs among Gramsci scholars. The risk is that inordinate amounts of meaning are attached to notes and asides that were included simply to remind the author of contiguous points, concepts or references.[21] The vulnerability of Gramsci's work to misinterpretation and misrepresentation is evident even immediately following his death, with the influence of Palmiro Togliatti and the PCI, who initially refused to recognise Gramsci as anything other than a devout Leninist and Bolshevik whose principal achievement was simply to place these teachings in an Italian framework.[22] Indeed, Femia laments the 'closing of context' that is an inevitable result of any interpretative stance, and promotes the need to 'know something of [Gramsci's] private world, as well as of the social and political conditions and controversies of his time and place'.[23] One of the clearest qualities of Henderson's analysis of the Italian Marxist is his prioritisation of the aforementioned 'private world' of the philosopher.

In his biography, Neat titles the chapter about the translation of the prison letters, 'The Disciple of Gramsci'.[24] It constitutes a pivotal phase in the narrative of formation that is central to this first volume of the biography and is situated chronologically, after extended sections dedicated to Henderson's experience of the War, his war poetry and the beginning of his friendship with MacDiarmid. As such, Henderson's discovery of Gramsci represents a culmination of these events and their effects, and a setting for the consolidation of the ideas which were to define the greater part of Henderson's working life. Neat opens this chapter with a reference to Piero Gobetti's profile of Gramsci, which was originally written in 1924 for *La Rivoluzione Liberale*.[25] Recognising Henderson's admiration for the passage, Neat cited its conclusion, which is reproduced below in Henderson and Nairn's translation:

> More than a tactician or a combatant, Gramsci is a *prophet*. In the only way possible today, that is: unheard of except by fate. Gramsci's eloquence will overturn no ministries. His catastrophic polemic, his desperate satire can expect no facile consolations. The whole of humanity, the whole of present-day here and now is suspect in his eyes. He demands justice from a ferocious future avenger. (emphasis added) (*PL*, p. 27)[26]

Before providing the reader with any other information on Gramsci's life, on his stature as a politician, as a political philosopher and as a writer, Neat focuses on this conception of Gramsci as a *prophet* and asserts that Henderson was a proud proponent of his imagined 'avenging future'.[27] Gobetti not only emphasises Gramsci's foresight; he describes an intellectual construction whereby the philosopher's penetrating gaze goes beyond the present, while simultaneously assessing the present by the criteria of a revolutionary future. Henderson celebrates the Gobetti profile as a document of 'exceptional interest',

> being the work of an observer who, although a close friend, was capable of standing back and viewing his subject dispassionately, even clinically. No-one reading the later prison letters of Gramsci can doubt that Gobetti had already put his finger, with prescient insight, on one of the principal reasons for Gramsci's tragic estrangement from his wife which is documented in such heart-breaking detail in the letters.
> (*PL*, p. 28n)

It may seem incongruous to emphasise the objectivity of an article that pronounces its subject as a prophet 'unheard of except by fate', but this is typical of Henderson's rhetoric. In this instance it helps us to understand his conception of an archetypal life and the political philosophy that defines it. Henderson's note emphasises the image of the committed and resilient radical, capable of great self-sacrifice. This personal and physical compromise is at once Gramsci's human tragedy and the basis of his celebrated martyrdom.

Those poets, politicians, singers, performers, philosophers and historical agents that appear in Henderson's various writings are never far abstracted from accounts of their lives and personalities. Henderson's interpretation of Gramsci's theoretical constructs cannot, for example, be separated from his understanding of Gramsci the man: his political martyrdom, and the image of the estranged father and husband writing letters and notebooks in his dark cell, a prisoner of the fascist regime he challenged with his work. In this sense the Gobetti profile can be helpfully contextualised: it shows that the early accolades of a contemporary Italian radical were still of rhetorical relevance to Henderson in formulating the language of his 'Gramscianism'.

The prophet-disciple dynamic is supported to some degree in Henderson's own writings and of course it provides an appealing framework for Neat as his biographer. However, this is a problematic framework if the intention is towards a more distanced critical analysis of Henderson's relationship with Gramsci: the man *and* the theorist. The conception of Gramsci as a prophet has purchase in the sense that the prophet is one who appears at a time of crisis, to forewarn of future events, or to give a message of hope and redemption. For those committed to socialist revolution, Europe in the 1920s and 1930s, and Italy in particular, was such a time and place: socialist revolutions had failed to materialise as fascist states grew in confidence and fostered imperialist ambitions. Henderson regarded Gramsci as a writer who made important observations on the likely legacy of this tumultuous period of European politics, and who sought to resolve the problems of the revolutionary ideal in countries of advanced capitalism. He did this at a time when the now celebrated *Prison Notebooks* had not yet reached a global audience.

Henderson's status as a 'disciple' suggests that he promoted the teachings of his 'prophet' and circulated the lessons of his life in a more comprehensive and authoritative manner than can be sensibly ascribed to the folklorist-poet. This 'disciple' role also implies that Henderson's work on Gramsci represented a baptism of sorts, a total immersion in Gramscian thought: a rebirth, a new beginning. Though Gramsci offered Henderson theoretical foundations that he had previously lacked, this influence did not displace the beliefs that had already begun to crystallise through his own engagement with socialism and his established passion for languages, poetry and folk-song; rather, it vindicated them.

Appearing on *Gramsci: Here and Now*, Henderson talked of his first encounter with the reputation of the Sardinian Marxist: a partisan's reference to the *Brigata Gramsci*, a *Garibaldini* brigade of freedom fighters who had taken inspiration from the 'great thinker'. In his article 'Gramsci and the Partisans' (*Cencrastus* 1996), Henderson later detailed the conflicts between the partisans and the fascists, emphasising the brutality with which the Germans suppressed the resistance forces, offering the massacre of 335 hostages at the Ardeatine caves as an example. Henderson goes on to credit Gramsci's notoriety to his prolific journalism in the early 1920s, and to the classes that he had organised for fellow inmates whilst in prison. This is the setting for his introduction to Gramsci, where the idea of the 'great thinker' was, in Henderson's own words, 'already floating in the air' (*AM*, pp. 339–44).

Henderson's relationship with Gramsci begins from this point, rooted in the Italian anti-fascist combatants of the Second World War, and in the secular canonisation of their former leader. In 1949, John Lehman, the prospective publisher of the prison letters, wrote to Henderson requesting 'proof' that he was 'equipped for the job' of translating these materials. Henderson responded with a long exposition on Gramsci's global significance, on the tragic and inspirational story of his political commitment and its consequences, and on the insights that would be afforded by his 'creative genius' with an English translation of the prison letters. He also provided a list of figures that he claimed shared elements of Gramsci's genius:

> the English seventeenth-century diarist John Evelyn (particularly his concern for his children), John MacLean [sic] (political activity leading to imprisonment, towering intellect and rich humanity), Norman Douglas (the Scottish pagan – for his omnivorous, Rabelaisian qualities), Thomas Carlyle (for his critique of an age), Walt Whitman (the prophet of democracy), Cavafy (the perverse and amoral Alexandrian), Croce (as a great Italian thinker), Oscar Wilde (the poet broken by imprisonment), Tomaso Campanella, 1568–1639 (27 years in a Naples prison, unbroken), Vincent van Gogh and Hugh MacDiarmid.[28]

This diverse list of names demonstrates Henderson's appreciation for Gramsci's versatility: he was a polymath and ought to be celebrated as a philosopher, political leader, writer, critic, and martyr. By listing these figures and the qualities they share with Gramsci, Henderson seems to suggest that his 'Gramsci' embodies a synthesis of the things that make these people significant, even where the actual point of comparison is seemingly arbitrary. For example, Gramsci shares the tragic experience of unjust imprisonment with Wilde and a concern for his children with Evelyn; but it is also clear that Henderson has chosen these figures for their standing in literary history and he suggests that Gramsci deserves a similar status. He finishes the letter with an observation on how to approach Gramsci's *Prison Letters*:

> Some people have read these letters as constituting a martyrology of a secular society . . . Gramsci's humanist vision was beyond party, law or imposed power – and he would not compromise the union he had constructed between his inner vision and external human need . . . Thus amongst the last sentences uttered by Gramsci some are very like those uttered by Christ on the cross: 'I have destroyed my own existence!'[29]

Gramsci is Christ-like in his embodiment of a perfect confluence of philosophy and life-course. He offers a message of sacrifice and redemption, which should be maintained and carried forward, free to adapt and re-engage with changing historical circumstances, like a folksong. Gramsci's 'martyrology' does not list saints and detail their suffering; it is an account of the life of the martyr written by his own hand. It is surely the prerogative of the martyr to externalise his or her philosophy and live it; even, and especially, where society has not yet recognised the value of the 'vision' for which he or she stands. It is in this sense that Gramsci was, in Gobetti's terms, a prophet 'unheard of except by fate'. He demanded justice from a 'future avenger': his diagnoses for the structural ills of society would not be given credence until long after his death, and the revolutionary moment that would see his philosophy realised lies further in the future still.

Neat's evocation of the prophet-disciple relationship might be seen as a gloss over the tensions Henderson found in Gramsci's work. It might also suggest that Henderson adhered absolutely to Gramsci's whole corpus, when we know that he was in fact highly selective in his reading. We might also note that it would be no easy feat to reconcile all of the 'great thinker's' works into a coherent position: Gramsci is, as the intervening years have demonstrated, infinitely contestable. However, this image is useful in describing the symbol that Henderson took Gramsci to be: a thinker who lived his philosophy, even in death.

Prison Letters

Henderson was the first to translate Gramsci into English. Having established an interest in the Sardinian Communist during the War, he was kept up to date with Italian publications of Gramsci's work by his friend, Amletto Micozzi, after his demobilisation. When Micozzi sent him the Einaudi edition of *Lettere dal Carcere* (1947), Henderson resolved to translate it. After Lehman decided in 1951, citing financial difficulties, not to publish the volume, Henderson was unable to find another publisher until 1974, when the *New Edinburgh Review* printed the letters alongside a selection of critical analyses.[30] The fact that Henderson chose to translate the letters rather than sections of the *Prison Notebooks*, which were also being published for the first time in this period, is testament to his interest in Gramsci's life as well as his work. The Einaudi letters won the Viareggio prize for non-fiction in 1947 and by

1953 they had been published in nine editions in Italy alone. The letters constituted the greater part of Gramsci's early reputation. Henderson was simply looking to export the existing account of Gramsci to a non-Italian audience. Nevertheless, Henderson continued to champion the personal dimension long after other, more abstracted, academic traditions had been established.

The translation was an explicitly symbiotic process: Gramsci's influence was keenly felt, but Henderson could not help but project something of his own cultural and political worldview onto the text. This challenge presents itself to any scholar trading in the currency of another's ideas, however, Henderson's case is distinctive because he makes no effort to resist this process, to conceal it, or even to defend it. Henderson set Gramsci into his own framework, endorsing the grounds on which the texts appealed to him personally. Like other translators, he recognised the value of the letters as texts that bound Gramsci's ideas to his experiences. Lynne Lawner's translation was published in 1975. Raymond Rosenthal's followed in 1994. In their respective introductions they place these exchanges in the appropriate historical contexts: the publishing history of the letters; the intellectual roots of Gramsci's Marxism; and his relationship with the Third International and the PCI. Though he touches on these elements, Henderson begins a chaotic yet illuminating introductory essay in the National Gallery of Modern Art in Edinburgh, with a Ken Currie painting.

'The Self Taught Man' was part of the exhibition *The Vigorous Imagination: New Scottish Art* (1987). It depicts a Clydeside worker reading at night under a bare light bulb. The book in his hands has 'Gramsci' clearly printed on the cover. Henderson surmises 'that a Scottish working-class intellectual – a stubborn survivor in Thatcher's Britain – should be interested in Gramsci's political thought in the 1980s is readily comprehensible'. He then turns to a recent docudrama, produced by Pelicula of Glasgow and broadcast on Channel Four television, titled *Gramsci: Everything that Concerns People* (1987). Henderson reflects on the possible contrivance of the director in retaining the Scottish accents of the actors who played Gramsci's Italian prison-mates, and read it as a gesture toward the cultural and political parallels between Scotland and Sardinia. He notes that the film premiered in the Filmhouse Theatre in Edinburgh a week after the opening of the exhibition in which Currie's painting appeared (*PL*, p. 1). The introduction to the letters is thereby set in a precise time and place: during August, festival-season, in Edinburgh, in the year of the fiftieth anniversary of Gramsci's death.

Henderson then lists these Scottish-Sardinian parallels: including their common 'intransigent ethnic folkways'; the importance of 'primitive rebels' (Eric Hobsbawm's term) such as Sardinia's nineteenth-century bandits Francesco Derosas and Giovanni Tolu, and Scotland's Rob Roy, Gilderoy and James MacPherson, all three outlaws and broadside-fodder; finally, a shared respect and reverence for education among the working class (*PL*, pp. 1–2). This sustained comparison represents an endorsement for Henderson's own national, cultural and political perspectives. Other commentators have noted Gramsci's fondness for his native Sardinia, its folklore, its language and its customs, particularly as evidenced in the letters, but for Henderson it had a special significance. Gramsci's first political commitment was to Sardinian nationalism and, though his sympathy for this regional outlook might be seen in the context of a still far from unified Italian national identity, it was convenient for Henderson to emphasise this dimension. Despite Henderson's appreciation for what he called the 'universalisation' of Gramsci's thought, he is always mindful of this, the first and least strategic tier of Gramsci's political identity (*TAN*, p. 131).

Henderson's introduction is also set apart from those of other editors and translators by the lynchpin of folk culture. While it initially arises as grounds for the comparison of Sardinian and Scottish cultural history, Henderson returns to it on several occasions. Gramsci is presented as a storyteller, acknowledging 'another well-attested Sard trait: the island storytellers are given to weaving fantastically convoluted folk tales, adapting the stock of international *Märchen*, and giving them a "local habitation and name"'. Examples of folk tales written in outline in the letters, to be 'fleshed out' and retold for Gramsci's sons are described in some detail and, in another Christological construction, Henderson emphasises the importance of Sardinian folk culture in helping to 'sustain [Gramsci] during the darkest days of the "long prison Calvary"' (*PL*, pp. 4–5).[31] This sentiment is reiterated throughout the introduction to the letters, as Henderson returns again and again to Gramsci's epistolary enquiries into the 'festas, folksongs, banners and ballads' of his native island (*PL*, p. 13). Henderson speculates further:

> Can one doubt that this was a conscious effort to add sap and savour to a life given point only by indomitable cerebral obduracy: to counter the rigours of an existence whose staying power was based (as he put it in one letter) exclusively on the will. (*PL*, p. 13)

Expanding this focus, Henderson works Gramsci into a framework of modern folklore studies both in Italy and the Anglophone world. He draws extensively on Moyra Byrne's article 'Antonio Gramsci's Contribution to Italian Folklore Studies' (1982) in this endeavour. The 'apparent paradox which seems inherent in Gramsci's view of folklore', and which is emphasised by Byrne, is described almost exactly in her terms: 'on the one hand he elevates folklore to the status of a world-view which demands serious study, and on the other hand he defines it as an *incoherent heap of detritus* which must be swept away by the class conscious broom of a future working-class hegemonic culture' (emphasis added).[32] Henderson continues:

> It is this fruitful thought-provoking dialectical confrontation that has incited several warring factions in Italy and elsewhere into controversy; these have, over the years, tried to make sense of and synthesise the seemingly ambivalent and contradictory Gramscian views of folk-culture. (*PL*, p. 11)

At this point Henderson turns characteristically to a 'personal reminiscence' detailing the arrival of Alan Lomax in Scotland in 1950 and his introduction of Gramsci's work to the American folklorist (*PL*, pp. 11–12). Much of Henderson's later retrospective writings concern the genesis of the folk revival in Scotland, as does Ailie Munro's *The Democratic Muse* (1996) and, as historians of the revival, both emphasise the significance of the singular event of Lomax's arrival in Scotland in the conception of the movement (*AM*, p. 16).[33] In this respect, Henderson consciously incorporates Gramsci into the formative events of the modern Scottish folk revival.

The extraordinary range of references in Henderson's introduction reflects his unsystematic approach to Gramsci. Unrestrained by the need to clarify his thinking or to account for its relevance, Henderson returns to Italy and to a phenomenon among young Italian intellectuals, one apparently recognised by both Roberto Leydi, the distinguished ethnomusicologist, and the novelist, Cesare Pavese: a fascination with 'the other America', that of the poverty-stricken and the marginalised, as represented by Steinbeck and Faulkner, and by pioneer folk revivalists like Woody Guthrie, the Weavers and Pete Seeger. From here Henderson expands on his folk culture tangent, considering 'oral history', the Mass Observation project in Britain, and Joe Gould's elusive study, *An Oral History of Our Time* – a huge, almost mythical, tome that was meant to capture 'the informal history of the shirt-sleeved multitudes' in New York City (*PL*, p. 12).[34] Henderson cites a short passage by a young William Saroyan celebrating Gould's work, and compares it in its appreciation for lucidity and directness to Togliatti's 1938 tribute to Gramsci. Togliatti writes: '[Gramsci] was a bitter enemy of the inflated tinselly eloquence which vitiates such a large part of Italian literature and culture, and has choked in so many literate Italians the fresh bubbling sources of popular inspiration' (*PL*, p. 20). Afterwards, the legacy of Gramsci's comments on folklore, and the application of his political philosophy to the study of folklore, is considered in relation to the work of the philosopher and anthropologist, Ernesto de Martino, and the generation of Italian scholars who followed. Drawing directly from Byrne's article, Henderson is primarily concerned with the model of the 'subaltern' and the 'hegemonic' in the conceptualisation of folk culture, and especially the political potential of 'folk' as a force in opposition to bourgeois 'high' culture (*PL*, p. 14). Leydi's celebration of working-class political song is evoked to this end and Henderson offers the anti-Polaris protest songs of 1960s Scotland as an example of this mode. Again, Henderson smuggles Gramsci into the history of the folk revival.

In an exposition of Gramsci's dedication to the study of 'all that concerns people', Henderson contends that, 'this must surely include the most ancient patrimony of human exploit and dream', that is, folk culture (*PL*, p. 15). Reflecting on the inclusiveness of Gramsci's studies, Henderson draws on more unlikely sources. He quotes extensively, for example, from a contemporary article from *The Guardian* detailing the plight of Leslie Hall Pinder, a Canadian lawyer explaining for a sceptical and dismissive judge, the cosmology and folk-beliefs of her clients, during the First Nations land claim cases in British Columbia. Henderson points to Pinder's support for Laurens van der Post's contention that, beyond governments and judicial systems, it remains that 'our rational, materialistic side has tried to kill an aspect of ourselves that is natural, intuitive, spiritual and creative' (*PL*, p. 15). Henderson proceeds with an exploration of Bruce Chatwin's central thesis in *The Songlines* (1987), which is concerned with the Aboriginal 'mapping' of space and time through song and oral transmission. Against this backdrop he then cites Gramsci's letter to his mother requesting that she send him the lyrics for Sardinian folksongs, and descriptions of local festivals. According to Henderson, such requests were part of Gramsci's '[fight] to assert his continued existence, and his will to execute a lasting work, *für ewig*' (*PL*, p. 16). It seems that Gramsci's notes to his mother are, for Henderson, evidence of his sensitivity towards our 'spiritual and creative' side and of his awareness of the importance that folk culture has in the way we conceive of landscape, history and community.

Thinking in terms of the *für ewig*, Henderson then moves on to the lyrical immortalisation of Gramsci in a modern Sardinian folksong written to an ancient lyric form. The song is titled *Quadernos Iscrittos in d'una Cella Oscura* ('Notebooks Written in a Dark Cell') and Henderson supplies a rough prose translation of the lyrics.[35] He provides a description of the traditional polyphonic performance style that relates to this type of song, its rhyme scheme, and the persistence and durability of its particular form through modern economic and social changes (*PL*, p. 16).[36] In the context of Henderson's introductory essay, 'Notebooks Written in a Dark Cell' is symbolic of his perspective on Gramsci. A folksong of traditional form, explicit in its concern with an international political landscape, modernistic in its language, like a call-to-arms in tone; it represents his fervent, folk-based rendering of Gramsci's life and thought.

In the concluding pages of Henderson's introduction, Togliatti is cited at length. The quotation is part of a famous passage celebrating the 'fighter's spirit' and 'iron will' of Italy's most influential socialist thinker:

> He had a profound knowledge of the life and customs of the Italian people, of the legends and stories which have been created by the people, and in which the people have expressed in ingenious and intuitive form their needs, their aspirations, their dreams of liberty and justice, their hatred of the possessor classes.
> (*PL*, p. 20)

Though set in a more internationalist and historicist framework, Henderson's 1949 letter to his publisher, Lehman, indicates a similar sentiment:

> Gramsci was a socialist who found fruitful difference among the un-differentiated mass . . . He made a special study of Italian popular culture, and if there are three words which epitomise what Gramsci was not – they are 'by invitation only' . . . He was very fond of [Romain] Rolland's phrase – 'a pessimist of the intellect, and optimist of the will', but it was Gramsci's intellect that strengthened his will.[37]

Togliatti represents another important element of Gramsci's legacy: his relationship with the Italian Left and divisions within the Third International, both during his lifetime and in the years after his death. Henderson does not neglect these factors, and gives particular emphasis to what he interprets as Gramsci's early recognition of the dangerous rise of authoritarianism in the CPSU. He cites Gramsci's letter, entrusted to Togliatti and addressed to the Central Committee of the CPSU. Written only a month before his arrest it advises that 'unity and discipline [in the party] cannot be mechanical and coercive; they must be loyal, and the result of conviction . . .' (*PL*, p. 9). Passages like this help to position Gramsci as a twentieth-century Marxist thinker untainted by the revelations of 1956 and Khrushchev's 'secret speech'.

As with the introductory essays of other collections of Gramsci's prison letters, Henderson gives considerable thought to his subject's intellectual formation: to the influence of Italian idealist humanism and Benedetto Croce in particular. Out of this contextualisation the letters come to represent the connecting thread between Gramsci's life-as-lived and his intellectual development. In the introduction to her translation, Lawner writes of this unity in Gramsci's work:

> where theory of the most complex kind emerged from an original experience – that is to say, an experience lived in an original way, where all of the elements constituting a particular experience were drawn upon and 'syntheses' reached only occasionally and hesitantly. Gramsci's contribution to culture lies in this very theorisation of experience, by which I mean above all *historical* experience, a direct participation in the problems posed by history.[38]

Henderson seems to support this analysis. While Gramsci's 'theorisation of experience' is given due attention, with biographical details and personal contexts for the letters, the other disparate references in his introduction go largely unexplained. Henderson's piece is replete with remarks on texts he happened to be reading at the time, and in this respect his stance is, though unorthodox, unusually reflexive. In discovering Gramsci, Henderson found a thinker who gave form and substance to the disparate collection of impressions and the few basic principles that had already begun to coalesce in his mind.

There is a pertinent example of this process in the closing passages of the introductory essay. Henderson writes of MacDiarmid's poem 'The Seamless Garment', in which the poet 'compares Lenin's political sure-footedness ... to Rilke's "Seamless Garment o' Music and thought", and calls on the Border weavers to pay heed to the produce of these other looms'. The three final stanzas of MacDiarmid's poem follow, but not before a reminder that 'at one point the great makar reverts to a richer canon of old Scots speech – much as Gramsci might have needed a full measure of Sardinian to express his deepest feelings'. The linguistic shift in question is '... fegs, hoo the auld / Emmle-deugs o' the past are curjute and devauld', which Henderson anglicises approximately as 'Lord, how the old "glad rags" of the past are cast off and discarded' (*PL*, p. 21).

Though this introduction was written for the 1988 edition of the letters, Henderson's concern with MacDiarmid and the linguistic mode of honest, emotional self-expression appeared almost forty years previously in his letter to the prospective publisher:

> [Gramsci] has a strange (Scottish) mixture of hardness and softness ... Sardinian is not really a dialect at all but a language, like Provencal and Lallans (no word can so well translate the Italian expletive 'Beh' as the vigorous Scots and Irish 'och'). There is a Celtic aspect to Gramscian culture – oral – casual – deep – he was the islander, '*l'isolano*'.[39]

This early impression of the cultural connections between the Sardinian and the Scot, as refracted through Gramsci, is present throughout Henderson's essay on the prison letters. He also included a 'poetic vignette' in the letter: a reworking of the final stanza of MacDiarmid's 'Second Hymn to Lenin', inspired by Gramsci:

> Unremitting, relentless
> Organised to the last degree –
> Though Lenin's politics is bairn's play
> To what a communist must be.[40]

While MacDiarmid's original had assured Lenin that politics was 'bairn's play' compared to the true work of the poet, Henderson's reworking suggests that Gramsci presents us with a model for what it is to be a *true* communist, beyond and before the fray of politicking, in every living decision. Drawing again from Byrne, Henderson describes the memories of Sardinian folk culture in the letters as representative of 'the exorbitant human need, as Diego Carpitella [an ethnomusicologist and an authority on Italian folk music] expressed it, to define and occupy "one's own territory"' (*PL*, p. 13). With this vast array of references to the study of folk culture, and in this final connection with his other major influence, MacDiarmid, there is no doubt that Henderson felt the same need, even in his treatment of Gramsci.

The translations of the letters themselves reflect the same interpretative posture. Firstly, Henderson's own linguistic register, and his tendency to pepper even his writings with conversational Scots, is prevalent. For example, 'wee' appears several times, making frequent appearances in the more playful letters addressed to Gramsci's children (pp. 143, 177, 239, 282, 285, 288). Terms like these convey the tonal quality of the letters as observed or imagined by Henderson. One especially telling instance of the casual Scots register is his use of the word 'daft' (p. 218) where Rosenthal employs the rather more formal 'stultified'. Henderson translates Gramsci's description of the 'Italian Jacobin' Carlo Cattaneo, as having 'bees in his bonnet' (p. 162), where Rosenthal conceives of the same sentiment as having a head 'full of fanciful ideas' and Lawner, with the rather poetic, 'too full of chimeras'.[41]

Henderson awards himself linguistic licence beyond the occasional 'wee', however. Gramsci's description of his own contribution to the study of Croce takes the form of a distinctly Scottish metaphor: 'another little stone to be added to the cairn where its million and one predecessors already lie' (p. 162). In this instance, Henderson's representation of the textual voice of Gramsci is situated within the very landscape of Scotland. Not only that, but it speaks of a sedimentary passing of time, the gradual accretion of artefacts of humankind's existence, all embodied by the 'cairn' – a sepulchral monument or a marker of geographical and topographical location. It is an evocative image. The corresponding phrasings in the other translations are: 'a trifle to be added to the millions upon millions of similar notes', and 'a tiny contribution to millions of commentaries'.[42]

Henderson's efforts to pull Gramsci's letters into a vaguely Scots linguistic field are part of a two-way process. While Scotticisms are incorporated through translation, Sardinian terms are also retained from the original. As Henderson makes clear in his introduction, Gramsci's conception of his Sardinian heritage is critical in understanding his cultural-political world view. Again, this can be seen at least in part, as a substantiation of Henderson's own cultural nationalism. Sardinian words are retained and furnished with explanatory footnotes; they are not supplanted in-text by their translations, as with standard Italian. Henderson thought that the letters' modes of expression were significant, even to the Anglophone reader (pp. 120–1, 165, 177–8). Sardinian terms sit in stark contrast to the surrounding English, as if to suggest that Gramsci's Italian is more commensurable with it. It is, like MacDiarmid's Scots, resistant to and diminished by translation. In a 1988 public debate on the language of Scottish poetry, Henderson referred to one of Gramsci's letters on this subject (*TAN*, pp. 276–7). In it Gramsci seeks to convince his sister to let her son speak Sardinian, rather than reinforcing the dominance of 'proper' Italian, which would 'damage intellectual development, and put a straightjacket on imagination' (*PL*, p. 47). This linguistic factor is part of the cultural distinctiveness that Henderson saw as implicit in Gramsci's intellectual development, as a *meridionale* (Southern Italian) and as a Sardinian.[43]

Gramsci asserted that languages embody world views and that folklore does the same (*PL*, p. 174).[44] Henderson's own perspective is reflected in his translation of the many instances of storytelling in the *Prison Letters*: personal histories and folk tales alike. It is clear from the careful paragraphing of these stories, that Henderson relished Gramsci's narrative prose. Moreover, these episodes are situated within a frame of reference informed by his interest in Scottish folk and literary culture. For example, Gramsci considers his sister's pet name for her child: '[it] could be the name of a brownie or a bogle' (p. 183), which, with Rosenthal becomes 'a zany or a sprite'.[45] Henderson's gloss brings to mind Burns' epigraph for 'Tam O'Shanter': 'Of Brownyis and of Bogillis full is this Buke', which was in turn borrowed from Gavin Douglas' *Eneados* (1513), the Middle Scots translation of Virgil's *Aeneid*. His explanatory notes also speak to this framework. Explaining the Sardinian term *moro cabbaru*, Henderson writes: 'Literally "black man wearing the hood", a macabre figure resembling the Devil in Scottish folklore (cf. Stevenson's *Thrawn Janet*)' (p. 127n), which might be compared to Rosenthal's concise commentary: '"Black cape", in Sardinian'.[46] Henderson uses the term 'flyting' to describe the work of a medieval Italian poet, Ciullo d'Alcamo, to whom Gramsci refers in one of his letters (p. 141n). The term is generally associated with the early Scottish 'makars', though it also came to characterise Henderson's own public debates with MacDiarmid. In the note for another of Gramsci's correspondences, Allan Ramsay's *The Gentle Shepherd* (1725) is evoked in an effort to explain something of the sense of 'gentle' – as in 'Gently born' – as it appears in the title of Pushkin's *The Gentle Peasant Girl* (p. 49n). In a remarkable echo of his introductory essay, Henderson also finds space for MacDiarmid. An explanatory note ostensibly written to give biographical detail on the figure of Prince Dimitri Mirsky (1880–1939) becomes an opportunity to write about the poet, whose 'First Hymn to Lenin' happened to have been dedicated to the Russian literary historian (p. 154n).

The key to understanding Gramsci's voice as rendered in Henderson's translation is perhaps contained within the text itself. In a letter to his wife, Gramsci wrote:

> For me literary expression . . . is a relationship between form and content: analysis shows me, or helps me to understand, if there is complete adhesion between form and content, or if there exist gaps, fissures, disguises etc. It's possible to be mistaken, especially if one tries to deduce too much, but if the critic has a certain criterion to judge by, he can comprehend a good deal – at any rate the general state of mind [of the writer]. (*PL*, p. 125)

Though this passage was directed at his wife's tendency to conceal in her letters the difficulties of life at home, or so Gramsci suspected – 'I'm writing all this to let you know that from now on you can and should write to me with extreme frankness' (Ibid.) – it might also apply to Henderson's translation. Disjuncture between form and content is an inevitable by-product of the act of translation but, if the 'gaps', 'fissures' and 'disguises' that make up this disconnect can be isolated and examined, perhaps the 'general state of mind' of the translator can also be inferred. The translator is tasked with negotiating between fidelity to the original text and the freedom that is required to best express the essence of the original. Translation is, in this respect at least, akin to the performance events that make up Henderson's 'folk process': when a song is taken on, adapted and reproduced, the life of the song is extended. Similarly, when a text is translated, though wholly transformed, something of the original is made available to a new audience. In this sense, Henderson's adaptation of Gramsci might be considered as one artefact in the vast complex of works inspired by the Sardinian. We can find Henderson in the space between the original and the translation.

While Henderson's own interests coloured his text, his translation should be taken in good faith. Above all, Henderson sought to replicate the prose he had found so affecting in the original Italian, and this meant inferring Gramsci's intended modes of expression from the original and reconstructing them in English. The tone he cultivates in the letters reflects this perspective: the playful use of 'wee' and the retention of Sardinian terms, for example, suggest a mindfulness of the conscious, or imagined, registers of Gramsci's correspondence. Henderson's is a successful translation in so far as it contains within it such careful modulations of tone. Whether it is a short note to one of Gramsci's young sons enquiring into some aspect of their day-to-day lives, or a more reflexive letter to his closest confidant, Tatiana, on some aspect of his studies, the translations were tasked with representing Gramsci's relationships. One of the later letters to his son Giuliano (referred to as 'Julik' in the letters) serves as a good example of the fluency of Henderson's translations:

> I liked your drawings a great deal, because they're yours. They're also very original; I don't imagine nature has ever created such astounding things as you have. The fourth drawing is of a really extraordinary animal; it can't be a beetle, because it's too big – and, indeed, like most animals, it's only got four legs. Yet what long legs they are! It can't be a horse, because it hasn't got any ears that I can see (the first animal you drew hadn't got ears either; neither had one of the men) . . . (*PL*, p. 279)

The corresponding letter in Rosenthal's translation is stilted and awkward by comparison, due to clumsy, formal syntax and the cold accuracy of terms like 'quadruped', where Henderson deploys 'it's only got four legs'.[47] Though it is not quite the difference between Dickens' Gradgrind and Sissy Jupe, Henderson does emphasise the doting father and playmate at the expense of the distant, teacherly tone of Rosenthal's. The syntactical structures in Henderson's translation give the letter a conversational quality and encourage the reader to envisage a playful guessing game between father and son. Rosenthal's may be more technically 'accurate'; nevertheless, Henderson's expresses more emotion, and is perhaps a more successful translation of Gramsci's intended modes of expression. Though only one small example, this passage represents something of the compelling voice Henderson gave Gramsci: it is sometimes assured and proclamatory, but often tender and melancholic. Its complexities and idiosyncrasies are not avoided or concealed; they are embellished and compounded by Henderson's own. In translating a text, a consideration of 'fidelity' to the original raises questions over what it is in the original that demands the faithfulness of the translation. In this case it seems that Henderson was loyal to the only impression of Gramsci's letters that he could honestly conceive of: his own.

'Folklore' and the Future Revolution

Gramsci's 'Observations on Folklore' were of prime importance to Henderson. Though they constitute only a few pages of the lengthy *Prison Notebooks*, they made a crucial contribution to his conception of folk culture, representing basic assertions that were to be redressed and reaffirmed throughout his lifelong engagement with Scottish folk revivalism. The force that these ideas held for Henderson is demonstrated by the conceptual proximity of his own writings to some of Gramsci's comments. Henderson celebrated folk-song as a 'process'. The transmission of folk-song and the implied qualities of those songs able to survive, adapt and disseminate among people, were for Henderson, the basis of the political potential of folk culture. In an early article asserting the status of a given example of 'contaminated' song, as a 'folksong', Henderson explained that it heralded the categorisation 'because the people have taken it, possessed themselves of it, gloried in it, recreated it, loved it' (*AM*, p. 50). In the 'Observations on Folklore', Gramsci set out a definition of 'popular song' on similar terms:

> those written neither by the people nor for the people, but which the people adopt because they conform to their way of thinking and feeling . . . since what distinguishes a popular song within the context of a nation and its culture is neither its artistic aspect nor its historical origin, but the way in which it conceives the world and life, in contrast with official society.[48]

In their respective considerations of these songs-of-the-people, Henderson and Gramsci emphasise the role of those who sustain and disseminate the material. They also remind us that the contribution of 'the people' towards the legacy of a given song is, in turn, contingent on the appeal of the conceptions of life captured in that song. Gramsci addresses 'popular song' in the quotation above, where Henderson writes of 'folksong' – for him the distinction was irrelevant.[49]

The most distinctive quality of Gramsci's understanding of 'folklore' is the expansive definition that he supposes for the term and, consequently, the broad range of applications it gains outside of what might be called the 'traditional' conception:

> One can say that until now folklore has been studied primarily as a 'picturesque' element . . . Folklore should instead be studied as a 'conception of the world and life' implicit to a large extent in determinate (in time and space) strata of society and in opposition . . . to 'official' conceptions of the world (or in a broader sense, the conceptions of the cultured parts of historically determinate societies) that have succeeded one another in the historical process.[50]

In Gramscian terms, 'folklore' as a world view is then necessarily 'subaltern' rather than 'hegemonic'; existing in opposition to '"official" conceptions of the world' and offering a counterpoint of perpetual resistance, due simply to the fact that it exists. Henderson reiterates this view in various adaptations. In his notes for a 1949 lecture with the Workers' Educational Association he writes:

> The real study of folk art – the art of the labouring classes, the work-songs of the community – how they come about, how they grow, what their energy and aesthetic force consists of – is still in its infancy; – for the very good reason that is has not suited the powers that be to further such studies. Folk art is an *implicit* – and in many aspects an explicit challenge to the ruling class way of looking at the world.[51]

Channelling Gramsci's theoretical framework, Henderson rearticulates the opposition between an 'official' world view ('the conceptions of the cultured parts of historically determinate societies') and a 'communal' world view, embodied by folk culture.

Similar constructions reappear throughout Henderson's work, often with direct reference to the promotion of the national folk revival. In an article entitled 'Enemies of Folk-song' (1955) Henderson wrote of the Scottish 'élite' and 'elect', and their entrenchment in 'all key positions of administration, religion and the organisation of culture . . . [who] deny just as long as they are able that anything so vulgar as popular culture exists' (*AM*, p. 46). He bemoans the efforts of this dominant cultural force to undermine folk culture, and in persistently politicised language he reinforces the opposition that Gramsci's passage implies:

> Realising that folk-song threw down a challenge to the culture of the élite, that it expressed with power and *élan* the communal creativeness of the people as against a

> book-song and art-poetry increasingly contracted and withdrawn from the life of the common people, the mandarins of official taste did their utmost to purvey a diluted spirit to the public. (*AM*, p. 46)

Henderson often described the condition of folk culture as in 'opposition' to the dominance of 'officialdom'. He saw folk arts as the manifestation of a rebel 'underground' and returned to this imagery repeatedly, inferring a counter-cultural and politically radical folk culture, from its embattled status. It is a characteristic common to his outwardly propagandistic articles of the fifties and sixties, such as 'Enemies of Folk-song' (1955) and 'The Underground of Song' (1963), *and* to his more tempered and nostalgic later writings, like 'The Voice of the People' (1989) and 'It Was In You That It A' Began' (1980) (*AM*, pp. 45–50, 31–6, 1–4).

Henderson explains the qualities of the 'rebel underground':

> whether it be the love-songs which reject the values and prejudices of a money-minded bourgeois society, or a hypocritical puritan religious set-up; the bawdy songs which frankly rejoice in the fun and comedy of sex; the 'Ding Dong Dollar' CND songs which pillory the antics of military bigwigs and the bonzes of imperialist power politics; the 'Sangs of the Stane' which send up the pretensions and absurdities of a stuffy royalist Establishment; the bothy songs which put on record the cheese-paring niggardliness of skinflint farmers – all share to a greater or lesser extent this rebel élan.[52]

In other articles Henderson developed more detailed arguments with regard to particular songs, and song types, that function well within this overarching construction of an 'underground' culture of perennial resistance. In particular, he notes that the Church of Scotland and its social legacy is the subject of many sardonic and condemnatory folksongs, a reflex of the fact that folk-song is regarded as 'the cult of the damned' under the tyranny of John Knox's Kirk (*AM*, p. 28). Henderson endlessly reiterates Gramsci's idea of folk-song as a radical, democratic worldview in opposition to an inflexible and self-serving 'officialdom'. However, Gramsci's original assertion is based on a broader philosophical foundation, to which Henderson also seems to have adhered.

Gramsci's conception of folklore as a worldview stands on the premise that 'all men are intellectuals . . . but not all men have in society the function of intellectuals'.[53] Elsewhere in the notebooks, Gramsci contends that all men are also 'philosophers' due to what he calls the 'spontaneous philosophy' exercised by everyone, at all times.[54] This 'spontaneous philosophy' is, he explains, contained in:

> 1. language itself, which is a totality of determined notions and concepts and not just of words grammatically devoid of content. 2. 'common sense' and 'good sense';

> 3. popular religion and, therefore, also in the entire system of beliefs, superstitions, opinions, ways of seeing things and of acting, which are collectively bundled together under the name of 'folklore'.[55]

Gramsci's use of the 'folklore' handle advocates its definition as a pervasive, collective term for the diverse complexities of those heuristic structures that one inherits from social and cultural contexts, and through historical 'processes'. This included the 'distillation' of scientific and philosophical advancements into popular knowledge and understanding.[56] In the quotation above, 'language', 'folklore', 'common sense' and 'good sense' function on common ground. Indeed, in another section of the *Notebooks* Gramsci elaborates on the idea of 'common sense' and describes it as the 'folklore of philosophy': '[it] always stands midway between folklore proper (folklore as it is normally understood) and the philosophy, science, and economics of the scientists. Common sense creates the folklore of the future, a relatively rigidified phase of popular knowledge in a given time and place'.[57] Gramsci's conception of 'folklore', which takes the term beyond the traditional usage, as a reference to the 'picturesque' element, is given just enough purchase to avoid dissolving into pure abstraction, while maintaining a broad frame of reference. It is a term as applicable to philosophy as it is to cultural heritage.

Gramsci insisted that folklore 'can be understood only as a reflection of the conditions of [the] cultural life of the people' and his discourses on this subject are reflected on two distinct levels in Henderson's work.[58] Firstly, the 'conditions of [the] cultural life of the people' are always present in Henderson's writings about folk-song, singers and tradition-bearers. The recordings and transcriptions from his research trips testify to this fact. Song performances and folk tale renditions are interspersed with Henderson's conversational rapport with informants, always characterised by a clear and direct investment in the 'ways of life' of his source-singers and by the social-historical bent of his questioning. In his preface to Kenneth S. Goldstein's landmark *A Guide for Field Workers in Folklore* (1964), Henderson describes the 'deeply humanistic' role of the folk-song collector. Any one of his articles on the subject could be cited in support of the methodological notion that folk-song represents a 'reflection' of the lives of those who foster it. For example, in his work among Scotland's indigenous travelling people, Henderson noted that the materials he collected 'have the authentic bloom of the open air on them . . . More important still, they carry the listener to the very centre of *a way of life* which, although profoundly alien to most industrialised Western society, has a permanent appeal, validity and attractiveness of its own' (emphasis added) (*AM*, pp. 102–3). The value of the songs is in the access that they afford to the heart of this 'way of life', to the complexities of these lived communities, and to the mode of hermeneutics that they inspired.

Henderson also adheres to the idea of 'folklore' as a 'conception of the world and life'.[59] While he recognised the interrelation between folk-song and the lives of those who are responsible for it, Henderson's own perspective seems to have been quite self-consciously embedded in this field of representation. In other words, Henderson appears to have purposefully stepped inside Gramsci's 'conception' of folklore by choosing to establish his 'view of the world and life' as one persistently framed by, and formulated through, folk culture. He once wrote of Calum Maclean, his former colleague at the School of Scottish Studies, that 'he took pride in sharing the beliefs and mental attitudes – and even maybe, at times, some of the wilful prejudices – of the ordinary folk among whom he worked' and this seems to have been as true of Henderson (*AM*, p. 203). His appreciation for F. Marian MacNeill's methodology in *The Silver Bough* (1957–68) reflects another aspect of this approach: '[she] enters into the spirit of the customs and events she is describing, and (as it were) dons guising gear herself to communicate the fun of the fair. Her books convey vividly the eager joy of the participant' (*AM*, p. 263). As a celebrated songwriter as well as song-collector, Henderson commented upon the vitality of folk-song from the perspective of the insider. His personal investment in this worldview can also be seen in his work on the prison letters. Folk culture is Henderson's referential touchstone, and it seems to be that regardless of the remit of a given article, interview, or public dispute; folk-song, as an expansive conception of the world, and of human history, bears down upon him and finds its own significance. Just as Gramsci's idea of 'folklore' cannot be addressed without taking into consideration its 'philosophical' basis, neither can it be analysed in relation to Henderson, in total isolation, separated from those other categories of Gramsci's study. Popular literature and comparative linguistics were among the other subjects of Gramsci's prison notebooks. As Henderson reminds us, the common principle behind all of these various studies was 'the creative spirit of the people'.[60]

The paradoxical aspect of Gramsci's 'folklore', which was addressed briefly with regard to Henderson's introduction to the *Prison Letters*, is only part of a broader tension in Gramsci's writings. Given his endorsement of Byrne's views on Gramsci's contribution to Italian folklore studies, it is clear that Henderson recognised the tension that is implicit in a conception of folklore that sees it as a subject worthy of serious study, that should be analysed as a system of interpreting the world, but at the same time concedes that folklore can have no place in the development of a working-class hegemony and, therefore, no place in the revolutionary future as imagined by a Gramscian Marxism. Gramsci fostered an expansive idea of folklore that could be mobilised as an interpretative framework for understanding the ways in which people conceive of their own lives in context. However, in some passages, he discerned a reactionary 'underground' of folklore that revealed itself as definitively 'subaltern', inherently defensive, and in perpetual opposition to the dominant hegemonic forces in society, even if those forces are revolutionary and aim for a new society couched in the interests of the proletariat:

> the state competes with and contradicts other explicit and implicit conceptions, and folklore is not among the least significant and tenacious of these; hence it must be 'overcome'. For the teacher, then, to know 'folklore' means to know what other conceptions of the world and of life are actually active in the intellectual and moral formation of young people, in order to uproot them and replace them with conceptions which are deemed to be superior.[61]

This need to overcome 'folklore' requires some qualification. Though it appears to be a direct challenge to the validity of folk culture and its perceived radical credentials, Gramsci's assertion is in fact less political than it seems. It is a disinterested claim, it does not specify the character of those educators of the state, nor does it elaborate upon the particular *hegemony* or the 'superior conceptions' that they represent. This is a process that occurs at any given historical juncture. Just as Gramsci envisaged a socialist revolution that must be aware of the need for 'coercive' and 'consensual' strategies – such as overcoming the obstacles of residual 'folklore' – so too must those who, for example, supported Mussolini's model of fascism. It is, in the first instance, a theory that describes how politics and culture are structured. To develop the idea into a programme for change is to tailor a politically neutral construct for a partisan agenda.

Gramsci's passive conception of 'folklore' both liberates and limits Henderson. While no singular notion can be totalising and absolute, 'folklore' becomes a cacophonic complex of worldviews where none has a greater claim to truth or knowledge than any other:

> This conception of the world [that of folklore] is not elaborated and systematic because, by definition the people (the sum total of the instrumental and subaltern of every form of society that has so far existed) cannot possess conceptions which are elaborated, systematic and politically organised and centralised in their albeit contradictory development. It is, rather, many-sided – not only because it includes different and juxtaposed elements, but also because it is stratified, from the more crude to the less crude . . .[62]

In one sense this passage presents us with the corrective for a socialism that would allow the cultural dimension of class-based politics to be homogenised or over-simplified. The political potential that Henderson celebrates in the 'underground of folksong' might therefore be undermined by an exposition of the cultural diversity of 'the people'. It is more difficult to promote an inherently political mode of coherent, communal artistic self-expression, when it is in fact characterised by a vast crowd of heterogeneous voices and belief-systems that refuse to be made uniform. In Gramsci's words, 'there is nothing more contradictory and fragmentary than folklore'.[63]

Gramsci's *Prison Notebooks* should, however, be interpreted with great caution. The hierarchy of his arguments on 'folklore' is typically unclear and his thesis is, in accordance with the rest of his writings, especially vulnerable to misrepresentation. One distinction that can be made in an effort to achieve a more precise reading of passages like those cited above is that 'folklore' should never be reduced to the popular, uncritical definition of 'traditional art forms and mythology'. Within this context it is clear that Gramsci's views on 'folklore' are divided, but not necessarily contradictory, and perhaps not even irreconcilable. Byrne recognises a series of 'levels' that constitute Gramsci's broader conception of 'folklore'; a reading that is based on passages like that cited above – stratification from the 'crude to the less crude'. The 'paradox' is exposed when we recognise the friction between ideas of folklore as fundamentally conservative or fundamentally progressive.[64] In his introduction to the *Prison Letters*, Henderson recognises an 'unresolved but creative clash of contradictions in Gramsci's approach' (*PL*, p. 15). Byrne summarises the anthropologist Ernesto de Martino's perspective on this 'paradox':

> On the one hand, their Gramscian-Marxist aim would be to determine the best means of accelerating the disappearance of this cultural relic [folksong] which is so 'disorganic' in relation to the modern world. On the other hand, an ethnographic operation aiming at a historico-religious reconstruction of a phenomenon depends on that phenomenon's persistence, and cannot *at the same time* be concerning itself with the means of eradicating it.[65]

More recently, Stephen Olbrys Gencarella has recognised this 'seeming contradiction' and ascribes it to a broader consideration of class and culture: 'he stands in solidarity with the working class and peasants, but calls them to aspirations beyond their immediate intellectual, social, and political environments'.[66] To overcome this difficulty Gencarella proposes 'critical folklore studies' that discerns between 'progressive' and 'conservative' folklore, and promotes the former while suppressing the latter. In response, José E. Limón asks 'how can we as folklorists possibly see our academic practice as one that should call for the eradication of our subject matter and, really, our subjects as creative people?'[67] The most obvious response to Gencarella's proposal might be that the remit of the folklorist does not extend so far as to include a strategic critical silence in relation to lore that cannot be easily reconciled with the scholar's political beliefs. Literature and lore ought to be studied and understood regardless of its political appeal to the academic. In fact, the apparent paradox that Gramsci's work describes can be overcome without retreating to this position.

If this 'creative clash of contradictions' is based on Gramsci's comments on the heterogeneity of folklore and on the need for folklore to be 'overcome', it seems that the 'contradictions' can be dissolved with relative ease. If 'folklore' is the broad network of various 'conceptions of the world', shared, yet adapted and manipulated by people within and between social groups, and if it includes the philosophical dimension of 'common sense', then the progressive and conservative elements can both comfortably inhabit the territory of 'folklore'. There are conceptions that must be 'overcome' and there are those that might be harnessed and developed, all within the broad forum of 'folklore'. This does not alter the fact that, in Gramsci's words, 'folklore . . . [is] something which is very serious and is to be taken seriously'.[68]

Henderson admired the fact that Gramsci championed the study of popular literature and linguistics within his remit of 'the creative spirit of the people in its diverse phases'. The philosopher's work in these fields explores tensions similar to those in his thoughts on 'folklore'. Gramsci laments the distinct lack of an indigenous popular literature in Italy, a fact that he attributes to the failure of the bourgeois cultural revolution in the country, and which he sees as indicative of a disconnection in the national literature with what he terms the 'national-popular'.[69] Henderson describes the 'national-popular' as 'the idea that the masses could achieve a "higher" national socio-cultural unity on the basis of a rejection of folkloric and provincial values' (*PL*, p. 14).[70] Gramsci recognised the importance of the study of popular and commercial literature: 'the success of a work of commercial literature indicates the "philosophy of the age", that is, the mass of feelings and conceptions of the world predominant among the "silent" majority. This literature is a popular "narcotic", an "opium".'[71] Writing of the formulation of a 'new' literary movement, Gramsci again stresses the imperative of the 'popular':

> The premiss of the new literature cannot but be historical, political and popular. It must aim at elaborating that which already is, whether polemically or in some other way does not matter. What does matter, though, is that it sink its roots into the humus of popular culture as it is, with its tastes and tendencies and with its moral and intellectual world, even if it is backward and conventional.[72]

As with 'folklore', Gramsci accounts for both *progressive* and *conservative* factors in his conception of literature. Qualitative judgements on the fundamental nature of 'popular literature' and 'folklore' are eschewed for a dispassionate recognition of the negative attributes that impede cultural hegemony – the 'backward and conventional' – and those that facilitate it – its rootedness in 'popular culture'.

Gramsci envisaged 'language' in similar terms: 'every language is an integral conception of the world and not simply a piece of clothing that can fit indifferently as form over any content'.[73] However, as is the case with 'folklore', the broad conceptual premise is a foundation for seemingly contradictory developments and it becomes another site for the paradox that, according to both Henderson and Byrne, plagued Italian folklorists. One of Henderson's most frequent references to Gramsci relates to language and dialect, and comes from one of the prison letters addressed to his sister Teresina. In it he asserts that Sardinian is a 'real' language rather than a dialect; that it ought to be encouraged as part of the linguistic development of his nephew Franco: 'I really do entreat you . . . allow your children to suck up all the "Sardism" they want, and let them develop spontaneously in the natural environment they were born into' (*PL*, p. 47). Henderson later offered an extract from this letter as 'food for thought to those Marxists . . . who would dismiss minority languages and the whole question of folk culture as insignificant', equating Gramsci's appreciation for his native Sardinian language with a political defence of the value of folk culture.[74]

Towards the end of his introduction to the *Prison Letters* Henderson reflects on the phenomenon that sees us return to the demotic when expressing the deepest, or most immediate, of our feelings. He provides a passage from MacDiarmid's 'Seamless Garment' as an example and suggests that Gramsci had a similar relationship with Sardinian (*PL*, p. 21). One of the letters seems to support this conjecture, as Gramsci recounts the reports of other prisoners who had witnessed his behaviour at a 'critical point' of illness and delirium: he spoke of 'the immortality of the soul in a realistic and historically-minded sort of way', of the 'inanity' of religion and of the 'universal historic process'; 'wanderings' which were, in his words, 'interspersed with long tirades in Sardinian dialect' (*PL*, p. 261). Gramsci's evidently subconscious relationship with his native language proves to be an obstacle for some of his other language-related proposals. In a note on 'normative grammar' he writes:

> it is rational to collaborate practically and willingly to welcome everything that may serve to create a common national language, the non-existence of which creates friction particularly in the popular masses among whom local particularisms and phenomena of a narrow and provincial mentality are more tenacious than is believed.[75]

Gramsci's endorsement of a standardisation of the national language is expressed as a force to overcome 'local particularisms' and provincialism.[76] Despite his enthusiasm for 'international languages' Gramsci did not support the Esperantists: '[how] could an international language take root when it is completely artificial and mechanical, completely ahistorical, not fed by great writers, lacking the expressive richness which comes from the variety of dialects, from the variety of forms assumed in different times?'[77] Gramsci appreciated the qualities of indigenous, regional languages and respected their organic connection with the communities in which they function; yet his 'rational' mind recognised the need for such forms to be subsumed into a greater, standardised register, for the sake of political and social progress. Similarly, Gramsci was fond of the traditional folk culture of his native Sardinia. Nevertheless, he foresaw that it needed to be 'overcome' as part of the implementation of a new hegemonic cultural force. We might interpret this 'paradox' as the compromise that is necessary in imagining a future revolutionary moment. It cannot be assumed that aspects of society or culture perceived as 'subaltern', or 'subversive', when viewed within a capitalist system, will be perceived the same way within an alternative social model. The 'subaltern' is defined by its relationship with the 'hegemonic'. As such, a revolutionary future is one that will need to 'overcome', or 'absorb', these aspects.

The tensions in Gramsci's thought can perhaps also be accounted for within the *Notebooks* themselves, as something inherent to the dialectical and discursive expression of his work. In a series of notes addressing the problems of criticism, Gramsci asserts that:

> critical activity must be based on the ability to make distinctions, to discover the difference underlying every superficial and apparent likeness, and on the ability to discover the essential unity underlying every apparent contrast and superficial differentiation.[78]

Gramsci sought to identify inconsistencies and contradictions, whilst conceiving of a greater, more abstract unity that might encapsulate these alleged differences. In the introduction to the letters Henderson addresses Gramsci's comments on folklore and the debates that they inspired:

> The passage [from one Gramsci's letters asking his mother about Sardinian folk culture], and others like it, served to a large extent to neutralise the effect of the long series of negative attributes which passages in the *Quaderni* attribute to folklore. In the past decade a certain equilibrium, a synthesis of speculation and experience, has been achieved in this whole disputed area, and some of the lesser-known remarks of Gramsci have acquired a fresh relevance. In addition, folklorists outside Italy have begun to tackle the job of examining their field of study from a class perspective, and the fresh controversies and 'flytings' which will inevitably surface can only benefit from the vigorous intellectual battles already fought.
> (*PL*, p. 17)

'Flyting' clearly evokes Henderson's own disputes with MacDiarmid. Gramsci featured throughout these exchanges, which took place after 1956, following the British Left's great disillusionment with the Soviet experience. In this context Gramsci provided an alternative intellectual tradition, untainted by the inhumanity of the Stalinist-Leninist line. In the first instance, Henderson cites Gramsci as an example of 'the universal genius' who appreciates the worth of the study of folk culture and popular culture, as distinct from MacDiarmid, who attacked the folk revival as a populist conspiracy of mediocrity against literary greatness and political purity (*TAN*, p. 131). The '1320 Club Flyting' was concerned with the strategy of the contemporary Home Rule movement. Henderson promoted the democratic process, based on party politics, while

MacDiarmid advocated a 'political vanguard' in the form of the eponymous club. Henderson derided what he called the 'self-elected Elect' of the organisation while MacDiarmid questioned why 'superior brains should acquiesce in the delimitation of their political and other objectives to conciliate the mass who cannot see beyond their noses?' Henderson drew upon Gramsci as a 'sociologist who found fruitful differences among the undifferentiated masses' and who stood in opposition to the kind of 'authoritarian strain' apparent in MacDiarmid's politics (*TAN*, pp. 164–6). In response, MacDiarmid presented his own claim to Gramsci, deploying his terminology in setting out a 'cultural front' in the 'war of position' – which the class struggle becomes, in periods following revolutionary activity. He proceeds to cite from the *Prison Notebooks*:

> In its most common form of economic superstition, the philosophy of praxis loses its cultural expansiveness in the upper sphere of the intellectual group, however much it acquires among the masses and among mediocre intellectuals who do not want to tire their brains but wish to appear very shrewd. (*TAN*, pp. 167–8)

Despite MacDiarmid's confidence, the Sardinian's proviso does not definitively support his argument. The economic and historical determinism that lies at the heart of undeveloped, popular conceptions of Marxism is under scrutiny in this passage, not those who seem to adhere to it. Rather than promoting the superiority of the intellectual cadre – in their ability to conceive of the vast complexity of the 'philosophy of praxis' – this passage encourages a more accessible, and foundational, Marxism that nevertheless avoids reductionist 'superstition'. Furthermore, MacDiarmid reads the 'intellectual' in a more conventional sense than that generally attributed to Gramsci, which is characterised as a far more mediatory and interpretative role than the isolated, vanguardist elite of MacDiarmid's model.[79]

This contest over Gramsci's support speaks of a tension that stretches through all of Henderson and MacDiarmid's 'Flytings'. Based on the opposition of the 'communal' and the 'individual' as cultural political agents, this tension is manifest in the earlier disputes, as an interrogation of the relationship between the folk arts and so-called literary art. In fact these debates signify the very points Gramsci sought to synthesise in the cultural focus of his notebooks: 'Marxism crowns the whole movement for intellectual and moral reform dialecticised in the contrast between popular and higher culture'.[80] In this sense, Henderson and MacDiarmid's disputes literally enact Gramsci's dialectics and glimpse the potential of a genuine *cultural* Marxism. The Sardinian philosopher's concept of 'contradictory consciousness' is formalised in relation to 'the active man of the masses' – a figure courted by both Henderson and MacDiarmid:

> We can almost say that he has two theoretical consciousnesses (or one contradictory consciousness), one implicit in his actions, which unites him with all his colleagues in the practical transformation of reality, and one superficially explicit or verbal which he has inherited from the past and which he accepts without criticism . . . this contradictory consciousness can result in a state of moral and political passivity.[81]

Gramsci offers an explanation for the difficulties the revolutionary vanguard incurs when trying to enlist the support of the 'masses': the impulse that arises from that consciousness that unites the individual with the many is frustrated by that which is inherited and goes unexamined. Henderson and MacDiarmid looked to resolve this 'contradictory consciousness' through art. MacDiarmid rejected the idea of appealing to the tastes of the masses as the patronising work of an 'interpreting class'; he called for a 'monumental' art aiming for nothing less than 'grand syntheses' for the times (*TAN*, pp. 127–9). Accordingly, his later poetic works are set at a level that refuses to conceal their complexity. Henderson, on the other hand, sought to harness the inherent power of folk culture, to synthesise it with the progressive elements of literary practice in Scotland and, in doing so, mobilise and politicise popular culture.

Henderson's efforts to resolve the 'contradictory consciousness' rested on the promotion of folk culture and the fostering of a new, genuinely popular culture. However, Henderson could not quite overcome the contradiction that arose in Gramsci's descriptions of 'folklore'. He tried to reconcile the traditional definition of folklore, the 'picturesque' element, with the broader conception of a 'way of conceiving of the world and of life'. Henderson is at once vindicated by Gramsci's letters and undermined by his notebooks: he is torn between the specificity of 'folk-song' as a body of material with a particular tradition, transmitted by particular means, and the abstraction of folklore as a *worldview*.

The Folk Revival as 'Gramsci in Action'

Alec Finlay describes Henderson as the 'principal strategist' of the Scottish folk revival, and in this capacity he frequently cited the importance of the Edinburgh People's Festival and, in particular the People's Festival Ceilidhs, as a catalyst for the movement (*AM*, p. xi). He later described these events as examples of 'Gramsci in action'.[82] In a televised discussion on Gramsci, Henderson explained the theoretical connection with the People's Festival: 'it was an attempt, in fact, to carry Gramscian ideas of infiltration, to put it bluntly, into the body politic'. The Festival was, in Henderson's words, about Scottish culture, not 'high-heid-yin culture'.[83] It was conceived as an alternative to the elitism and 'high-culture' focus of the International Festival established in 1947. The slogan attached to the original People's Festival, 'By Working People For Working People', certainly evokes a political perspective in keeping with Gramsci's focus on 'the creative spirit of the people'. Trades unions, Labour Party organisations, the Workers' Music Association, the Musicians' Union and the Edinburgh Trades Council were all represented in the Committee for the Festival, which set out its aims in the first programme:

> To initiate action designed to bring the Edinburgh International Festival closer to the people as a whole and to make it serve more fully the cause of international understanding and good will; and also to initiate action such as will more generally make what is best in the cultural life of our country more accessible to working people, and will secure further facilities for the development of the cultural activities of working people.[84]

Over the first two years the Festival's programme covered a broad spectrum of social, political and cultural issues: there were lectures on Beethoven, James Connolly, Scottish folk-song, MacDiarmid, David Lyndsay, and the 'Radical Tradition in Scottish Culture'. There were choirs, art exhibitions and theatre productions including Ewan MacColl's *Uranium 235* and *The Travellers*, and Joe Corrie's *In Time of Strife*. In its first year, the Festival also hosted a day conference entitled 'Towards a People's Culture'.[85]

Henderson celebrated the People's Festival Ceilidhs in particular as a site of 'Gramsci in action'.[86] The programme for the first ceilidh articulates an aim to 'restore Scottish folksong to the ordinary people, not merely as a bobby-soxer vogue, but deeply and integrally'.[87] The second was held in honour of MacDiarmid's sixtieth birthday and, as Henderson later recalled, the poet gave a vote of thanks that became a staunch defence of the folk culture represented at the event:

> One thing must have struck you, I think, in the programme tonight – that is, the extent to which all the items on the programme have been correlated to the lives of the common people, to the work of common people, the daily darg of the common people.
>
> We are not going to be taken from that – we're not going to be persuaded by the advocates of snob art, that some mystical palaver is better than that which comes from the working life of our own people. (*AM*, p. 395)

The diversity of the Festival's programmes and the staging of both 'high' and 'low' culture, adheres to what Henderson often referred to as a constant 'cross-fertilisation' between folk and literary cultures (*AM*, pp. 4, 27, 427). Gramsci offered an explanation for this phenomenon: 'folklore has always been tied to the culture of the dominant class and, in its own way, has drawn from it the motifs which have then become inserted into combinations with the previous traditions'.[88]

The ceilidhs brought together several of the source-singers Henderson had 'discovered' on his early recording trips. These recordings, and the ceilidhs themselves, played a vital role in energising a new generation of folk singers and song collectors, many of whom were then inspired to take the material to schools, folk workshops and, in later years, folk clubs, disseminating previously unheard examples of an invaluable indigenous folk culture.[89] Gramsci writes: 'If the cultural world for which one is fighting is a living and necessary fact, its expansiveness will be irresistible and it will find its artists'.[90] The agency of a given 'culture', as something real and active though not necessarily realised *en masse*, correlates with Henderson's conception of folk-song and with the project of the revival. Henderson and his peers sought out source-singers; the field recordings and Festival ceilidhs that resulted put in motion a revival that literally 'found' its artists. Countless people with unrealised potential as 'tradition-bearers' and creative artists, were given a mode of self-expression that appealed to them and legitimised their voices.

Henderson saw the revival as an attempt to put into action Gramsci's proposal that the teaching of folklore would bring about 'the birth of a *new culture among the popular masses*, so that the separation between modern culture and popular culture of folklore will disappear' (emphasis added). Gramsci went on to state that, in the sense of appealing to the masses and relating to their conceptions of the world, action of this sort would 'correspond on the intellectual plane to what the Reformation was in Protestant countries'.[91] The steadily increasing momentum of the revival was realised through traditional 'oral transmission', at ceilidhs and at folk-clubs; by the passing around of field recordings; through articles such as those written by Henderson exploring folksong threads and defending the programme of revivalism; and by the establishment of folk music festivals and the formation of bodies like the School of Scottish Studies. These elements represent prime examples of what Gramsci referred to when he wrote:

> Creating a new culture does not only mean one's own 'original' discoveries. It also, and most particularly, means the diffusion in a critical form of truths already discovered, their 'socialisation' as it were, and even making them the basis of vital action, an element of co-ordination and intellectual and moral order.[92]

The 'socialisation' of the 'truths' of the folk revival was, if anywhere, realised in these channels of dissemination and popularisation. Henderson's description of the Edinburgh People's Festival as 'Gramsci in action' might therefore be extended to apply to the whole of the modern Scottish folk revival.

Most Gramsci scholarship has focused on his overarching political philosophical concepts: 'cultural hegemony', 'national-popular' and 'traditional and organic intellectuals'. In Henderson's response to Gramsci these terms are conspicuous only in their absence. Instead, Henderson's relationship with Gramsci must be understood through its various incarnations: in the image of the political martyr and socialist prophet; in the imagined registers of prison letters; in the bold assertions on the importance of folk culture, and on the revolutionary future that jeopardises its political value. On one level, the folk revival that Henderson promoted can be understood as an instance of 'Gramsci in action', where many of Gramsci's notes on culture are enacted in the public sphere. On another, Henderson adopted 'folklore' as a 'world-view', just as Gramsci had described it: he dedicated himself to the folk arts on these terms and constantly negotiated with the tensions that arise from Gramsci's cultural politics. He advocated Gramsci in practice and wrestled with Gramsci in theory.

As this chapter has shown, Henderson was sensitive to the distinctiveness of Scotland's culture and politics, just as Gramsci had been to those of Sardinia. Like the British New Left, Henderson responded to Gramsci's emphasis on the cultural dimensions of the political struggle: in his case, formulating a conception of folk culture as perennially subaltern. Like the 'Scottish Gramscians', he used Gramsci to negotiate between the particularities of a local or national cultural-political framework and the broader structures of an internationalist socialist perspective of history. In his introduction to the prison letters Henderson wrote at length about the Italian folklorists and ethnomusicologists who sought to reconcile Gramsci with their research and with their commitment to traditional arts and to the 'folk process'. The 'moral and methodological dilemma' that this caused was perhaps closer to Henderson's experience of Gramsci than any other avenue of the 'great thinker's' scholarly legacy.[93]

Gramsci's influence continues to expand in several directions. Ernesto Laclau and Chantal Mouffe's celebrated *Hegemony and Socialist Strategy* (1985), which sets out a post-Marxist theoretical framework of 'universals', and formalises a theory of 'radical democratic politics', is founded on an extended conception of Gramscian 'hegemony'. Likewise, Gayatri Chakravorty Spivak's influential essay, 'Can the Subaltern Speak?' (1988), engages with the concept of the 'subaltern' as it had been discovered in Gramsci's notebooks and adopted in analyses of the postcolonial condition. More recently, Peter Ives has revisited Gramsci's politics through his parallel study of linguistics, and connects his work to that of the Bakhtin circle and the Frankfurt School in *Gramsci's Politics of Language* (2004). This chapter cannot be extended to include a detailed exploration of the legacy of Gramsci's ideas in all disciplines; however, the selection mentioned above is sufficient to show that Henderson's 'Gramsci' is unique. Beginning among the Italian *Resistenza*, Henderson's relationship with the Sardinian was heavily influenced by the idealised image of the prophet and the political martyr, but also by a conscientious reading of the prison letters, and by a friendship with many of Gramsci's friends and family. In 1968, Henderson reserved a special place for Gramsci in his blueprint for a poetry that could 'become people', where 'the self-sacrificing political champion of the *rossa bandiera*' would be the central figure.[94]

Henderson's absorption of Gramsci was unsystematic. In the '1320 Club

Flyting', MacDiarmid isolated a passage from Gramsci's early writings. This was consistent with his renowned magpie tendencies: citing a whole range of thinkers at length and implying that the most esteemed of the intelligentsia could always be drawn upon to support his position (cf. *Lucky Poet*). On the other hand, Henderson was as likely to point to Gramsci's prison life, and to his heightened appetite for the folk culture of his native island, as he was to cite a passage of the *Prison Notebooks* and follow its logic through the contemporary political and cultural landscape. Gramsci's influence is coded into the texture of Henderson's work, though it is never acknowledged fully. Henderson's relationship with Gramsci cannot be fully understood by constraining him in a corner of the bibliography, alongside the Italian folklorists or the New Left, for example. Instead, as this chapter describes, the influence of the 'great thinker' is realised in various works to varying degrees of subtlety. At this juncture, we might return to Gramsci's own words: 'if the cultural world for which one is fighting is a living and necessary fact, its expansiveness will be irresistible and it will find its artists'.[95] The same might be said of Gramsci's influence on Henderson: Gramsci's legacy bore down on Henderson as a 'living and necessary fact' and found its realisation, its art, in his work.

Notes

1. MacDiarmid, *Complete Poems*, p. 745.
2. See Srivastava and Bhattacharya, *The Postcolonial Gramsci*; Green, *Rethinking Gramsci*; Ives and Lacorte, *Gramsci, Language, and Translation*; and Martin, *Antonio Gramsci: Critical Assessments of Leading Political Philosophers*.
3. Forgacs, 'Gramsci and Marxism in Britain', pp. 72–3.
4. See Forgacs, 'Gramsci and Marxism in Britain', p. 75; and Davidson, 'Gramsci's Reception in Scotland', p. 38.
5. Forgacs, 'Gramsci and Marxism in Britain', pp. 75–6.
6. 'Gramsci and Marxism in Britain', p. 74. Here, Forgacs was likely thinking of texts like Thompson's 'Socialist Humanism' and *The Making of the English Working Class* (1963), and Williams' *Culture and Society* (1958) and *The Long Revolution* (1961).
7. Chun, *The British New Left*, p. 26. See Williams, *Marxism and Literature*, pp. 108–14, and 'Base and Superstructure in Marxist Cultural Theory'; Thompson, 'Patrician Society, Plebeian Culture'; Hobsbawm, 'Gramsci and Political Theory'; and Hall, 'Gramsci and Us'.
8. Unless otherwise stated, the volume of Gramsci's letters from prison referred to throughout this chapter is Henderson's translation, *Prison Letters* (1996).
9. *Gramsci: Here and Now* was made by Scottish Television and broadcast in 1987, the fiftieth anniversary of Gramsci's death. Henderson appeared alongside the other panel members: Lidia Curti, Stuart Hall and John Reid.
10. Davidson, 'Gramsci's Reception in Scotland', p. 36.

11. Ibid., pp. 39–41.
12. Burnett, 'Scotland and Antonio Gramsci', p. 12.
13. Calder, *Revolving Culture*, pp. 229–42.
14. Brown, *The Red Paper on Scotland*, p. 18.
15. In particular, Davidson discusses Harvie's *Scotland and Nationalism* and Young's *The Rousing of the Scottish Working Class*, pp. 45–9.
16. See Finlay, 'A River That Flows On: A critical overview of Hamish Henderson's life and work', pp. 313–14; Sassi, 'Hamish Henderson: Un Gramsciano a Edimburgo'; Neat, *Making of the Poet*, pp. 242–55; and Featherstone, '"Gramsci in Action": Space, Politics, and the Making of Solidarities', pp. 76–9.
17. Henderson, 'Edinburgh People's Festival, 1951–54', p. 165.
18. An earlier, condensed version of this chapter was published as '"Gramsci in Action": Antonio Gramsci and Hamish Henderson's Folk Revivalism'.
19. Gramsci, *Cultural Writings*, pp. 9–11.
20. Antonio Labriola (1843–1904) was the first to describe Marxism as a 'philosophy of praxis' (*filosofia della prassi*), and is generally recognised as Gramsci's source for the epithet.
21. Femia, *Gramsci's Political Thought*, pp. 8–9.
22. Femia, *Gramsci's Political Thought*, pp. 10–11. See Piccone's 'Gramsci's Marxism: Beyond Lenin and Togliatti' for an account of Togliatti as 'the main architect of the myth of Gramsci as brilliant theoretical footnote to Lenin' (p. 489). In later years Togliatti espoused a more developed appreciation of Gramsci's thought, though he was consistent in his focus on the Italian contexts of Gramsci's work. See Togliatti, *On Gramsci and Other Writings*.
23. Femia, *Gramsci's Political Thought*, pp. 16–19.
24. Neat, *Making of the Poet*, pp. 242–55.
25. Piero Gobetti was a radical liberal journalist and activist. He founded *La Rivoluzione Liberale* in 1922. Like Gramsci, he was greatly influenced by Croce's idealist philosophy. See Henderson's explanatory note (*PL*, pp. 27–8n).
26. Neat cites *La Rivoluzione Liberale* directly, and translates some terms differently, *Making of the Poet*, pp. 242–3.
27. Neat, *Making of the Poet*, p. 243.
28. Ibid., p. 246.
29. Ibid., p. 246.
30. Neat suggests that Lehman's decision might have been part of a conspiracy to silence Henderson, following his politically motivated expulsion from Italy in 1950, *Making of the Poet*, pp. 253–4. The papers published in the *New Edinburgh Review* were a selection of those presented at a day conference held in Edinburgh. Contributors included Gwyn A. Williams, Stephen White, Anne Showstack, V. G. Kiernan, C. K. Maisels and Arturo Labriola.
31. Henderson attributes the phrase 'long prison Calvary' to Giuseppe Fiori, who wrote a biography of Gramsci, *Vita di Antonio Gramsci*, which was later translated by Tom Nairn as *Antonio Gramsci: Life of a Revolutionary*.

32. Only the 'class conscious broom' is Henderson's own in this quotation, the rest is taken wholesale from Byrne, though it is not directly accredited to her.
33. Munro, *Democratic Muse*, pp. 26–7.
34. See Hubble's *Mass Observation and Everyday Life* for a history of the research organisation. Joe Gould, referred to in popular folk memory as 'Professor Seagull', was a homeless bohemian and a self-proclaimed social historian. Joseph Mitchell describes him and his great life's work in detail in *Joe Gould's Secret*.
35. 'Notebooks written in a dark cell by a wise man light up the world. Life is still hard because exploited people don't yet fight for their sacred rights. Gramsci left his mother in Sardinia, his master in Turin, his wife in Russia. With immortal fame, more than any star, shines forth the light of unity that he established. Through the merit of Lenin, every nation wants communism to lead them to glory. Against the aggression of imperialism, the victory will lie with the forces of Ho Chi Minh' (*PL*, p. 16).
36. These observations are largely accredited to A. L. Lloyd in the footnotes, and are probably taken from the *New Edinburgh Review* edition of Henderson's translated letters (1974).
37. Neat, *Making of the Poet*, p. 244.
38. Lawner, trans. *Letters from Prison*, pp. 6–7.
39. Neat, *Making of the Poet*, p. 246.
40. Ibid., p. 246.
41. Rosenthal, trans. *Letters from Prison Vol. II*, pp. 175, 67; Lawner, trans. *Letters from Prison*, p. 205.
42. Rosenthal, trans. *Letters from Prison Vol. II*, p. 68; Lawner, trans. *Letters from Prison*, p. 205.
43. Citing Cammett's *Antonio Gramsci and the Origins of Italian Communism* (1967), and Oscar Büdel's work on the Nobel laureate Luigi Pirandello, Henderson describes how Gramsci's identity as a Sardinian and as a southerner seems to be in keeping with the dialectical thought that characterised his political philosophy (*PL*, p. 275n).
44. Gramsci, *Modern Prince*, p. 60.
45. Rosenthal, trans. *Letters from Prison Vol. II*, p. 112.
46. Rosenthal, trans. *Letters from Prison Vol. I*, p. 363.
47. Rosenthal, trans. *Letters from Prison Vol. II*, pp. 386–7.
48. Gramsci, *Cultural Writings*, p. 195.
49. Henderson, 'It Was In You That It A' Began', p. 13.
50. This citation is from the segment of Gramsci's 'observations' that were concerned with the work of an Italian folklorist, Giovanni Crocioni (*Cultural Writings*, pp. 188–9).
51. Neat, *Making of the Poet*, pp. 235–6.
52. Henderson, 'It Was In You That It A' Began', p. 8.
53. Gramsci, *Selections from the Prison Notebooks*, p. 9.
54. Gencarella, in his work on Gramsci's significance in the study of folklore, redresses

this 'spontaneous philosophy' and suggests 'vernacular philosophy' as a more appropriate term, 'Gramsci, Good Sense, and Critical Folklore Studies', p. 228.

55. Gramsci, *Selections from the Prison Notebooks*, p. 323.
56. Gramsci, *Selections from the Prison Notebooks*, pp. 325–6; *Cultural Writings*, pp. 189–90.
57. Gramsci, *Cultural Writings*, p. 421.
58. Ibid., p. 190.
59. Ibid., pp. 188–9.
60. Henderson, 'It Was In You That It A' Began', p. 14.
61. Gramsci, *Cultural Writings*, p. 191.
62. Ibid., p. 189.
63. Ibid., p. 194.
64. Byrne, 'Antonio Gramsci's Contribution to Italian Folklore Studies', p. 72.
65. Ibid., pp. 72–3.
66. Gencarella, 'Gramsci, Good Sense, and Critical Folklore Studies', p. 226.
67. Limón, 'Breaking with Gramsci', p. 254.
68. Gramsci, *Cultural Writings*, p. 191.
69. Ibid., p. 275, 342.
70. See Forgacs, 'National-Popular: Genealogy of a Concept' (1984).
71. Gramsci, *Cultural Writings*, p. 348.
72. Ibid., p. 102.
73. Ibid., p. 226.
74. Henderson, 'It Was In You That It A' Began', pp. 14–15.
75. Gramsci, *Cultural Writings*, p. 182.
76. Efforts to standardise a national Italian language had been underway since the *Risorgimento* in the mid-nineteenth century.
77. Gramsci, *Cultural Writings*, p. 29
78. Ibid., p. 134.
79. Gramsci, *Selections from the Prison Notebooks*, pp. 12–23.
80. Gramsci, *Modern Prince*, p. 86.
81. Ibid., p. 66.
82. Henderson, 'The Edinburgh People's Festival, 1951–54', p. 165.
83. *Gramsci: Here and Now.*
84. Henderson, 'The Edinburgh People's Festival, 1951–54', p. 165.
85. The People's Festival down-sized in its later years due to funding issues, which many, including Henderson, saw as the effect of a McCarthy-esque climate of distrust and suspicion of the political Left. The Labour Party in particular was criticised for its disassociation from the Festival. See 'The Edinburgh People's Festival, 1951–54'.
86. See *1951 Edinburgh People's Festival Ceilidh*, which is part of the 'Alan Lomax Collection', for a full recording of the first ceilidh. Also, Eberhand Bord, ed., *'Tis Sixty Years Since.*
87. Henderson, 'The Edinburgh People's Festival, 1951–54', p. 168.

88. Gramsci, *Cultural Writings*, p. 194.
89. Henderson, 'It Was In You That It A' Began', p. 14.
90. Gramsci, *Cultural Writings*, p. 109.
91. Ibid., p. 191.
92. Gramsci, *Selections from the Prison Notebooks*, p. 325.
93. Byrne, 'Antonio Gramsci's Contribution to Italian Folklore Studies', p. 72.
94. Henderson, 'Freedom Becomes People', p. 1.
95. Gramsci, *Cultural Writings*, p. 109.

CHAPTER

4

POETRY AND THE PEOPLE

I have come to set greater store by my songs 'in the idiom of the people' than by other kinds of poetry that I have tried to write. By working in the folksong revival, therefore, I am paying what is probably congenital tribute to the 'honour'd shade' of the most famous Crochallan Fencible.
(Henderson, extract from a letter to *The Scotsman* during the '*Honour'd Shade* Flyting', 28 November 1959) (*TAN*, p. 88)

In the quotation above Henderson defends the perceived turn in his creative efforts away from the art-poetry of his *Elegies for the Dead in Cyrenaica* (1948) and towards folk-song. By this time Henderson was established as a central figure in the Scottish folk revival: collecting, cataloguing and disseminating Scottish folk culture; tracing the byways of the oral tradition; profiling the songs and tale-types of regions and peoples; and reinvesting in the 'carrying stream' of this tradition through his own songs. Besides the *Elegies*, his poetry was not well known and had only appeared as scattered contributions to literary magazines. Henderson's exclusion from the *Honour'd Shade* (1959), an anthology of new Scottish poetry published to mark the bicentenary of the birth of Burns, was noted by a reviewer for *The Scotsman*, and became part of the ensuing debate in the opinion columns. Henderson, and the other poets who were positioned outside the Rose Street circle presented a challenge to the editorial stance of the collection.[1]

The debate questioned how literary value should be determined and how the 'best' of Scottish poetry should be represented. Henderson was also concerned with his own standing as a poet in lieu of these discussions. The comment above is an attempt to validate his shift towards the folk idiom, based on a broad political affiliation with 'the people' and the form of their creative, communal self-expression. The 'congenital tribute' Henderson describes implies his faithfulness to an aspect of Burns' legacy that is neglected by his peers. It is also an admission that his 'other kinds of poetry' had been less successful. This concession does, however, come with its own subtle qualification: the allowance he makes for the failings of his *other kinds* of poetry makes space for his songs as a legitimate 'kind of poetry' in themselves. Henderson's tentative defence, and his staking a claim on the 'honour'd shade' of the national poet, required that he also renegotiate his place among the poets. In the context of these disputes and, according to MacDiarmid's analyses, to ally oneself with Burns was certainly not an inherent claim to literary quality or political incisiveness. The hyperbole of the contributors and Henderson's self-conscious attempts to voice his disapproval without insisting too strongly on his own literary standing, make it difficult to find a compelling account of his distinctiveness as a poet in these exchanges.

This chapter will explore Henderson's approach to poetry in his own terms, as a search for the 'voice of the people'. Though there was a discernable second wave of Scottish Renaissance writers in the post-war years, many began to reject the poetic models associated with the interwar generation. By the 1960s, MacDiarmid, the old man of Scottish letters, was pitted against formal innovators like Alexander Trocchi, Edwin Morgan and Ian Hamilton Finlay. Henderson adhered to the cultural-political agenda that came out of the Renaissance, but his conception of the kinds of poetry that might be realised in keeping with this agenda was far more flexible and inclusive than MacDiarmid's.

The elder poet's diagnosis for Scotland's cultural and political malaise, and his promotion of a politically-framed, national conception of literary culture, was of paramount importance in Henderson's understanding of the role of the artist in society. In the late 1940s Henderson began to disassociate himself with the so-called 'Lallans Makars' and, instead, promoted the work of the 'Clyde Group': a loose faction of poets who also drew their inspiration from MacDiarmid but who dismissed the linguistic experimentation of the 'makars' as a distraction. Instead, they focused their efforts on a genuinely political poetry, which sought to represent the lives of 'the people' in late-capitalist Scotland.

In surveying the Scottish literary landscape Henderson also adhered to a radical national tradition embodied by the figure of John Maclean (1879–1923) – the Clydeside socialist leader and Bolshevik consul – in the minds of many Scottish poets. Despite investing so much symbolic capital in a named individual, Henderson also believed in the political potency of literary anonymity and pseudonymity. His conception of 'Alias MacAlias' as a phenomenon that represents the debatable land between the folk-song tradition and the literary tradition in Scotland, is a crucial element in his apparent drift towards poetic strategies informed by folk culture. Finally, this chapter will sketch out some of the ways in which Henderson's own poems and songs, and the works of other poets and performers that he admired, are successful in melding the folkloristic and the literary, and in finding a poetry that is in some sense also faithful to a conception of the (singular) voice of the (collective) people.

The immediate post-war years marked a turning point in Henderson's art. Alec Finlay describes the period as a 'journey of transition' from poetry to song, and in explanation he paraphrases a passage from Henderson's sixth war elegy (*TAN*, p. 310): 'the words that I have looked for, and must go on looking for, / are words of whole love, which can slowly gain the power / to reconcile and heal. Other words would be pointless' (*EDC*, p. 38). In their original context, these lines speak of the impossible task set by the poet who seeks to offer a 'true and valued testament' for the war-dead (*EDC*, p. 17); in this new setting they describe Henderson's conception of the artist's need to 'try to reach completeness' and his call for the 'the poet and the community [to] be threaded together again'.[2] While this search for 'words' can be used to describe Henderson's increasing commitment to the field of folk culture as the sphere in which a return to 'the people' might be realised, it is also a search informed by contemporary circumstances.

In 1951 Henderson embarked on his first tour as a folksong collector and in the following year he became one of the first full-time staff with the School of Scottish Studies, a position he was to hold in one form or another for almost forty years. This 'transition' saw Henderson's creative practices and political philosophies converge in his role as strategist and theorist for the modern Scottish folk revival. Henderson's biographer, Timothy Neat, reflects something of this 'turn' in the two volumes of his work. The first, *The Making of the Poet* (2007), describes Henderson's childhood, education and wartime experiences. It ends in the mid 1950s with its subject poised to 'embark on the second half of his life's long journey – as a folklorist'. The second book sees this 'journey' as the culmination of Henderson's formative years, an enactment of his cultural-political philosophy enshrined in the title, *Poetry Becomes People* (2009).[3]

While this apparent shift in Henderson's focus can be explained by his awakening to the political potential of a reinvestment in the folk idiom, it can also be understood as a simple recognition of the fact that his own abilities were better placed to proceed in this direction than in the pursuit of 'art-poetry'. Tessa Ransford notes that the *Elegies* were both Henderson's 'garland and his albatross';[4] they fuelled expectations for his literary career and later encouraged comparisons with his work in folk-song. While Henderson often wrote of his refusal to distinguish between poetry and song, commentators in the 'Flytings' and elsewhere felt that poetry and folk-song ought not to be evaluated according to the same criteria. Henderson promoted the dissolution of borders between these forms of lyrical expression, while he published works that, on the surface, stood on either side of this distinguishing line: compare the 'art-poetry' of the *Elegies* with the soldiers' songs of *Ballads of World War*

II. The broader trajectory of Henderson's work as a poet, the responsibilities that he ascribed to that occupation, and the common ideas that informed even his most diverse compositions, require further explanation.

Henderson's career was marked by unfinished projects and unrealised ambitions. The publication of his Gramsci translation was delayed by twenty years, denying him his place in the history of political theory and philosophy as the first to introduce these works to an Anglophone audience. Furthermore, there are several accounts of unfinished poem sequences and book ideas that were never pursued.[5] Until the publication of his selected writings, letters, and collected poetry and songs in the 1990s and 2000s, Henderson was under-represented in print. There is no single great literary work and no seminal piece of folklore scholarship with which his name is popularly associated. Indeed, it is through his songs that he is usually celebrated. Henderson's reputation has been forged through narratives like that of the literary poet who 'turned' to that other art, 'in the idiom of the people'. His story has been collated out of a vast constellation of writings, anecdotes, memories and songs. When Henderson is discussed as a poet, the most commonly noted aspects of his cultural position are his refusal to distinguish between song and poetry, and his associated preference for the anonymous streams of folk culture over publishing under the singular accreditation of the 'author'. Raymond J. Ross's comments in the introduction to the *Collected Poems and Songs* are typical:

> [it is] the long held belief of a poet steeped in the oral tradition that the first speaking of a poem – or the singing of a song – counts as much towards publication as its first appearance in print [. . .] Dr Henderson often declared, when pressed by others to make more of his own poetry, that he had put all his 'eggs in one basket', referring to his commitment to the Folk Revival . . . Hence, and with characteristic modesty, he was often blate (as opposed to late) when it came to publishing his own poems. (*CPS*, pp. 7–8)

This ethos can be read as a convenient excuse for the paucity of published material. It can also be interpreted as an account of the most distinctive aspect of Henderson's aesthetics: his effort to understand, and gain access to, the forms of authorship and transmission that characterise folk culture.

In an interview in 1964, Henderson was asked: 'Do you see yourself then more nearly as a troubadour, a minstrel, than an intellectual poet sitting down and wanting to have his words regarded on the printed page?' To this he responded:

> I think that is a false antithesis . . . I don't think it is possible for a Scottish poet to make this sort of schizophrenic split . . . I think of myself as a lyric poet, a satiric poet, a ribald poet, at times a bawdy poet, who thinks not only in terms of words but in terms of music. If at the present moment lyricism, ribaldry, bawdry have been

> separated from music, it is a passing phenomenon. We are in the preliminary stages of an enormous revival of oral tradition. Everyone knows that. A lot of people don't *like* it, but everyone can see it, and in so far as my poems are part of the beginning of this, I am pleased at the idea. (*AM*, p. 451)

Henderson presents his position as a challenge to the *temporary divergence* of poetry and music. He ascribes himself a prophetic role as one able to recognise fundamental truths about human self-expression and the enduring unity of lyric and song. Henderson's commitment to a poetry that could engage with 'the people' was constant, yet, consistently renegotiated. Though this aim is often associated with Henderson's 'turn', or else with the 'enormous revival' he anticipated, it was manifested in other ways, stretching back to his creative responses to the War and forward to his part-autobiographical sketches, part-critical essays, on literary history and folk culture. To understand the cultural-political position that might be distilled in the epithet 'poetry becomes people', it is necessary to comprehend the scope of Henderson's relationship with the literary landscape and the national paradigm.

The Renaissance and the 'Lallans Makars'

In 'To Hugh MacDiarmid: On Reading *Lucky Poet*', Henderson's poetic endorsement comes with an important qualification: '*If there were just two choices . . . / mine would be yours, MacDiarmid!* (*CPS*, p. 119). This qualified solidarity with MacDiarmid is analogous to Henderson's relationship with broader literary landscapes. Regularly listed as one of the acolytes of the Scottish Literary Renaissance, Henderson expressed his impatience with the developments of poetry in Scots as early as 1948.[6] Later, after the inception of the folk revival, he came to regret the influence of the 'renaissance establishment', and of the 'Rose Street Group' in particular, actively resisting their restrictive prescriptions of literary value. Defending modes of traditional literature against the perceived elitism of MacDiarmid and MacCaig, Henderson found common cause with those working in areas of Scottish literary practice that had been attacked on similar terms.

In the 'Flytings' Henderson set out a conception of literary value distinguished by its breadth and inclusivity. Excluding no literary form or genre outright, he pronounced as valid any work that succeeded on its own terms. Henderson later contextualised the debates with a sketch of the divisions that arose between MacDiarmid and 'the folkies', and gestured toward more profound hostilities between the 'Scottish Renaissance Establishment' and the various literary figures who belonged outside of this group. He cites Allan Riddell, Robert Garioch, Edwin Morgan, Ian Hamilton Finlay and Alexander Trocchi as allies, being writers who had also been targeted by MacDiarmid and his 'ill-tempered epistolary potshots' (*AM*, p. 407).[7] With a contemptuous disregard for the differences between their work, MacDiarmid grouped Henderson with these writers, due to his supposed 'wish to scrap all learning and all literature as hitherto defined': 'He is presumably at home among beatniks and beatchiks' (*TAN*, p. 97).

The divide that Henderson perceived between the 'literary gents and their onhangers' and the 'folkies' developed in a geographical capacity in Edinburgh, with the former frequenting the Abbotsford Bar and Milne's Bar in the city's New Town, and the latter gravitating towards Sandy Bell's, the unofficial headquarters of the folk revival (*AM*, p. 396).[8] MacDiarmid became increasingly alienated from younger writers; a problem that Henderson put down to a broader generational dynamic that had repeated itself throughout Scotland's history:

> Scotland hates and fears its creative writers. Why is there here this conspiracy of the old against the young – which you get everywhere – but which with us is so blatantly tyrannical? It goes back to the fantastic theocratic tyranny of the seventeenth century and the attempts to divide the nation into a small, elect elite and the damned mass . . . This brings us back to MacDiarmid, for his vision of literature grows out of this tyrannical division – there is an artistic elite and there is folk culture. But Christ died for all men and Scots literature arises out of the whole Scots people. (Henderson, unpublished notes)[9]

On this basis, the older generation's resistance to the innovations of the young is inevitable; there will always be an insurrection against the tyranny of past literary frameworks. Indeed, Finlay has suggested an Oedipal dimension to Henderson and MacDiarmid's relationship, 'a mixture of devotion and rebellion . . . against the stern father-figure he chose' (*TAN*, p. 301), whilst Neat points to an unpublished note from the 'Flytings' period: 'MacDiarmid fears his sons will kill him'.[10] These comments emphasise Henderson's struggle with MacDiarmid as a figure who provided him with the foundations for his own cultural-political programme but who also represented the most concerted and vocal opposition to the agenda he pursued. Neat goes so far as to conceive of Henderson as MacDiarmid's successor – the poet who would 'engender the second Enlightenment and the New Scotland he [MacDiarmid] dreamed of'.[11] Henderson wrestled not only with MacDiarmid's words, but also with the 'Renaissance Establishment' that had grown around him. This faction had demonstrated in the '*Honour'd Shade* Flyting' that they held their own prescriptions of literary value to be absolute. For Henderson, a broader unity of purpose – the exploration of Scottish literary voices of all kinds 'rising out of the whole people' – was betrayed by short-sightedness.

Despite these altercations, Henderson championed the poets of the Renaissance: he endorsed their uses of Scots, their politics, the scale of their ambition, and their value as assertive critical voices in Scottish letters. He hoped that the folk revival might come to be regarded as an extension of this cultural Renaissance (*AM*, p. 50). Both movements represented political ideologies that Henderson adhered to: he recognised the literary Renaissance as the 'counterpoint in letters' of Scottish Nationalism (*AM*, p. 315) and envisaged the folk revival as a step towards a genuine 'people's culture' – a confident expression of the lives of the masses and a path to a culturally inflected class-consciousness. In one interview, he proclaimed his closeness to Goodsir Smith, and to the MacDiarmid of the early Scots lyrics and *A Drunk Man Looks at the Thistle*, as opposed to the prevalent English poets of the 1960s, including Ted Hughes, Thom Gunn, Edward Lucie-Smith and Peter Porter (*AM*, p. 452).

In the late 1940s Henderson spoke out in defence of the advancement of so-called 'Plastic Scots'. He was in broad agreement with many of the prevailing values in discussions of Scottish literary life: linguistic experimentation; the simultaneous insistence on a national literary canon and the imperative of an internationalist perspective; a generally leftist and nationalistic political standing; and a sensitivity to the problem of connecting art with the people. This climate of consensus was, from Henderson's perspective, not only the result of the relatively small group of writers who regularly contributed to the same publications on the same subjects, it was also a consequence of the cultural Renaissance which had laid waste to 'Kailyard' nostalgia and sentimentality and encouraged a more critical and politicised engagement with modernity in Scotland.

Maurice Lindsay's 1948 pamphlet, *The Scottish Renaissance*, provides a contemporary account of the movement that aligns closely with Henderson's.[12] Lindsay celebrated the fact that the Renaissance poets were able to 'close the gap' between poetry and the public; he traced this capacity back through the 'series of inter-linked peaks' of the Scottish literary tradition, which he described as fundamentally 'popular (*i.e.* of the people)' as opposed to the 'rarefied, aesthetic varieties' of the English literary tradition. He wrote of 'the broad mass of the folk from which all vital art must draw its sap' and insisted on the ability of great art to always 'proclaim its nationality together with its universality in a hundred different ways'. In a tone similar to that used by Henderson to describe the genuine 'people's culture' he hoped to foster through the folk revival, Lindsay concluded: 'when the Scottish people do become completely conscious of this new poetry which has grown up out of them, the Scottish Renaissance will have achieved fruition, and new life may come to Scotland, the nation'.[13] Henderson shared Lindsay's belief that future incarnations of the Scottish Renaissance could bring these principles to bear.

The parameters of the Literary Renaissance cannot be easily defined. To list its adherents, or to provide a conclusive set of formal or theoretical principles that constitute it, would be to misrepresent the complexity and disunity of the movement. Henderson's association with the Renaissance is in this sense arbitrary; it cannot as a fact in itself reveal anything about his conception of poetry, his politics, or his attitude to Scots language. If the 'Renaissance' is considered as a 'revival', as it was by George Bruce in his 1968 anthology, it might simply indicate a period of popularisation, but the constant presence of the national descriptor transforms these potentially empirical terms into a tangle of political and historical claims, and an implied cultural exceptionalism. Henderson proposed that the folk revival become an extension of the cultural Renaissance within an assumed national framework. He acknowledged the importance of MacDiarmid's clarification of 'the relation of the cultural revival to the political struggle' (*AM*, p. 376) articulating his commitment to those twin 'gospels': 'Nationalism and Communism'.[14] In an essay like 'Scotland's Alamein', the political will for a Scottish republic is not disguised or transmuted into other cultural forms; but in writings focused on the literary aspect, these political principles are expressed in the effort to imagine a national tradition, and in the frequently contested forms that the extension of this tradition ought to take.

This renewed emphasis on the national framework brought with it an enthusiasm for literary connections with Europe. In his potted history of the 'cultural revival' of the interwar period, Henderson echoes MacDiarmid's aim to bring 'Scottish Literature into closer touch with current European tendencies in technique and ideation',[15] pointing out the advantages of the 're-orientation of our intellectual contacts in the direction of the continent'. He cited MacDiarmid's early translations of Blok and Rilke ('years before the "New Signatures" group in Oxford made such a song and dance about "discovering" them'), and Douglas Young's Scots translations of the verse of 'a dozen assorted languages', as examples of this new international perspective (*AM*, p. 375). His own contribution to the migration of ideas between the continent and Scotland can be identified with his work on Gramsci's *Prison Letters*, while in the literary field he produced translations and adaptations of the work of contemporary Italian poets, which appeared in small magazines and journals throughout the late 1940s.[16] Through his renderings of Eugenio Montale, Dino Campana, Salvatore Quasimodo, Alfonzo Gatto, Corrado Govoni and Vincenzo Cardarelli, Henderson was among the first to import many of the most celebrated voices in twentieth-century Italian poetry for the readers of Scotland's literary magazines.[17] The literary transference that Henderson documents was to be continued in Robert Garioch's translations of Giuseppe Belli, in Morgan's work on Mayakovsky and in countless other partnerships.[18] Translation, as a manifestation of the movement of 'technique and ideation' between nations, signifies the porous quality of the national framework as imagined by MacDiarmid and Henderson.

The language question, which had dominated Scottish literary discourse throughout the early twentieth century, still held sway with Henderson in the immediate post-war years. In his 1919 review essay 'Was There a Scottish Literature?' Eliot wrote of a literature overtaken and absorbed by the English tradition and pointed to lack of 'continuity in language' as evidence of this fact. In *Scott and Scotland* (1936), Edwin Muir famously described the 'curse' of Scottish literature as 'the lack of a whole language, which finally means the lack of a whole mind', and concluded that Scotland could only create a national literature by writing in English.[19] Though he countered these assertions in his prose, and showed in his early verse what could be achieved in a Scots register, MacDiarmid had largely abandoned 'synthetic Scots' by the mid-1930s. Nevertheless, he continued to support the creative choices of those still writing in various vernaculars. It was well understood that the veracity of Scots as a literary language in the modern world was an issue tied closely to the idea of a 'Scottish literature' and, therefore, to a continuing claim to cultural and political autonomy. However, by the time Henderson was involved directly in the controversies, it was as a contributor to the 'Plastic Scots' debates of the late 1940s, which were concerned principally with poetry and with the formal qualities of the work of the so-called 'Lallans Makars'. Nevertheless, the potency of the issue remained, especially since claims for the potential of this 'synthetic Scots' towards successful art-poetry – termed 'plastic Scots' by some of its detractors, after James Fergusson in a BBC broadcast in 1946 – could be substantiated with the work of MacDiarmid and others, even while its artificiality, its archaism and its relevance in modern Scotland were contested. In a postcard sent to MacDiarmid in 1947, Goodsir Smith set out a response in verse to this dispute: 'Makars are born and Critics made- / The latter, of course, synthetical.'[20]

Henderson expressed his belief in the artistic potential of a revived Scots literature by hailing the highest achievements of MacDiarmid: 'rescuing the Scots tongue from the slough of havering provincialism into which it had fallen, he demonstrated incontrovertibly . . . that it was still capable of carrying art poetry' (*AM*, p. 375). The debate had, however, drifted from the question of whether Scottish writers could or should write in Scots to whether the Scots they did employ was permissible in terms of intelligibility and authenticity. In a contemporary pamphlet exploring the 'Plastic Scots' controversies within the context of a long national literary tradition, Douglas Young describes the varying degrees of support for the use of Scots, from those who would restrict it to 'humour, pathos, and our native philosophy', to those who 'championed it as a medium for the "highest matters of poetry'.[21] In one short stream of contributions to the *Glasgow Herald* throughout November 1946, the debate around 'Plastic Scots' was pulled in all directions. It became a question of the fundamentally synthetic quality of all modern languages (MacDiarmid, 11 November); in another contribution, the popularity of the poetry was enough to validate it (Young, 16 November); one commentator reminded readers that 'a cult is not culture' (Andrew Shanks, 18 November); while another called for 'a legitimate language, not a bastard one' (James Fergusson, 25 November). Some saw pronunciation and spoken performances as the principal requirements for intelligibility and therefore the validity of the form (R. Crombie

Saunders, 19 November; Maurice Lindsay, 21 November; R. Maxwell, 22 November), while others lamented the fact that writers were 'feverishly engaged in evolving a hotch-potch synthetic gibberish to convince the world that we do not have an inferiority complex' (Murdo Ewan MacDonald, 26 November).

Among these questions of legitimacy, of underlying political motives and the freedom of the artist to manipulate language, Henderson did not initially lay claim to any original line of argument. He was briefly a member of Douglas Young's 'Makars' Club', and as such he was one of the signatories of a letter published in *The Scotsman* in April 1948 in response to comments made by the playwright James Bridie.[22] In a public lecture in St. Andrews, Bridie had objected to the work of 'the modern Makars' and reportedly stated that 'a really ambitious writer is better employed in enriching English, than by discarding it'. The response of the 'Makars' Club' confirmed that 'the Scots literary tradition in Lallans . . . ought to be extended'. They concluded: 'the pure Scots spirit must continue to be distilled if Scotland is to contribute any potent element to a polyglot international medium' (*TAN*, pp. 24–5). According to this analysis, accession to the international sphere requires that poets cultivate a strong, distinctive national style, rather than an affected, self-conscious cosmopolitanism. Scottish writers were to find their place in the modern literary world by continuing to distil this 'pure Scots spirit'; that is, they were to defer to a certain conception of the Scottish literary tradition. However, less than a year after the 'Makar's Club' letter was published, Henderson rejected the argument from 'tradition' in favour of a more candid approach:

> no one who walks through Scotland with his ears washed out can doubt that the speech of the people is still a helluva lot nearer to the language of Burns than to the stringy metropolitan argot of the BBC announcer. Which means that there is still a living foundation for poetry in 'the raucle tongue' . . . Surely no man of sense will waste his time speculating which exactly of the blubber-lipped buccaneers who invaded our shores were the first to call a cuddie a cuddie. (*AM*, p. 378)

Henderson went on to single out his fellow 'Makars' Club' members: 'I propose to cut out all the literary-historical cross-talk so beloved of Mr Douglas Young, which in the main I regard as so much nonsense-value' (Ibid.). He described the 'so-called "Lallans Makars"', 'Maurice Lindsay and his maudlin mates', as 'bourgeois nationalists, hopelessly hobbled from the start by their political gormlessness' (*AM*, p. 379). While he conceded that the makars' original work had helped overcome the 'Kailyard', Henderson believed that their usefulness had been exhausted long before 1949. Pre-empting his argument for the 'living' folk-song tradition, Henderson set out to remind readers that tradition alone was no basis for a concerted cultural revival: the contemporary lives of the people must already be at home with that which is to be revived, be it

Scots language or folk culture. Henderson had shown his support in response to common detractors but his views on the language issue saw him diverge dramatically from his sometime allies.

The Editorial Diarist for the *Glasgow Herald* inspired the debate on 'synthetic Scots' in November 1946, with his satirical column, 'Short Course in Plastic Scots' which included pointers such as, 'Your subjects need be few – Hugh MacDiarmid, Glasgow, the Highlands, the English, love, drink and Hugh MacDiarmid'; 'It is not necessary for what you write to have no meaning, but it is vital to conceal your meaning, if any, as much as possible'; and a whole host of 'other effective ways of disguising the fact that you think in English'.[23] The piece roused equally heavy-handed responses, though in this instance Henderson was unusually reserved, using the example of the eighteenth-century Italian poet, Vittorio Alfieri (1749–1803) and his relationship with Piedmontese dialect, Tuscan and French, to account for the universality of the problems inherent in choosing a language in which to write (*TAN*, p. 10). Henderson concluded by expressing his confidence in the existing support for literature in Scots, but also in the need for further innovation of these forms:

> In spite of the sneers of linguistic Quislings, who find it convenient to side with the big battalions of London press lords and Glasgow Englishmen, Scottish poets will find more and more support now in erecting a dam against the 'mór-shruth na Beurla'. Most of them realise this, and realise too that it is not enough merely to use the 'language of the outlaw' like their compeers of former ages, they must also recreate and reshape it. (*TAN*, pp. 10–11)

Though this passage seems reserved when compared to Henderson's polemics elsewhere (compare, for example, with 'Scotland's Alamein'), we can still trace an uncompromising ideological perspective in the terms he employs. 'Quisling', for example, had only recently been coined. Defined as 'a person cooperating with an occupying enemy force; a collaborator; a traitor', it was a reference to the Norwegian diplomat, Major Vidkun Quisling, who had collaborated with the Nazis during the occupation (*OED*). Reference to the 'big battalions of London press lords' further establishes the militaristic, embattled territory of the language question, and strikes the same point as the opening remarks of another of Henderson's articles from this period, in which he decries the fact that 'the indigenous traditions of the people, both Gaelic and Lallans, seemed to have been left tattered and defenceless before the *big battalions* of alien aggression ['the English Imperialist Ascendancy']' (emphasis added) (*AM*, p. 374). The Gaelic phrase, *mór-shruth na Beurla*, meaning 'big flood of English', also appeared as the first line of a short poem written by Brendan Behan in the same period.[24] In Behan's use it is part of a call to arms to resist the cultural influence of the British in Ireland by politicising the Irish language. Here, the same principles are invoked with Gaelic, for Scotland –

Henderson signed as *Seumas mac Eanruig* (*TAN*, p. 11). Furthermore, the phrase 'language of the outlaw', which also features in Henderson's letter, refers to the title of a pamphlet by Sir Roger Casement setting out the nature of those incursions on the Irish language, and the need for, and inevitability of, its resurgence: 'The language of a people is a fortress which the enemy first assails; and once that fortress is captured and its stones levelled with the ground, every other stronghold of nationality must inevitably fall'.[25] Unacknowledged references and evocative word-choice contribute to Henderson's implicit suggestion that the conditions of Scotland's struggle for cultural and political autonomy were comparable in nature to those of the Irish campaign. In MacDiarmid's writings the parallel of the politics of language in Scotland and Ireland goes back at least as far as 1929.[26] In 'English Ascendancy in British Literature' (1931) MacDiarmid developed these ideas and set out a conception of Scottish literature delineated by the incursions that English language and literature had made upon it.[27]

In a later contribution to the controversies arising from Bridie's comments, Henderson set out a more precise and comprehensive argument for the work of the 'Lallans Makars'. Firstly, he points out that the makars are condemned not because they write in Lallans, but because 'they form an *avant garde*' (*TAN*, p. 25). He deigned to undermine the authority of the critics by presenting them as a faction resistant to the direction of historical progress: writers in the forefront will be vindicated by subsequent developments. This account also abstracts the Lallans issue from its own terms: the 'language question' is no longer relevant; it is simply the medium through which a literary vanguard has seen fit to respond to the conditions of modernity. It might easily have been a development in any other formal aspect. Secondly, Henderson redresses the mistaken impression that the language the makars use is archaic, by claiming that it is 'no longer the "done thing" to speak it' (Ibid.). This rhetorical manoeuvring seems intended to undermine the critics by revealing the subtleties and nuances that they, in their ignorance, have overlooked. In this manner, the problem of the makars' language is elided by the predicament of the '*avant garde*', and its seeming archaism is derisively accredited to the fact that it has merely fallen out of fashion.

The remainder of the letter relies on more substantive arguments. Henderson cites the undeniable success of MacDiarmid's poem, 'The Eemis Stane', and its use of 'the modern idiom'. He concludes:

> After countless inroads the old Scots tongue now stands like a great ruined broch, with the rubble of centuries lying round it. Stones from that rubble have for too long gone to nothing higher than the building of dykes around lowly kailyards . . . an attempt has at last been made to put stone on stone, to rebuild the tower . . . Of course, they may fail . . . But history will at any rate give them credit for bringing the Scottish cultural predicament ruthlessly into the light of day. (*TAN*, p. 26)

It is not clear exactly how Henderson envisages the *illumination* of the Lallans poets' work, but it is apparent that whether or not they succeeded in 'rebuilding' the tower of the 'old Scots tongue' is of less significance than the fact that they force us to confront the disjuncture between accepted literary and linguistic traditions, and the reality of life in modern Scotland.

Promoting the 'Clyde Group'

Henderson recognised that the language question was only one aspect of the relationship between modern Scotland and its poetry. In the 'Clyde Group' he found a new school of poets who sought to redress the gap between the artist and society more consciously and directly. The group emerged in the late 1940s and, according to Henderson, set out like MacDiarmid to identify their work with 'the *present* difficulties and tasks of the people' and to thereby help Scottish poetry 'recover its true identity' (*AM*, p. 376).[28] Henderson had been enthusiastic about the trajectory of the Renaissance, which promised to expose Scotland's identity crises, and thereby clear the path for new ways of imagining the nation. However, he began to feel betrayed by those who prioritised 'literary-historical cross-talk', who obsessed about the validity of Lallans poetry but neglected to relate it to the lives of Scots. Poets and commentators like these risked slipping into the very parochialism that they had, after MacDiarmid's example, originally rallied against.

Two of Henderson's earliest articles on the condition of contemporary Scottish literature, 'Flower and Iron of the Truth' (*Our Time* 1948) and 'Lallans and all that' (*Conflict* 1949), document his admiration for the 'Clyde Group' in the context of this creeping disillusionment. Henderson acknowledged two distinct groups of poets which each inherited different aspects of MacDiarmid's aesthetics. The 'Lallans Makars' responded to the 'revelation of the potentialities of the "aul leid"' and were principally concerned with advocating the capacity of Scots language for great poetry. He lists these 'makars' as Albert Mackie, Goodsir Smith, Maurice Lindsay and Douglas Young. The 'Clyde Group' picked up MacDiarmid's commitment to the cause of the Scottish proletariat and 'resolved to carry a stage further [his] application of Marxism to the Scottish predicament . . . [and] to produce work which will interpret more immediately the reality of the Scottish people' (*AM*, p. 376). In this 'group', Henderson lists John Kincaid, Thurso Berwick (pseudonym of Morris Blythman), George Todd and, as affiliates: the miner and Fife poet, T. S. Law, and the poet and University of Glasgow lecturer, Alexander Scott (*AM*, pp. 379–80). He summarised their project by noting that they had 'comprehended the need for a literature of *presentification*'. The italicisation suggests its connection with the previous passage detailing MacDiarmid's concern with 'the *present* difficulties and tasks of the people' (*AM*, p. 376). The term is useful in describing the immediacy of the poetry (literally 'making something present'), both in terms of its relation to the lives of contemporary urban Scots but also to the spoken quality of the language, its constant evocation of an audible poetic voice and the directness with which its subjects are often explored.

Their efforts to interpret the realities of the people, 'of the commons of Alba, the industrial proletariat, the dockers, the miners and shipyard workers, the Highland remnant', were to drag Scots poetry from its depoliticised landscapes, its pastoral associations and the general 'archaism [of its] subject-matter' (Ibid.). In George Todd's poem, 'Embro Makars', the 'Clyde Group' are distinguished both geographically and, in terms of poetic form, from the 'Makars, / Thae verbalan cakers' (according to the appended glossary, literally, 'those excreters of words'):

Wi muckle complaisance
Thir's talk o Renaissance;
At the lear o' the scrievers ye'd gowk;
Bit they're ettlan ti soom
In a river gey toom
Gin they leave oot the wants o the fowk.[29]

Just as Henderson was to remind MacDiarmid in the 'Flytings' that he had failed to do what he ought to have done if his poems were not 'spoken in the factories and fields, / In the streets o' the toon',[30] the 'Clyde Group' identified the learning ('lear') of the modern Renaissance poets with their intention to swim ('soom') in an empty river, by neglecting the 'wants' – the poverty as well as the desires – of the people. The poem goes on to remark that 'It's Sydney [Goodsir Smith] has lichtit oor view', and his radicalism among the 'Embro Makars' is described: 'Sae luk roon, luk roon / In Embro Toon, [. . .] Ye'se aa been tauld / There's a tod [fox] i the fauld / An he's merkit ye aa in a raw'.

According to Henderson, the 'Clyde Group' blamed the 'Lallans Makars' for 'the tendency of the Scottish public to equate Lallans poetry with a predilection for the grotesque: a taking wing on Jamieson's battered broomstick to riotous, non-stop Walpugisnacht'.[31] He heralds the young poets' rejection of 'Mahoun' (the devil, 'a darling of Scottish literature') in favour of 'Maclean' (John Maclean). The danger, as Henderson saw it, was that Scots poetry would turn into a 'mere academic exercise, a field for Alexandrian virtuosity – a "pluralism of superstructures" above a life with which it has lost all contact' (*AM*, pp. 376–7). 'Mahoun', as a concentrated image of all that was wrong with the established forms of Lallans verse, is problematic. 'Mahoun-mongering', as Henderson called it, risked relegating poetry to the scholarly and the derivative, fostering a disconnection from the lives of any potential popular audience. However, 'Mahoun' also evokes the stock-in-trade imagery of Scottish folklore, and the devil's place in this formulation, as one embodying the regressive forces in Scottish poetry, perhaps demonstrates that Henderson had not yet reconciled the processes of folk-song with a committed political poetry seeking to reconnect with society.[32] The devil, this mystifying and insufficiently political character, in fact featured in the title poem, and prolegomenon, of Goodsir Smith's contemporary collection *The Deevil's Waltz* (1946). Henderson and the 'Clyde Group' celebrated Goodsir Smith for his 'rebellious sympathy with the forces for political progress' (*AM*, p. 380) and yet his 'Mahoun' stood next to John Maclean as permissible subject matter. At this point, the poetry that might 'become people' was intended to make contact with the realities of life in Govan or Hamilton and even Comrie or Lochboisdale (*AM*, p. 376). In short, it was to avoid the tropes of folklore as diversionary and insufficiently radical, and commit to representations of the lived consequences of the political structure.

In Thurso Berwick Henderson found a poet who, like Mayakovsky, could take his poetry to audiences of all sizes. In John Kincaid, he saw signs of a 'diction which will command immediate response from working-class gatherings' (*AM*, p. 379). Kincaid's *Setterday Nicht Symphony* is singled out in both of these early articles as proof of 'the beauty that can be struck from the forbidding grey whinstone of Glasgow tenement life' (*AM*, p. 377). Looking out on the whole of Glasgow, the opening stanzas imagine inhabitants of all ages expressing in various ways the fact of their lives, and their parts in the great 'symphonie' of the city's 'nicht, lang prayed fur bi aa'. Glasgow is incited to dance, to relieve itself from the exploitation and wage-slavery of the working week: 'Ay, whirl awa citie, ye've swat lang eneuch, / yuir week's wark huis made a braw tocher for some'.[33] After exploring the nerves, frustrations and thrills of the 'Luvers', and, in the pub, addressing the 'nicht wan wise men peddle staurs' and the heads of the drinkers are 'aa birlan wi thi infinite', the poem concludes with another passage on the 'Citie': 'yuir Setterday's lauchan wull ding doun thi deils / thit lowp frae thi stanes as men bigg thur roads'.[34] The eponymous 'Symphonie' expresses the joy of the weekly release and its importance for the wellbeing of the people, but at the same time it implies the limitations of this celebration, and calls upon the reader to ask why so much of value to human life – from genuine human companionship to thoughts of the metaphysical and spiritual – must be concentrated in this weekly carnival. The dizzy cinematic sweep through the city's streets provides Henderson with a standard-bearer for the movement's potential to represent the realities of life in modern industrialised Scotland by portraying a wealth of human potential curtailed by socio-temporal structures.

In his introduction to *Fowrsom Reel* (1949), a collection of poetry published for the 'Clyde Group', MacDiarmid echoes Henderson's forecast for these poets, as writers who might 'make the political sympathies of our literature identical with our interests'.[35] He expresses his regret that the recent

Lallans controversies diverted attention from the 'content' of the new poetry, which, 'in keeping with our traditions, has been largely concerned with the problems of our people, with current political issues, with anti-imperialism and anti-militarism'. MacDiarmid praised the poets for their 'pioneering' work in this field in which 'the most important developments in Scottish poetry in the immediate future . . . *must* take place', namely, 'debourgeoisification', 'deAnglification' and 'scientisation'.[36] These overwrought watchwords for the new Scottish poetry represent MacDiarmid's proposals for the contemporary fulfilment of that 'traditional' concern with the lives of the people and the political structures that create them and are imposed on them. In their own way, the 'Clyde Group' developed this aspect of MacDiarmid's aesthetic project and, in his promotion of their poetry, Henderson offered his support to this vision of a committed socialist poetry.

During the War, Henderson transcribed songs and poems, and wrote many of his own that bore out a genuine connection with the lives of the servicemen. Whether it was in their treatment of the minutiae of life on the North African Front, the pathos of his meditations on death and loss, or else in the bawdy and satirical songs that trivialised the discomforts of war and showed contempt for 'official' accounts of the conflict, this material showed the qualities that Henderson and MacDiarmid celebrated in the work of the 'Clyde Group', but within the circumscription of the War. This kind of direct, contextualised artistic response was repeated in 1948, during the same period in which Henderson first publicised the work of Berwick, Todd, Law and Kincaid. In 'Ballad for the Men of Knoydart', he produced a folksong that told the story of the ultimately unsuccessful land seizures of the 'Seven Men of Knoydart' (who had all served in the War) on the estate of Nazi-supporter and absentee landlord, Lord Brocket (1904–67). According to Neat, Henderson wrote the song in December 1948, the day after having met the 'Clyde Group' in Glasgow.[37] It was published the following January in MacDiarmid's *National Weekly*, which had followed the story closely since the initial land raids in November, and showed unstinting support for the cause of the crofters.[38] The song itself, described by Neat as a 'modern "rabble-rouser"', portrays an imagined dialogue with the crofters asserting the Highlander's 'right to Scottish land', and Lord Brocket launching furious verbal attacks: 'You're a crowd of Tartan Bolshies!' (*CPS*, p. 128). The final stanza, recognising the cultural currency of the nineteenth-century Clearances and the Land Wars of the 1880s, transposed to this modern context, imagines a future where this isolated site of resistance might stand as a symbol for a far greater movement of reclamation and redistribution: 'Roll on the day when The Knoydart Way / Is Scotland's battle song' (*CPS*, p. 129).

By reaching out to the conflicts of the dispossessed in the Knoydart peninsula (often described as Britain's 'last wilderness'), the song takes very literally the idea of an art that speaks to the realities of life in all the corners of the country, from Govan to Lochboisdale (*AM*, p. 377). The clear moral outrage, the ridiculousness of Brocket's protestations, and the prophetic ending, are not perhaps what Henderson and MacDiarmid had in mind in the model they attributed to the 'Clyde Group'. However, the immediacy of the song, published alongside journalistic accounts of the events as they unfolded, establishes it as a poetic inflection on agitprop and the 'living newspaper', and a precursor of the kind of protest song that was to become popular throughout the 1950s and 1960s. Henderson also contributed to this form in response to the docking of American nuclear submarines at Holy Loch, in *Ding Dong Dollar*; and in his call for the release of Nelson Mandela, in 'Rivonia' (*CPS*, p. 150).

Henderson celebrates those writers who are able to instil MacDiarmid's 'gospels' of Nationalism and Communism into their work, and criticises those who neglect these principles. At the root of the national literary framework that Henderson advocates, there is a contingent appeal to an international cultural sphere in which Scottish voices might find legitimacy in the modern world and expel any traces of parochialism. For Henderson these international connections were demonstrated in translation work and in the universality of the debates arising around the language question. However, this 're-orientation' of the national framework from the Scottish perspective also relied on a more openly political construction that was embodied by the figure of the Clydeside socialist, John Maclean.

John Maclean and the Radical National Tradition

> Not they who died
> in the hauteur of Inverkeithing,
> in spite of valour and pride,
> the high head of our story,
> but he who was in Glasgow
> the battlepost of the poor,
> great John Maclean,
> the top and hem of our story.
> (Sorley MacLean, 'Clan Maclean')[39]

In his 1948 survey of contemporary Scottish writing, 'Flower and Iron of the Truth', Henderson set the 'cultural revival' in its historical context. Writing of the campaigns against increased rent rates in the early years of the First World War and the resistance to conscription in 1916, he identified 'the growth to political maturity of the Scottish working class' as a factor that could not be divorced from the literary developments that followed. The political movement gave rise to a 'leader of genius' in John Maclean:

> It would be hard to overestimate Maclean's service to Scotland; not only did he use his profound knowledge of Marxism to train a whole generation of activists, not only did he transform the workers' struggle in the industrial belt of Scotland and make the Clyde an embattled outpost of the European proletariat – he also, by a correct interpretation of the national problem, showed the workers and crofters of our country that the Scottish past was their rightful heritage. (*AM*, p. 374)

In this brief article setting out the literary terrain of contemporary Scotland for the readership of an internationally-minded, London-based socialist magazine, *Our Time*, the Glasgow schoolmaster stands as a political leader praised by both William Gallacher (co-founder of the CPGB and Communist MP) and Lenin; as an educator who identified a radical national tradition that might be adopted and extended by the contemporary working class; and as a man whose 'legend' was to be one of the principal formative influences on MacDiarmid and his 'Renaissance' (*AM*, p. 375). Henderson's portrayal of Maclean was in turn informed by MacDiarmid's sustained promotion of what he called the 'Maclean line', or the 'Red Scotland Thesis', throughout the 1930s and 1940s. Maclean's interpretations of Scottish history, of Lenin's proposals on the self-determination of nations, and of the dictates of the Third International, prompted his campaign for a 'Scottish Workers' Republic'.[40] Proclaiming the need for a 'Scottish Communist Party' as opposed to the subsumed membership of a 'British' movement, Maclean stood for Home Rule as a committed Marxist and Internationalist. Though the Scottish Party did not appear in the form Maclean had hoped for, the idea of a 'Scottish Workers' Republic' remained a mobilising cause among those on the Left in the face of a dismissive and sometimes hostile British Communist movement.[41]

In 1936, Routledge, who had formerly agreed to publish MacDiarmid's book *Red Scotland*, finally decided to suppress it. Originally titled 'What Lenin has Meant to Scotland', the work drew heavily on Maclean's declarations for a Scottish Workers' Republic.[42] In the first edition of his magazine, *The Voice of Scotland*, in June/August 1938, MacDiarmid included a piece setting out his political project, 'The Red Scotland Thesis: Forward to the John Maclean Line'.[43] Henderson showed his support for this 'line' in a 1948 letter to MacDiarmid, sent while he was studying to become a modern languages teacher at Moray House College of Education in Edinburgh. He assured the poet that 'at least one generation of students will get the John Maclean line with their religious instruction. *And* like it, by Christ!' (*TAN*, p. 22).

Among his early manuscript translations of Gramsci's prison letters, there is an extended passage by Henderson on the failings of the Communist Party in Scotland in relation to the national question. He lamented that the 'CP in Scotland' 'don't sing "Scots Wha Hae" as the French Communist Party sings to Marseillaise; it has never displayed the Lion Rampant or the Saltire as the Italian Party displays [images of] . . . Garibaldi or the Republican tricolour'. Opposed to the so-called 'Maclean Line', Scottish Party members had, in Henderson's estimation, failed to interpret 'the national cause with the working-class movement, as had happened (for example) in Vietnam, [and] the German Democratic Republic'.[44] In Maclean's construction, commitment to Home Rule was both the inevitable result of a considered Marxist analysis and the continuation of a tradition of working-class radicalism in Scotland. In a speech titled 'All Hail, the Scottish Workers' Republic!' (1920) Maclean set out his position on Scottish independence with reference to contemporary examples of the British power imbalance, such as 'the English government's intention to rely mainly on Scottish troops to murder the Irish race'. He also evoked a long history of manipulation and exploitation orchestrated through the collusion of London elites and those Henderson and MacDiarmid would later conceive as 'Anglo-Scottish Quislings'. These included the Edinburgh lawyers who brokered the Union, Scottish Hanoverian forces, Highland chiefs corrupted with English education, and the Dukes of Sutherland and Argyll, who 'proceeded with the English landlord policy of land clearances'.[45] Maclean envisaged a Scotland whereby 'the communism of the clans must be re-established on a modern basis . . . the country must have but one clan, as it were'. Conceiving of a past 'Celtic or communistic system' that had escaped the horrors of feudalism, Maclean felt that in Scotland, he could quite accurately make the pronouncement, 'back to communism and forward to communism'.[46]

Adopting a similar interpretation of Scotland's imagined past, Henderson later spoke of 'Scots Ballads' as inspiring a 'mythological view of . . . some sort of classless society of the past', 'a romantic idea; but nevertheless . . . perfectly tenable ground on which to proceed'.[47] In this sense, the folk revival harnessed essentially romantic notions of the national past, which could be turned toward a more expedient political agenda in the contemporary cultural sphere. Henderson seems to recognise the usefulness of 'romantic' ideas of the national past, and in this sense his outlook is in line with Maclean's idiosyncratic views on Scotland's social history, and on the utopian reinvention of the clan system in particular. However, this aspect of Maclean's thought is at odds with the remit of MacDiarmid's Renaissance. Writing of the 'Clyde Group', Henderson and MacDiarmid had both envisaged a new poetic form based emphatically on the *reality* of the lives of the people, which meant rejecting 'romantic' notions of the past in favour of a committed poetry of the present. The 'Maclean line' was useful in articulating a vision of a Scottish political radicalism but it was not only the substance of Maclean's ideas that appealed to MacDiarmid and, subsequently, to Henderson; it was also the popular political currency of his name.

Having died at only forty-four due to the sustained maltreatment he suffered serving prison sentences for sedition, Maclean's name loomed large in the folk memory of the working class movement. His international reputation as an anti-war agitator, his standing in Soviet Russia and popular accounts of his historical significance as a Marxist martyr akin to figures like Rosa Luxemburg, Karl Liebknecht and Gramsci, helped to elevate Maclean and make him a symbol of the same political struggle in the Scottish tradition that he had asserted in his lifetime (*AM*, p. 349). He became the Scottish contingent of the international stuggle. In a letter to *Justice* (17 September 1914) Maclean made his position on the War very clear, and gave an example of the kind of proclamation that made him so attractive to later Scottish poets, as a compatriot in this body of political martyrs borne out of the twentieth century's struggles:

> it is our business as Socialists to develop a 'class patriotism', refusing to murder one another for a sordid world capitalism . . . Let the propertied class, old and young alike, go out and defend their blessed property. When they have all been disposed of, we of the working class will have something to defend, and we shall do it.[48]

In 1948, in an echo of the thousands who had lined the streets for his funeral procession, a mass meeting was organised by the Scottish-USSR Society to mark the twenty-fifth anniversary of Maclean's death. Henderson presided over the rally, and oversaw poetry recitations and speeches by Goodsir Smith, Sorley Maclean, Berwick, Kincaid and MacDiarmid, as well as performances by folksingers, pipers, the Young Communist League Choir and the Glasgow Unity Theatre. Almost all of those poets associated with the 'Clyde Group' were in attendance. In an article describing the proceedings, MacDiarmid paraphrased Henderson's opening remarks:

> The common people cannot raise to its heroes the monuments which organised hypocrisy erects for the 'Fallen' – the fallen in wars which are always costly and often totally unjustifiable. But the commons of Scotland have made for Maclean a surer and more lasting monument in their minds and hearts . . .[49]

The 'lasting monument' for this man who had become a 'symbol of all that is best in our national tradition and the only real guarantee of our national future' was to be built and maintained by Scotland's writers. Detailing the influence Maclean had on young authors, MacDiarmid described a Scottish literary tradition that 'up to the death of Burns . . . was mainly a literature of the whole people as English literature has never been'. Out of a modern concern with the 'gap between literature and the great masses of the people' and after the lessons of the Bolshevik Revolution and the Spanish Civil War, writers in 'civilised' countries, wrote MacDiarmid, had to choose between the left and the right. The fact that the 'majority of significant writers' in Scotland had devoted themselves to the left is attributed to Maclean's legacy.[50]

Fowrsom Reel supported MacDiarmid's analysis. Dedicated to Maclean, the publication's epigrams include an extract from *Lucky Poet* that calls for a 'Scottish Movement' that might give 'a mortal blow to the greatest Empire in the world', alongside lines from Goodsir Smith's 'Ballant o John Maclean' and Henderson's 'The John Maclean March'. The collection includes Kincaid's dramatic dialogue 'The Accuser', which depicts a discussion in Scots verse between 'Alba' – 'the lass o Scotland', the 'Worker' and a resurrected Maclean (the eponymous 'Accuser'),[51] and Berwick's 'The Citie o John Maclean', which also calls for its hero to 'rise again'.[52] The political and cultural programme of the 'Clyde Group' stood as a prize example of the renewed literature that Henderson and MacDiarmid envisaged in 1948.

The commemorative meeting that saw this united front of Scottish literary figures performing together under a common muse grew in later years to represent more than a fleeting consensus among poets. Morris Blythman later referred to the event as the 'first swallow of the [Folk] Revival' (*CPS*, p. 162n) and, alongside the Edinburgh People's Festivals (1951–4), the Maclean memorial was one of the earliest manifestations of what Henderson was later to articulate in his call for a folk revival that could be 'a powerful component part of the Scottish Renaissance' (*AM*, p. 50). In these historical moments, folksongs and poems shared stages and common political programmes. The proximity of their performances and their common subject matter were, however, not the only factors that thrust these creative forms together. Blythman's talent for presenting his work to mass audiences, which was demonstrated at the memorial meeting, and which reminded Henderson of Mayakovsky, was later explained in terms of the 'oral' quality that his work shared with that of the other members of the 'Clyde Group'. Years later Henderson acknowledged that the 'vigorous spoken poetry of *Fowrsom Reel* . . . [was] a potent agent in the contemporary folk-song revival' (*AM*, pp. 379, 447). The poets of the memorial rally, whose political credentials had been so emphatically celebrated by Henderson throughout the late 1940s, had inadvertently brought about conditions – a new model of Scottish literature orientated towards the 'Maclean line' – whereby the first shoots of the folk revival could flourish.

Blythman ('Thurso Berwick') perhaps best embodied this particular era of 'cross-fertilisation between "high-art" and the native demotic tradition', as in Henderson's eyes he was both a 'literary poet' and 'the unrivalled chief and brigade-major of the anti-Polaris balladeers' (*AM*, p. 3). In the 'Scottish Issue' of *Our Time*, which Henderson edited in 1948 he stated that, in the context of the memorial meeting, the headline might have been 'A World Issue'. Though all of the content was concerned with Scottish culture and politics, he posited that 'the separation of art from life and of artists from their audience is . . . the one crucial issue for all people whose great interest is Art Today, to whatever country they may belong, alike to artists and to the audience those artists would serve with their art'. In this sense Maclean comes to embody the nexus between the national and the international and, in this particular context, he gains symbolic value for those who seek to reconcile art and society in contemporary Scotland.

A further twenty-five years after his death Maclean was honoured by the John Maclean Society (est. 1968) with a collection of songs and poems titled *Homage to John Maclean* (1973). It showed how Maclean's appeal had extended beyond MacDiarmid, Henderson and the 'Clyde Group', and reached writers as disparate as Matt McGinn, Edwin Morgan, Alan Bold, Andrew Tannahill and Ruaraidh MacThomais (Derick Thomson). Edited by T. S. Law and Berwick, the collection included folksongs like McGinn's 'Dominie, Dominie', Henderson's 'The John Maclean March', and Ian Davison's 'Remember John Maclean', alongside a broadsheet election ballad from 1918, 'Mr John Maclean, M.P.', and Berwick's own 'Shout!' – a 'loud-speaker election song' of 1967. Like Henderson's *Ballads of World War II* and later song collections published during the folk revival (cf. *The Rebels' Ceilidh Song Book*), *Homage* does not attribute its pieces to their respective authors in the main body of the text. The provenance and authorship of each work are set out in endnotes. The effect on the page is that the materials seem to come from a vast anonymous resource, and the body of work, with all its variance, therefore implies a claim to speak with the authority of a collective that is representative of more than a roll-call of individual artists. Indeed, songs such as those written by McGinn and Henderson intimate this kind of collective foundation. In each case the lyric voice comes from among the crowd waiting to welcome the hero home after his release from Peterhead prison: 'Oor John Maclean has come hame tae the Clyde'.[53]

Featuring poems in Gaelic, English and various registers of Scots, the collection reveals a range of approaches to Maclean's legacy. While Sorely MacLean considers the lineage of his surname, setting his Clydeside namesake above those who died at Inverkeithing at the hands of Cromwell's New Model Army in 1651, MacDiarmid writes of the Russian word 'krassivy', 'which means / Both beautiful and red', which described Lenin in 1917 and Maclean in modern Scotland.[54] Meanwhile, Morgan imagines 'the rock of nations / like the rock of ages, saw-toothed, half-submerged' with the ships 'Workingclass Solidarity' and 'International Brotherhood' wrecked around it, as Maclean 'painfully trimmed the lighthouse lamp', and sought out a 'Scottish Socialism' whereby nationhood might illuminate the ships' journeys and further their ideals.[55]

Maclean was frequently cited as a symbol of the 'Scottish Socialism' he had conjured from the nation's history. After his death he was exalted as the 'top and hem' of a long tradition of individuals who embodied these principles. In *The Company I've Kept* MacDiarmid brackets Maclean's name with those of John Murdoch 'the crofters' leader – Maclean's agrarian counterpart', Thomas Muir, and John Swinton 'who aided the Negroes in South Carolina before the Civil War, became a friend of Walt Whitman, and knew Karl Marx' as Scots 'of far more consequence than most of those who figure prominently in our history books'.[56] MacDiarmid himself was, for Henderson at least, another embodiment of 'the true traditions of the Scottish people'. Henderson professed that 'it is to the radical and republican tradition of Scotland, an unbroken line from Burns and Muir to Maclean and MacDiarmid, that the youth of our nation is now looking'.[57] Indeed it was MacDiarmid's influence that helped to crystallise 'the Maclean line' as a commitment to Scottish Republicanism. Gallacher, Maclean's contemporary on the Scottish Left, downplayed his 'Nationalist deviation' and his refusal to join the CPGB, attributing these perceived failings to a mental instability that came out of the hardships of his later life.[58]

In the introduction to *Homage*, the editors showed their admiration for MacDiarmid's role in having 'countermanded the betrayal of Maclean' by squaring his legacy with his belief that the future of socialism would be formulated by small nations.[59] In the verses that follow, Maclean is steeped in Christological imagery: he preaches, is betrayed, crucified and resurrected. He is presented in the company of figures like William Wallace, Burns and Thomas Muir. Berwick lists him among those who demonstrated George Buchanan's 'Perfervidum Ingenium Scotorum' (translated in *Homage* as 'The Ardent Spirit of the Scots'), a revival of which might secure national independence.[60] In George Hardie's contribution, 'Sic a Land as This', quotations from David Lyndsay, John Barbour and Robert Fergusson are recast as prophesies of Maclean's coming. In short, he becomes the figure under whom radical national traditions converge, and the result is a demand for the fulfilment of his political aims in the future. In this sense, the 'Maclean line' was both a policy – the demand for a Scottish Workers' Republic – and a line of descent, a tradition that Maclean belonged to and exemplified. As the editors of *Homage* remind us in their introduction, 'in the matter of whom do we remember and how do we remember him, the poets always have the last word'.[61]

Both Henderson and MacDiarmid wrote of a democratic instinct in the Scottish literary tradition, accommodating the political principles of socialism and nationalist republicanism, even where it predates the development of these schools of thought. Henderson later clarified his position by positing that 'Scots literary and folk traditions through the centuries have been constantly and inextricably intertwined' (*AM*, p. 9). This model provided an interface between literary production and the field of popular culture, and opened up individual artefacts to the benefits of a 'communal recreation' (*AM*, p. 48). In *The Very Bastards of Creation* (1996), James D. Young attempts a 'biographical study' of 'Scottish International Radicalism' from the Union of Parliaments to the late twentieth century. Citing sources from the period of the American Revolution, through to Alasdair Gray and James Kelman, Young plots a route through this tradition. In Maclean he identifies a form of socialist-humanism, a defining commitment to 'the people', that, he alleges, MacDiarmid neglected in favour of contemplating 'consciousness' and the implications of an 'abstract world culture'.[62] Young's contention seems to have been influenced by Henderson's work: not only is folk-song frequently drawn upon to indicate a 'rebellious underground', a kind of unofficial history that is suppressed by documented narratives, but MacDiarmid's elitism and his leanings toward a 'scientific' socialism are contested with a desire to reconnect with the lives of the people.[63] In line with Maclean's own reclamation of the Scottish past as the 'rightful heritage' of the people, Henderson held that the conception of a national radical tradition was fundamental to realising 'the potentialities of a genuine "people's culture"'. In this short manifesto for a poetry that might 'become people', Henderson emphasised the need to 'go back to school with the folksingers'; but in considering the poem he would write to argue these ideas, he identified the need for a central figure, 'the self-sacrificing political champion of the *rossa bandiera*', a 'hero and martyr' like Gramsci, or Maclean.[64]

In his formula for a poetry that might 'pass into the mass itself, into the lowest strata of society, and become people' (Heine as cited by Henderson), Henderson proposed that both the anonymous processes of the folksingers and the symbolic heroes and martyrs of the socialist-humanist cause would be needed. The currency of Maclean's reputation in this context was bolstered by his call for Scotland to gather under 'one clan', which was in turn supported by the national synthesis represented in his own life. As MacDiarmid wrote: 'he was of Highland stock, his work lay in the great industrial belt in the Lowlands, and he married a Border woman. The unification of Scotland – Highland and Lowland, rural and urban – was complete in himself'.[65] However, the totemic folk hero sits at odds with Henderson's faith in the power of the anonymity of the masses, particularly as demonstrated in the 'folk process'. Henderson committed to the dictum 'when you become *Anon*, you've arrived'.[66] Though this principle might be used to explain the relative dearth of published verse throughout much of his career, with the development of his conception of the 'folk process' and its political potential Henderson gloried in the thought of his work acceding to the hallmark, *Anon*.

Anonyms, Pseudonyms and 'Alias MacAlias'

Henderson's understanding of the processes of the anonymous folk tradition, and his demonstrable belief in the symbolic value of names like Maclean's, were brought together by MacDiarmid's poetics. In one sense this 'doyen of the Scottish movement' had, under his pseudonym, come to represent the confluence of nationalism and internationalism (*AM*, p. 375). In Henderson's words, he was a 'standing stone – or (better yet) a sort of glorified totem-pole of the tribe, a new and in many ways more potent cult-figure than Scotland's superannuated "Loved One", poor stuffed, cosmeticised and mummified Rabbie'. Henderson recognised that the 'characters' Grieve took on were often *noms de guerre* rather than *noms de plume* (*AM*, pp. 436–7) and his responses to 'MacDiarmid' were made in full acknowledgement of this fact (cf. The 'Flytings'). In reference to the later poetry, Henderson posits that 'MacDiarmid' had in fact transcended the pseudonym and become a 'trade mark which appears stamped on such items as the poet considers worthy of being displayed to the public in the trundling top-heavy co-op pantechnicon which transports his productions' (*AM*, p. 438). 'MacDiarmid' stood not only as a pseudonym for Grieve but for all of the sources from which he borrowed words, phrases, entire passages, and even philosophic and scientific theories.

Though Henderson saw in MacDiarmid a 'genius who ransacks everything from the folk idiom to the latest edition of the encyclopaedia' (*AM*, p. 437), he did not consider this approach unusual in the Scottish tradition:

> It is never easy to draw a hard and fast line between the 'popular' arts and the 'elite' arts of individual excellence. Owing to the constant fruitful interaction of folk-song and art literature in our tradition . . . A sort of friendly communal cannibalisation has . . . been the rule rather than the exception in Scottish literature. 'Art' poets have operated like 'folk' poets in appropriating lines or even whole stanzas from earlier or contemporary authors – or, of course, from Anon – and using them as a basis for their own productions. (Ibid.)

Henderson called this phenomenon 'Alias MacAlias'. In an effort to avoid becoming a 'MacAlias' himself, he acknowledged that it was a term first coined by Moray McLaren in the *New Statesman*. In the original article, 'MacAliases', McLaren describes his personal discovery of the pervasiveness of 'Scottish anonymists and pseudonymists'. In his efforts to understand whether this practice is particularly common among Scottish writers, McLaren consulted *The Bibliographical History of Anonyma and Pseudonyma*, from which he concluded that, 'for the last 200 years MacAlias is well ahead, with Poland (possibly for political reasons) a runner-up'. Having begun by considering Scott's identity as 'the author of Waverley', McLaren goes on to list a whole range of writers from the hundred years previous to 1960, including Ian Maclaren (or Reverend Dr John Watson), Lewis Grassic Gibbon (James Leslie Mitchell) and even 'Saki' (Hector Hugh Munro). McLaren used the example of MacDiarmid's honorary doctorate from the University of Edinburgh to highlight the potential for the absurd. It was obligatory to use the recipient's legal name for the ceremony, and so 'they were compelled to neglect the internationally known poet of genius, and honour the writer of indifferent prose'. McLaren describes Scottish writers' tendency towards the 'MacAlias' as symptomatic of 'our fear of giving ourselves away'. To sign a work is to expose 'the intimate matter of your personal judgement of emotion'. Referring specifically to the Edinburgh bourgeoisie, McLaren writes, 'Dr Jekyll (or more usually Mr

Jekyll, Advocate) does not give himself away. And if, despite himself, the heart in him bursts out in the expression of anything in which there is a shred of beauty, he will publish it under the name of Mr Hyde'.

Henderson's conception of 'Alias MacAlias' was altogether more analytical and owed a great deal to MacDiarmid as its principal proponent. Setting out his interpretation in 1969, Henderson did not attribute the phenomenon to the neuroses and niggardliness of the Scot, as McLaren had done. Instead, he explained the reach for anonymity and pseudonymity as another expression of the long held interrelationship between the folk and literary traditions. Just as there could be no distinct border between '"popular" arts and the "elite" arts of individual excellence', he insists that 'no one can say for sure where MacAlias ends and Anon begins'. The difference between 'MacAlias' and 'Anon.' is ostensibly the difference between the pseudonymous and the anonymous. However, in Henderson's model, each reaches out from the respective territories of literature and folk-song, meeting one another in a 'gey debatable land' in between (*AM*, p. 437). Furthermore, the sense of the 'MacAlias' is not comparable to pseudonyms like George Eliot's, for example. It is centred on the adoption of an alternative name as, at least in part, a cover for creative plagiarism. While Henderson notes that '"Ossian" MacPherson' reversed the usual process of an 'art' poet appropriating lines for his or her own productions by writing a piece of original work and attributing it to an imagined other, the 'MacAlias' he writes of is centred on MacDiarmid's example, where 'The Kind of Poetry I Want = The Kind of Poetry I Take' (*AM*, pp. 437, 439).[67] Henderson cites the poem 'Perfect' as an example. In this instance MacDiarmid is not only a pseudonym for Grieve but for Glyn Jones, the Welsh novelist whose words were 'given poetic shape' (*AM*, p. 438).[68] Gibbon is recognised as having much the same approach, having taken 'the stuffing out of a clumsy German mattress in order to produce a much superior article of his own', which is a reference to Gustav Frenssen's *Jörn Uhl* (1901) and its influence on *Sunset Song* (1932). In Henderson's view, 'plagiarists of genius are the justified sinners of literature' (*AM*, p. 439).[69]

In a later article for *Cencrastus*, titled 'Zeus and the Curly Snake: The Chthonian Image' (1995), Henderson developed 'Alias MacAlias' to reconcile MacDiarmid's poetics with his own cultural-politics. The purported aim of the paper was to justify Henderson's use of MacDiarmid's 'Depth and the Chthonian Image' in the introductory essay for an album of 'Child' ballads, *Muckle Sangs* (1975), produced by the School of Scottish Studies. Henderson's argument proceeds along familiar lines: he details the 'fruitful cross-fertilisation in the fields of literary and "folk" poetry in [the] Scottish cultural tradition' and contends that 'art-poets forage in the communal bin just like folk-poets' (*AM*, pp. 427, 430). Again, the figures of 'MacAlias' and 'Anon.' work in symmetry with one another, blurring the borders of individual and communal authorship. Lines lifted from MacDiarmid's poem are inserted to validate these ideas throughout the article, demonstrating that 'art-poetry' can also be conscious of its relationship with these processes. Henderson notes MacDiarmid's response to this use of his verse: 'the various quotations from my poems are very relevant, and no matter how what I've said on occasions may have been interpreted, I of course stand by what I wrote in these quotations' (*AM*, p. 431). Henderson interprets this as 'at least a partial intellectual – as well as personal – reconciliation' after the entrenched opposition of the 'Flytings' (*AM*, p. 435). In an effort to bolster the significance of this confluence of ideas between MacDiarmid and himself, Henderson also considers the poet's estimation of 'Depth and the Chthonian Image': '[it provides a] perfectly clear and comprehensive expression of my whole aesthetic, political and general position' (*AM*, p. 432).

Henderson's close reading of 'Depth and the Chthonian Image' unearths two specific examples of MacDiarmid's 'MacAlias' tendencies. As these original sources are unpacked, they substantiate, and elaborate on, his argument for the combined processes of the literary and folk traditions in MacDiarmid's aesthetic. The first source is Jane Ellen Harrison's *Prolegomena to the Study of Greek Religion* (1908), particularly its first chapter, 'Olympian and Chthonic Ritual'.[70] Henderson does not trace precisely how this work influenced MacDiarmid's poem, instead, he delves into the body of Harrison's work and uncovers those elements that most clearly inform *his* understanding of MacDiarmid's poetic project. He points out the influence of anthropology and archaeology on Hellenists of Harrison's generation, and describes the author herself as a 'St Just-like Jacobin' in the 'revolution of ideas' that the comparative study of religion had brought to Classics. In Henderson's words, 'Jane's great service was to explore the dark underworld of Greek religion – the Chthonian deities who still lurked under and behind the shining figures of the Olympian gods'. The article celebrates Harrison's emphasis on the 'ritual' behind the constructs of Greek religious belief: 'The *thing done*, the rite, is before the *myth* which explains it – ritual before theology – and literature last of all' (*AM*, p. 433).

Illustrating how these ideas are borne out in the book, Henderson cites Harrison:

> We are brought face to face with the astounding fact that Zeus, father of gods and men, is figured by his worshippers as a snake . . . It is these rites of purification, belonging to the lower stratum – primitive and barbarous as they often are – that furnished ultimately the material out of which 'Mysteries' are made: mysteries which, when informed by the new spirit of the religion of Dionysus and Orpheus, lent to Greece its deepest and most enduring religious impulse. (*AM*, p. 433)

In these lines Henderson found a 'theme' that had a remarkable parallel in the 'curious dualities' of the Scottish literary tradition:

> 'Olympians' being the established 'greats' like Dunbar, Henryson and Gavin Douglas – plus Burns, Scott, Fergusson and Garioch – and the 'underworld' being the vast anonymous treasure-house of balladry and folksong – with all the manifold possibilities that existed and exist of constant interfusion. (Ibid.)

Harrison's methodology was groundbreaking. She based her study of Ancient Greek theology on the tangible elements of religious practice: the Athenian festivals and their 'rituals'. These 'things done', as Henderson refers to them, are seen as both reflections of, and formative contributions to, the nature of religious belief in classical Greece. In passages like that above, the whole tenor of Greek Mythology is borne out of a synthesis between the rites and rituals 'belonging to the lower stratum' and the Olympian gods. According to Henderson's reading, the central theme of Harrison's work is 'the superimposing of the official cults on the primitive Chthonian nature-cults'. The evolution of Greek religion relied on the 'interfusion' between these two sources and Henderson discovered that in the best of MacDiarmid's work (and in the passages he cites in his notes for *Muckle Sangs* in particular), the same process was at work (*AM*, pp. 433–4). Harrison's thesis provided Henderson with a metaphor for his conception of the interlinked folk-literary traditions in Scotland. It also provided a nuanced archetype of the 'MacAlias' in action. The Olympians are 'superimposed' and the myths of the underworld are 'superseded'. When this dynamic is transferred to the Scottish cultural tradition, the established greats are in one sense only *placed over* the vast anonymous folk-song that lies beneath, while the same body of lore is in another sense *replaced* by those literary names. The 'nature-cults' and folk-song are not substituted wholesale for Olympians and 'established greats' of the literary world. Nor are they simply repackaged. To return to the metaphor of the ritual and the myth: each aspect validates the other and, in this sense, Zeus (the myth) is a 'MacAlias' for the curly snake that consumes its own tail, and for the ritual that gives it meaning.

The second source for the poem relates to the passage that begins '*Ein Mann aus dem Volke* – weel I ken / Nae man or movement's worth a damn unless / The movement'ud gang on withoot him if / He de'ed the morn'.[71] The verse that follows is, it transpires, a thinly disguised adaptation of a passage from Wyndham Lewis's *Hitler* (1931) ('Hitler is just a very typical *Mann aus dem Volke* . . . one feels, should he fall tomorrow, the movement could still proceed without him'). Henderson notes that even with the poet's 1923 proposals for 'Scottish Fascism' in mind, MacDiarmid's borrowing from Lewis's eulogy is 'hard to stomach'. Nevertheless, he insists that his use of MacDiarmid's verse was entirely appropriate. The 'movement' to which the poem refers was, in Henderson's estimation, 'the great carrying stream of folk poetry and balladry, which survives and burgeons irrespective of the life or death of its foremost practitioners'. Henderson closes his article with a reminder of MacDiarmid's achievements in composing 'immortal poetry' that had also been 'swept irresistibly into the carrying stream' (*AM*, pp. 434–5). In this analysis, *Einn Mann aus dem Volke* ('A man of – or out of – the people') who can stand for the 'movement' but is not needed for its continuance, is a title as applicable to MacDiarmid as to the folksingers. The relationship between 'MacAlias' and 'Anon.' is, like that between the 'Olympians' and the myths of the 'underworld', tipped in favour of the 'superseded', anonymous masses. Their ineluctable folk process will persist, even when those who seem to stand apart from it die. By sacrificing individualised identity to be part of the anonymous collective, contributors to the 'folk process' become part of a greater body that is more resilient than any singular author. It is a remarkable irony that these particular texts, so closely tied to the modernist galaxy of ideas and influences – one by the co-founder of the *Vorticist* movement and the other of such vital importance to Virginia Woolf's thinking – should provide Henderson with an opportunity to demonstrate how the folk process subsumes all.

Henderson's ambition to *become* Anon. is in keeping with his insistence that 'poetry becomes everyone, and should *be* everyone'.[72] If a poet can dissolve his or her authorial identity in the body of the anonymous, a body that stretches back through history to claim classical literary fragments and scraps of folksong and lore alike, then that poet's work has, at least on the level of its authorship, *become* people. Henderson satisfied this ambition in many of his folksongs and was thrilled to hear singers carry his own work forward in new forms (*AM*, p. 429). Though he was to successfully set new songs on the 'carrying stream' Henderson also invested directly in the expressive freedom afforded by pseudonyms, particularly in his early career.

At Dulwich College Henderson edited the school magazine, *The Alleynian*. He assumed many pseudonyms: 'Agrippa' (after the Roman statesman and general), 'Polonius' (after *Hamlet*), 'Baralipton' (the term for a mnemonic used to memorise a syllogism) and even 'Omega'. His most frequent *nom de plume* was 'Z. Marcas', after Balzac's novel of the same name. In the last copy of the magazine under his editorship, Henderson included a poem entitled 'Ballade des Noms de Plume', which cited all of his pseudonyms and finished with an acrostic verse spelling out 'H-A-M-I-S-H'. The epigram to the poem is made up of a series of passages from Balzac's novel in the original French. In these segments Marcas considers his two-syllable name and the sinister meaning he suspects it holds. This experimentation with pen names can be put down to Henderson's efforts to fill the pages of the magazine with his own work, and to generate the kinds of discourses he thought ought to be promoted in the school, given that in another article he celebrates the 'literary Renaissance' that had bloomed under his editorship. It also shows his awareness of the potency of a named author. Though they are full of overblown language and convey a youthful pomposity, Henderson's schoolboy writings prefigure his later newspaper 'Flytings' in his adeptness for self-promotion and public criticism.

While the school model suggests a supreme confidence in his exaggerated presence as a whole series of disguised individual authors, Henderson later formulated a more nuanced and considered approach to his authorial designations. His trust in the 'folk process', and his aspiration to become another constituent of *Anon.*, is often heralded as a politically motivated decision and part of the perceived 'turn' toward folk-song and away from the career of an 'art-poet'. Neat describes this strategy: 'He would not seek public success. He would do something quieter, more subversive, more revolutionary: he would dissolve himself into the bloodstream of his people, like salt in water'.[73]

In 1951 Henderson wrote 'The Song of the Gillie More'. Its title was taken from the Gaelic, *Gillie Mór*, or the 'Big Fellow'. Conceived as an expression of 'fraternal good wishes', 'from the Blacksmiths of Leith to the Blacksmiths of Kiev', Henderson sought to express 'the reality of Scottish-Soviet "solidarity"' by conjuring up 'the figure of the "Big Fellow", familiar in the folklore of many trades – the superhuman individual who is really the sum total of the men who make up the union and give it its communal strength' (*AM*, pp. 17–18). Henderson noted that when Eric Winters compared his creation, the Gillie More, to John Henry (the American industrial-era folk hero) he wrote: '[the song] poses the ability of men acting collectively to transcend human frailty, and the power of human brotherhood to over-reach frontiers' (*AM*, p. 18). The identity of the 'Gillie More' as a figure representative of the collective becomes increasingly clear throughout the song, which ends with the celebratory lines 'You an' me: the man, the brither! / Me an' you: the Gillie More' (*CPS*, p. 137). As a folk hero who is at once national (named in a language unique to Scotland) and international (extending his representation to include the smiths of Kiev), Henderson's 'Gillie More' is not unlike his 'John Maclean'.

By publishing his 'writings on songs, folk and literature' under the title 'Alias MacAlias', Henderson and his editor, Alec Finlay, made a statement about how he conceived of these subjects and how he understood his authorial identity. In his introduction to the first edition, Angus Calder recognises the title's tribute to MacDiarmid (*AM*, p. xiv), while Neat quotes Henderson's intention as wanting readers to think about 'the communality of life and artistic production'.[74] Henderson's 'MacAlias' speaks of the long-established, mutually contaminative relationship between the folk and literary traditions in Scotland. This 'friendly communal cannibalisation' was most powerfully demonstrated by MacDiarmid (*AM*, p. 437). However, it is the title of his own collected writings and so Henderson is implicated, too. While the body of the text is filled with his work, it relies on countless others: their words, their worldviews, their songs and their poems. 'Alias MacAlias' therefore becomes a lens through which the individual's relationship with the many might be understood: it becomes difficult to tell where Henderson ends and where the mass of his subjects begins.

A Synthesis of Folk-song and Literature

Writing of that most urgent task, 'to make poetry "become people"', Henderson proposed that writers 'go to school with the folksingers' as it is their work that has consistently achieved such an accession to the 'people'.[75] This articulation of Henderson's vision of the synthesis of folk-song and literature is legitimised by a long history of 'interconnection' and 'cross-fertilisation' and, in his view, ought to have been extended and adapted for modern Scotland, bringing the artist and society together.

Elaborating his argument for poetry that would 'become people', Henderson called on Yeats: 'Before the night ends you will meet the music. There is a singer, a piper and a drummer. I have picked them up here and there about the street, and I will teach them, if I live, the music of the beggar man, Homer's music' (from *Death of Cuchulain*).[76] The nobility and timelessness attributed to this 'music of the beggar man' presents the desire to make poetry 'become people' as an integral characteristic of the Western tradition. In his opening contribution to the 'Folksong Flyting', Henderson's ally David Craig ridiculed MacCaig for his claim that folk-song was beneath him – 'he had read Homer' after all – reminding the poet that the two works attributed to Homer were very probably 'pieced together out of short lays chanted by minstrels at the Aegean courts'. He asserted that Scotland's own lays were the ballads, and that at their best they were equal 'in quality, in beauty and truth if not in scale' to the great European epics (*TAN*, p. 118).[77] These debates over the literary value of Scottish folk-song in the mid-twentieth century were thereby contested in the furthest regions of European literary history. Henderson laid claim to Barbour's *The Bruce* (1375), 'Scotland's *Iliad* and *Odyssey* rolled into one', and the fount of the Scottish vernacular tradition as an early example of the 'cross-fertilisation' of folk culture and literature.[78] Given the form and content of the poem, Henderson writes, 'one cannot help but surmising that echoes of actual balladry have occasionally found their way into the narrative' (*AM*, p. 79).[79] In his manifesto, 'Freedom Becomes People', Henderson also identified Burns as a 'forerunner in the practice of this strategy' – who 'transformed . . . our whole conception of the meaning of traditional art for society'. Angus Calder, in his introduction to *Alias MacAlias*, summarised Henderson's view: 'all the major Scottish writers since before Dunbar and Lindsay . . . can be heard as distinctive voices arising within, not separate from, a continuous strong flow of language and music in which labourers and scholars have swum together' (p. xv).

Henderson's idea of the Scottish literary tradition as an extended interplay between the individual author and the great unnamed reveals a grand unifying idea of authorship and, therefore, of the relationship between the artist and society. By recognising a juncture between the singular author and *Anon.*, but at the same time promoting a theory of the creative processes that pushes the a writer into a 'debatable land', towards the anonymous and the pseudonymous ('Alias MacAlias'), Henderson spoke of the complex dynamic between the artist and the world he or she seeks to interpret. The author mediates their own relationship with society by organising and rearranging innumerable influences. The act of writing is also, in this understanding, akin to broadcasting or singing in that it presupposes an audience. Henderson's proposal for a folk-literary synthesis recognises the distinctiveness of the forms of authorship associated with each of these fields only to insist on their mutual affinity. He theorised folk-song as an irrepressible reflex of human society, always capable of finding new forms. However, as a strategist of the folk revival, he was part of a calculated intervention in the ways traditional arts were recorded, performed and circulated. In orchestrating the conditions for a revival, Henderson had to incite a process that he believed was naturally occurring. Similarly, he imagined a Scottish literary tradition that had, through its interrelations with the folk tradition, consistently 'become people', and yet he called for this historical precedent to be consciously replicated and invoked in modern poetry.

To argue for the extension of a cultural tradition is to admit to some degree to its precariousness in the present. The immediate circumstances of literary practice in Scotland were Henderson's main grounds for concern. His distrust of MacDiarmid's 'quasi-solipsistic elitism',[80] and his impatience with the posturing of 'bourgeois nationalist' Lallans Makars (*AM*, p. 379), mark the parameters of the poetry Henderson envisaged: it could not be dismissive of 'the man in the street', neither could it pander to popular tastes or novelty and lose its political vitality. Finlay proposes that Henderson and the 'Clyde Group' be seen as part of a modern tradition of figures seeking out the same route; one that includes the Unity Theatre, the Glasgow Folk Club, folk-singers like Matt McGinn and the protest songs of the 'Ding Dong Dollar' anti-Polaris demonstrations (*TAN*, p. 309). Henderson identified various contemporary artists and cultural projects that overcame the problem of the isolation of the artist in society by implementing aspects of the 'folk process'. With the inception of the modern revival he acknowledged a generation of 'masterly poet-songmakers' who made the connection with traditional literatures more explicit (*AM*, p. 3).

One of the 'poet-songmakers', or 'folk-poets', that Henderson celebrated was McGinn, whose works 'blurred' the lines between 'tradition and revival' and between 'art' and 'folk'. McGinn melded the influence of the Glasgow music hall tradition with the 'gallus sardonic verve' of the Gallowgate area to which he belonged, and composed topical songs that often disguised their political incisiveness with humour and a disarming tenderness (Ibid.). In his song, 'Red Yo Yo', for example, a little girl loses her yo-yo and, after telling the janitor at the school, the missing toy quickly becomes a concern for the police, the government, the monarchy and, finally, world leaders, from Paris to Peking. In the final verse the search is called off: 'finally Annie announced that her Granny / Had bought her another Yo-Yo'.[81] Despite its playful narrative, the song summons a compelling sense of scale: the child from west central Scotland and her missing yo-yo are, in a few short lyrics, dwarfed by the power structures of world politics, all cooperating in the search. Written at the height of the Cold War, both Lyndon Johnson and Alexi Kosygin appear and are confounded by the problem, and the absurdity at the heart of the joke relies on the reality of an utter dislocation between these most extreme ends of the spectrum of power. In another of his well-known songs, 'Coorie Doon', McGinn plays with the double meaning of the title, which can be read as to crouch or stoop down, or to nestle or 'cuddle in'. A father sings his daughter to sleep in this 'miner's lullaby', describing the 'darkness, dust and damp' that he endures: 'but we must have oor heat, oor light, / Oor fire and oor lamp'. The father's resignation to his work, and the tenderness he expresses for his daughter, are elided in the dual meaning of 'coorie doon':

> Your daddy coories doon my darling,
> Doon in a three foot seam,
> So you can coorie doon my darling,
> Coorie doon and dream.[82]

The conjunctive 'so' further complicates the final verse. The father's self-sacrifice conceivably brings about the conditions whereby the child might sleep peacefully, but it also sustains her, so that she might 'dream' in an escapist or aspirational sense; that is, to imagine removing herself from the kind of toil her father tolerates daily. These songs represent a political reality through tender portraits of human relationships, and in doing so they achieve something of Henderson's aim to make poetry 'become people'.[83]

Henderson also listed Ewan MacColl among the 'poet-songmakers'. In collaboration with Peggy Seeger and Charles Parker, MacColl had conceived of a new creative form in the 'Radio Ballads' series broadcast between 1958 and 1964. Conscientious social documentary, field interviews and custom-written folksongs were combined to produce these 'ballads', which each focused on the lives of a different group of contemporaries: railwaymen, road-workers, fishermen, coal miners, polio sufferers, teenagers, professional boxers and travelling people.[84] Developments in mobile recording technology enabled MacColl, Seeger and Parker to broadcast the voices of working-class people and the soundscapes they inhabited. Their term for these was 'actuality recordings'.[85] Their production techniques – including the use of songs written especially to fit the recorded material – helped them to profile people's lives in their own words and in context, whilst also referring to the greater narratives that connect their lives to those of their peers. In short, they aim, like Henderson, for reconciliation between the singular and plural, between the individual agent and the nameless many. During the 'Flytings' Henderson's ally, Craig, wrote of a 'New Wave . . . that would find creative uses for the music-hall, the folksong, the vernacular tale, the tough-guy novel, and the radio documentary'. Among its members he lists Brendan Behan, John Osborne, Joan Littlewood, Arnold Wesker, John Arden, Alan Sillitoe, David Storey and the creators of the 'Radio Ballad'. Pointing out the alternative to MacDiarmid's intellectual isolationism, Craig emphasises these figures' attempts to 'bridge the modern cultural gulfs and to reach people' (*TAN*, p. 121).

Henderson saw the Edinburgh People's Festival Committee as a forerunner of Arnold Wesker's 'Centre 42' (*AM*, p. 9). In terms of achieving a truly integrated art that could re-engage the artist with society, the People's Festival furnished Henderson with a testing ground for these ideas. Referring to the combination of academic lectures, poetry readings, theatre performances and ceilidhs that made up the festival, Henderson later stated that the 1952 programme was, in many ways, his 'finest work of art'.[86] The comparison with 'Centre 42' is borne out quite clearly. Conceived after resolution 42 of the Trades Union Congress of 1958, which called for greater access to the arts, 'Centre 42' set out to work with the Labour movement and trade councils to organise events that would begin to 're-establish the tradition of art in society'.[87] Like Henderson, Wesker wanted to see art genuinely democratised and looked forward to a day when the social structures that bring about opposing forms of philistinism, of the 'street' and of the 'boudoir', would be no longer. In his essay 'Fear of Fragmentation' Wesker details his conception of 'fragmentary' thought, whereby we 'elevate each . . . fragment of understanding we reach, to the level of totality'. Consequently, the 'democracy' we have created incites an 'acceptance of mediocrity at all levels of that democratic life' by pandering to what is easily understood or what appeals to the instincts of the people.[88] The integrated art that Wesker proposes as a solution to this malaise, and an antidote to the 'fear of fragmentation', is not unlike Henderson's evocation of MacDiarmid's lines from the 'Third Hymn to Lenin' during the 'Folksong Flyting': 'Our concern is with human *wholeness*' (emphasis added) (*TAN*, p. 132).

Describing the world that would be made possible through the 'Centre 42' Arts Festivals, Wesker wrote:

> You start off with a picture: orchestras tucked away in valleys, people stopping Auden in the street to thank him for their favourite poem, teenagers around the jukebox arguing about my last play, miners flocking to their own Opera House; a picture of a nation thirsting for all the riches their artists can excite them with . . .[89]

The sentiment here is remarkably close to that expressed by MacDiarmid in his poem 'Glasgow, 1960', where a record-breaking crowd head to Ibrox to witness a great debate on the psychologist Émile Coué's notion of *la loi de l'effort converti* (the law of converted effort), rather than a football match.[90]

Henderson later wrote that MacDiarmid himself had achieved an equivalent feat with his own poetry (*AM*, p. 442). The Edinburgh People's Festival sought to overcome the isolation of the artist and the exclusivity of the arts by initiating action 'designed to bring the Edinburgh International Festival closer to the people as a whole', to 'make what is best in the cultural life of our country more accessible to working people', and to 'secure further facilities for the development of the cultural activities of working people'.[91] The Festival illustrated how a programme for the reconciliation of art and society might look in practice. Henderson also stated that the work of figures like Alan Jackson, Tom Leonard and Matt McGinn, was inspired by the 'blend of oral poetry and traditional Scottish song' encouraged at the Festival (*AM*, p. 97). Henderson conceived of a nationally framed, folk-orientated programme that shared many of its aims with bodies like 'Centre 42', the Unity Theatre and Joan Littlewood's Theatre Workshop, and with writers like the 'Angry Young Men'. However, his particular conception came with its own theoretical basis.

During the '*Honour'd Shade* Flyting' Henderson insisted that it was the folk revival that offered the 'best hope for a genuine popular poetry'. He posited that poets would feel a 'thrill of liberation' when they realised that 'the primary question facing them is not so much one of language as one of idiom' (*TAN*, p. 96). This emphasis on 'idiom', which was repeated in Henderson's assessments of his own creative work, 'in the idiom of the people' is of central importance in understanding the distinctiveness of his proposals for reconciling art and society. Not only does the term denote a mode of expression that is *natural* to a language or a group of people, it also refers to phrases that gain particular meanings *through usage* that cannot be gleaned from their constituent words. In this sense 'idiom' gestures towards the 'folk process' as Henderson understood it: as a mode of cultural expression that is defined by its 'usage' or transmission through the oral tradition. Folksongs are born when they accede to this process and win the approval of the people who carry and transmit them. Neat refers to this concept as Henderson's 'underground methodology',[92] and it is evident throughout Henderson's writings on Scotland's folk culture, with repeated references to the 'underground of folksong', presenting a challenge to established tastes and to the purveyors of so-called 'art-culture' (*AM*, pp. 31–6, 45–50).

As Neat has recognised, this 'methodology' informed *The People's Past: Scottish Folk, Scottish History* (1980), a collection of essays to which Henderson contributed, under the editorship of the historian Edward J. Cowan.[93] In his postscript, Henderson writes at length about the historical framework for his own 'song-poem', 'Glasclune and Drumlochy' – itself a product of the folk revival which 'grew and developed as spoken (and sung) poetry at Edinburgh Festival readings in the mid-sixties'.[94] The Glasclune and Drumlochy of the title relate to the estates of two feuding families who feature in an historical tale Henderson had heard as a child in Glenshee. He explores the prominence of these estates in medieval Scottish history, drawing from Andrew Wyntoun's *Original Cronykil of Scotland* (c.1420) and Walter Bower's *Scotichronicon* (1447); and presents his song-poem with the kind of detailed historical context that might be expected in the work of an antiquarian or a song collector. However, as Henderson reminds us, his poem is a contemporary reimagining of the historical; it is informed as much by a twentieth-century perspective of the grand trajectory of Scottish history as it is by the long-dead protagonists of the violent conflict it describes.

Henderson's preamble reinforces this point, and encourages us to read 'Glasclune and Drumlochy' as a piece that, like McGinn's work, combines tradition and revival: 'art' and 'folk'. The ruins of the castle of Glasclune become 'a symbol like the mill which MacDiarmid apostrophises in "Depth and the Chthonian Image"': 'The mills o' God grind sma', but they / In you maun crumble imperceptibly tae'.[95] We are instructed to find the creative and destructive forces of the universe and their passage through human history in the image of the Glasclune ruin. In the poem itself Glasclune represents the 'progressive' but dishonourable side of the conflict, which ultimately destroys Drumlochy with a newly bought canon:

Then shame, black shame, ay, shame on the bluidy Blairs!
Shame on the Blairs, an' sic wuddifu races.
They think nae sin
when they put the boot in
In the eyes of all ceevilized *folk tae disgrace us.*[96]

Henderson's poem, which combines spoken parts with 'ballad pastiche' sections, is said to 'echo' the 'old warfare' that has marked Scotland's history, 'as it still pulsates in the folk memory'. The poem is to function like folk-song, as the principal medium by which such conflicts have survived in the popular consciousness (cf. 'The Battle of Otterburn', Child no. 161). Henderson writes that the 'clannish confine' – those familial divisions and regionalised hostilities – lie 'in jagged outline across Scottish history'. This concept is elevated to relate to the 'millennial internecine conflict of humankind, which in our century bids fair to write *finis* to the "hail clanjamfrie"'.[97] The rhythm of countless feuds, battles and wars is repeated and exaggerated down through the generations to Henderson's century, in which two world wars and the policy of mutually assured destruction threaten to end everything in total annihilation. 'Hail clanjamfrie' is an evocation of MacDiarmid's 'The Bonnie Broukit Bairn', in which the tears of Earth, the poor neglected child, threaten to drown the other celestial bodies along with all their pageantry and finery. Henderson addresses what he referred to in his wartime poetry as 'our human civil war' (*EDC*, p. 15). He harnesses folk-song as a tool for remembrance, as it has historically given form to the ways in which past conflicts are imagined. He also appeals directly to the metaphysical depth of MacDiarmid's poetry by explicitly and implicitly comparing the imagery of the poem to those of 'The Bonnie Broukit Bairn' and 'Depth and the Chthonian Image'.

Henderson comes closest to fully synthesising these strategies of folk-song and literature in the final stanza:

Ochone Drumlochy
Glasclune and Drumlochy –
Twa herts on ae shiv

An a shitten larach.[98]

An expression of sorrow or lamentation, 'ochone' establishes the tone of these closing lines. Derived from Gaelic, one of the first recorded uses of the term is in Henryson's *Testament of Cresseid* (c.1505). Though they come to embody all human conflict, Glasclune and Drumlochy are represented as 'twa herts on ae shiv': the narrow confines of their distrust and antagonism and the lack of foresight this generates has left both families impaled on a single blade. Following the pause after this penultimate line, Henderson returns to the ruin of Glasclune, which is the only surviving marker for this tale. 'Shitten' is defined as 'defiled with excrement', and 'larach' as another Gaelic-derived term meaning 'the site of a building or habitation' (*OED*). The site has been superseded by the folk tradition and by Henderson's creative agency, whereby the conflict is immortalised and elevated as a symbol of the transhistorical 'human civil war'. The ruin becomes a contemptible monument to humanity's inhumanity.

'Glasclune and Drumlochy' is one example among many of Henderson's creative work elaborating on the blueprint of his cultural politics. Similarly, in 'Here's to the Maiden' he recasts an episode from Scottish history through contemporary concerns. Beginning with the note, 'in 1331 the heads of fifty executed "misdoaris" decorated the castle of Eilean Donnan', Henderson's poem shows regret for those who lost their lives over meagre, unremarkable indiscretions and suggests that the walls might have been better adorned with the heads of '*oor* Scottish quislings' ('Ye'll see them shinin the Southron's shoes'). Written in the immediate post-war years, Henderson's poem finishes:

The heids o a score o *Vichy Scots*
wad suit these partisan days
and mak mair sense as an ornament
than dizzens o wild MacRaes.
(*CPS*, p. 123)

In the spirit of his contemporary article, 'Scotland's Alamein', Henderson calls for the rooting out of those who would impede the progress of Scotland's political self-determinism. He asks that the ire of people in the 'partisan days' of the late 1940s be directed at those who betray his implied political principles (those 'quislings' who betray Scotland as the Vichy betrayed France), rather than at petty criminals or simple 'misdoaris', as was the historical want.

In 'Brosnachadh', Henderson applied the Gaelic term for a poetic 'incitement to battle' (or 'incitement to rise' as it is noted in the *Collected Poems and Songs*), to the concerns of a post-war international movement for peace. Henderson was a delegate at the International Peace Congress in Paris in 1949, the second of several annual meetings of the 'Partisans for Peace' to whom this poem was dedicated, after their inaugural in Wrocław in 1948. The poem is a direct plea to those who belong to the cause, to 'tell of the rebellious truth', to 'face the imperative choice' and to 'prove that with us is no "villainy of hatred", / and history will uphold us – / justify and forgive' (*CPS*, pp. 130–1). Burns' 'Scots Wha Hae' is rendered in Gaelic as 'Brosnachadh Bhruis', literally, 'Bruce's call to arms'. In this sense the imperatives of the internationally minded 'Partisans for Peace', who looked out on the prospects of a protracted Cold War, were to be realised through Henderson's reference to that period of Scotland's history when a vigorous claim to national autonomy was most forcefully made. This association comes close to the 'one clan' ideology that Maclean had proposed: the adoption of a perceived characteristic of Scotland's civic past to negotiate with the political conditions of the twentieth century, which had seen two *World* Wars.

Henderson's most celebrated song, 'The Freedom Come-All-Ye', is often touted as an alternative national anthem. Among Henderson's creative works, it is perhaps the most compelling example of his conception of a poetry that 'becomes people'. Written in 1960, and often associated with his CND campaigning (it was recorded for the *Ding Dong Dollar* record in 1962) the song combines contemporary international causes with a dense framework of Scottish historical and geographical references. The opening stanza's warning: 'there's mair nor a roch wind blawin / Through the great glen o' the warld the day', also reads as revolutionary fervour: a great sea change in history swelling up beneath the speaker, the audience and their times (*CPS*, p. 143). The Great Glen, that separates the Grampians from the Northwest Highlands, becomes a symbol of global division. And some commentators have interpreted the 'roch wind' as a reference to Harold Macmillan's 'Winds of Change' speech, in which the Tory Prime Minister appealed to the emerging nationalist movements in Africa to choose the path of the 'Free World' over that of Communism.[99] The final dissolution of Western Imperialism and especially Scotland's complicity in it, is keenly anticipated throughout the song for the sake of domestic and overseas victims alike. Henderson looks forward to the day when 'Broken faimlies in lands we've herriet, / Will curse Scotland the Brave nae mair . . .' (*CPS*, p. 143). Evoking Scotland's military reputation as an engine of empire and the popular song that celebrates this heritage ('Scotland the Brave'), Henderson awaits an improvement in Scotland's sense of itself, and in the image it projects to the rest of the world. Imagining all that must be overcome, the poem envisages a time when 'black and white, ane til ither mairriet [will] mak the vile barracks o' their maisters bare' (Ibid.). This image at once suggests the great scale of the task at hand – the reconciliation of races and continents – whilst also suggesting that the foundations of such profound progress will be set at an intimate human level, as in marriage. This kind of connection is all that is needed to empty the 'barracks' of the 'masters' who have orchestrated this alienation of humankind from itself.

The doomsayers, or 'hoodies' (carrion crows), who 'croak for doom', are described in language that suggests their equivalence with the malign crows and ravens of Scottish folklore, symbolising death, and the kind of Calvinistic predestination that seems to make no allowances for the change that can be affected by collective human will. Those 'at hame wi Freedom' are encouraged to disregard their 'croaks' and look to a world where 'a' the bairns o' Adam / Can find breid, barley-bree and painted room'. The final lines picture the spirit of Maclean reunited with his 'freens in Springburn', his political vision reintegrated into the Scottish working class: an event that will incite all the flowers to bloom, 'and a black boy frae yont Nyanga / Dings the fell gallows o' the burghers doon' (Ibid.). Finally, Henderson looks back to South Africa, and to one of the townships outside Cape Town, where the ANC first established its resistance to the Apartheid regime. Here, the apparatus of the class system (the 'burghers', the comfortable middle classes, the bourgeoisie) and of all oppressive societal structures, will be torn down.

The 'come-all-ye' form is common to both Scottish and Irish folk-song. It can be a poetic device with which to gather the imagined figures who populate the song ('Come all ye tramps and hawkers . . .'), but it can also be a direct plea for a like-minded audience ('Come all ye faithful . . .' or 'Come all ye at hame wi' Freedom'). Henderson claims this song type as an appropriate medium for the expression of Freedom and with the definite article he points to the universality of the message behind '*The Freedom* Come-All-Ye'. Like 'Brosnachadh', it is an incitement to rise. In the notes to *Ding Dong Dollar*, its style is categorised as 'rebel-bardic'.[100] Indeed, in relation to this 'bardic' form, Adam McNaughtan has noted that the perfect matching of text and song is a quality not easily accounted for by the literary critic.[101] Sung to the pipe tune 'The Bloody Fields of Flanders', the song retains a connection to the fallen of the First World War, where the proletariat eschewed class allegiance and slaughtered themselves in service of the power structures Henderson looks to overthrow.

The ballad Scots in which the song is written also conjures rich associations with the linguistic landscape of a national past. Rather than compromising the contemporary relevance of the song, this approach seems to commit its sentiments to a kind of timelessness that could not have been achieved with the ever-changing, highly regionalised vernacular. John Mitchell wrote of the song's 'balance between "intellect" and "emotion"', and its prescience in pointing to a 'significant way forward out of the dilemma in which contemporary . . . poetry finds itself', as one built 'on the culture of the people'.[102] An explicit attempt to reconcile the national with the international; a perspective of the past with one of the future; and literature with folk, 'Freedom Come-All-Ye' shows in content and form how Henderson's proposals might be realised.

Mario Relich has noted that in his 'undeviating focus on common humanity', Henderson's later poetry in 'a more populist balladic form' challenged the 'aesthetics of confessional poetry' and 'self-absorbed verse' that had taken hold in this period.[103] In practice, this position was not arrived at easily. The mid-century 'turn' that is said to mark Henderson's career was not characterised by a wholehearted break from the aesthetics of art-poetry and the figure of the artist isolated from society, towards the integrated model of folk culture. Henderson assures us that his cultural-political programme is faithful to the ideas underlying the best of MacDiarmid's work; he tested its principles against the 'Plastic Scots' debates, and found writers putting it into action among the 'Clyde Group'. In Maclean, Henderson discovered a potent symbol for the radical tradition he sought to extend, and in the anonymous masses who constitute the 'carrying stream' of folk culture, he identified a field of political potential where author and audience are indistinguishable: *Anon.* and 'Alias MacAlias' were to be understood as articulations of the same space, between artist and society. A synthesis of folk-song and literature is always at the centre of these appraisals and is revealed in various formulations: it is made apparent in literature that demonstrates, in form or content, a closeness to the lives of the people; in an attitude to authorship whereby sources and influences go unacknowledged; in the conscious reunification of poetry and song, which have been too long separated; and in an extension of the radical national tradition that has its cultural counterpart in a literature for, and out of, the 'whole people'. His movement toward work 'in the idiom of the people' (as cited at the beginning of this chapter) was not indicative of a break, but a deepening in his analysis of the role of the artist. Henderson's manifesto, in which he suggested poets go to school with the folksingers, was in fact a call to return to the fundamental truth of literary production as he conceived of it: its capacity to 'become people'.

When he was asked about the nature of the satisfaction he got from writing poetry, Henderson paraphrases Wilde's *De Profundis*:

> the object of love is to love. To feel itself in the joy of its own being. To a certain extent this is poetry too: one shouldn't divide it between the moment of creation and the created completed thing . . . [the most important thing is] to have this sensation of the thing moving and being and in existence, and not dead and flailing. (*AM*, p. 453)

Henderson conceived of the 'carrying stream' of the folk tradition in similar terms, as a channel for 'living' works that applied equally to his folksongs as to MacDiarmid's verse. One of the ways in which this quality could be attained was through the synthesis of folk literature and art literature. In his introduction to *The Red Paper on Scotland* (1975), Gordon Brown wrote:

> The vision of the early socialists was of a society which had abolished for ever [sic] the dichotomy – the split personality caused by people's unequal control over their social development – between man's personal and collective existence, by substituting communal co-operation for the divisive forces of competition.[104]

It is this same division between 'personal and collective existence' that Henderson sought to overcome with his cultural-political programme. While this project could do little to solve the rift Brown describes in the economic sense, an art that was truly integrated in society, that recognised the blurred line between an artist and his or her audience, could, Henderson hoped, bring about a 'genuine people's culture'. Late in his life, Henderson wrote of MacDiarmid: 'in the shadow of this colossus the so-called Left Wing poets of today – half declassed and wholly introverted, wrapped up in the saving of their own neurotic little spiritual skins – will collapse unheeded to dust, the seeds of their own destruction being already within them' (*AM*, p. 316). The reason for MacDiarmid's supremacy over other poets is explained in a passage from his poem 'Etika Preobrazhennavo Erosa' (as cited by Henderson):

> It is easy to cry
> I am one with the working classes
> But no task in this world surpasses
> In difficulty his who would try,
> Must try since he is not, succeed or die.
> Miseducated and more articulate,
> Sensitised by what numbs their fate
> And raised up by what keeps them down,
> Only by the severest intellectual discipline
> Can one of the bourgeois intelligentsia win
> Up to the level of the proletariat
> On this side of the grave or that
> – The only goal worth aiming at.
> (*AM*, pp. 316–17)[105]

This is the task that Henderson set himself. His notion of becoming *Anon.*, and his ideal of a poetry that could 'become people' constitute his methods for 'winning up to the level of the proletariat' and singing from among them.

Notes

1. MacCaig edited the anthology. The other poets noted for their absence were Alan Riddell, T. S. Law, David McEwan and T. T. Kilbucho (pseudonym of Tom Todd). Henderson also noted the exclusion of the poets behind the *Fowrsom Reel* (1949) (John Kincaid, George Todd, F. J. Anderson and Thurso Berwick), and *Four Part Song* (1950) (Arthur James Arthur, Martin Gray, Alasdair Thompson and George Kay) (*TAN*, pp. 79–100).
2. Neat, *Making of the Poet*, pp. 235–6.
3. Neat, *Making of the Poet*, p. 348. Glen coined the phrase in his essay 'Hamish Henderson: Poetry Becomes People' (1988), though it paraphrases Henderson's short manifesto of 1968, 'Freedom Becomes People'.
4. Ransford, 'Encompass the Crossed-Sword Blades', p. 144.
5. Neat reports that Henderson intended to produce a book of memoirs based on his wartime service, entitled 'German Interrogator' (*Making of the Poet*, p. 70). From the early 1950s Henderson's poems appeared less frequently in print and many did not find their final shape until their publication in the collected works, decades after their original composition.
6. Henderson's work is included in George Bruce's 1968 anthology *The Scottish Literary Revival*, and in Maurice Lindsay's *Modern Scottish Poetry: An Anthology of the Scottish Renaissance, 1925–1975*.
7. See 'Tangling with the Langholm Byspale' and 'Flytings Galore: MacDiarmid v. The Folkies' (*AM*, pp. 381–404, 405–26) originally published in consecutive issues of *Cencrastus* in 1994. Henderson supported Finlay's magazine *Poor.Old. Tired.Horse.* in the 1960s and, in the 1980s, he came to Finlay's defence in the well-documented controversies over his art. See Neat, *Poetry Becomes People*, pp. 172–5, 313–16; Thomas, 'Turning their Fey Shoulders to the Wheel: Edwin Morgan's letters to Hamish Henderson'; and James McGonigal, *Beyond the Last Dragon*, pp. 334–6.
8. Henderson acknowledged the fact that MacDiarmid, MacCaig and Goodsir Smith became a kind of 'literary triumvirate' referred to by the city's columnists as the 'Rose St Poets' (*AM*, p. 397). Alec Finlay has written of Henderson, Morgan and his father, Ian Hamilton Finlay, as forming a nexus resistant to the 'high modernism' of MacDiarmid and his followers (*TAN*, pp. 341–3).
9. Neat, *Poetry Becomes People*, p. 330.
10. Ibid., p. 145.
11. Neat, *Making of the Poet*, p. 348.
12. MacDiarmid showed his support for Lindsay's exposition on the Renaissance in his editorial for *National Weekly* (1. 21, 5 February 1949, p. 5).
13. Lindsay, *The Scottish Renaissance*, pp. 5, 6, 8, 28.
14. Goodsir Smith, 'MacDiarmid's *Three Hymns to Lenin*', p. 144.
15. McCulloch, *Modernism and Nationalism*, p. xii.
16. Henderson also translated and adapted the work of the nineteenth-century

German poets, Hölderlin and Heine. Furthermore, after the War he produced English versions of the work of Czech-German writer Louis Fürnberg.

17. See *The Obscure Voice*, which includes Henderson's translations of Montale, Quasimodo, Cardarelli and Campana.
18. See Corbett, *Written in the Language of the Scottish Nation*, and Bill Findlay, *Frae Ither Tongues: Essays on Modern Translations into Scots*.
19. Eliot, 'Was There a Scottish Literature?'; Muir, *Scott and Scotland*, pp. 9, 111.
20. Edinburgh University Library, *Hugh MacDiarmid and Company*, p. 15.
21. Young, *Plastic Scots*, p. 28.
22. The other signatories were Albert D. Mackie, Maurice Lindsay, J. Ritchie, Alexander Scott, Goodsir Smith and Douglas Young.
23. 'An Editorial Diary: Short Course in Plastic Scots', p. 4.
24. *Letters of Brendan Behan*, p. 37.
25. Casement, 'The Language of the Outlaw', p. 113.
26. Lyall, *Hugh MacDiarmid's Poetry and Politics of Place*, p. 96.
27. MacDiarmid, *Selected Prose*, pp. 61–80.
28. The 'Clyde Group' also had its equivalent in visual art. In a manifesto published in MacDiarmid's *National Weekly* titled 'The Working Class And The Arts: Clyde Group Festival and Exhibition' this group declared that they would not engage in 'escapist' paintings because, 'We are artists who are working for the Community, and, among other things, show through our Art the desire of mankind to LIVE, and LIVE DECENTLY and IN PEACE.'
29. Kincaid, et al., *Fowrsom Reel*, p. 44.
30. 'Second Hymn to Lenin', *Complete Poems*, p. 323.
31. *Jamieson's Dictionary of the Scottish Language* (1867). 'Walpugisnacht' refers to the German folk belief associated with May Day, where witches meet in council with the devil in the Harz Mountains. The festival also features in Goethe's *Faust*.
32. See Burns' 'The Deil's Awa Wi' Th' Exciseman' and Dunbar's 'The Dance of the Sevin Deidly Synnis'.
33. Kincaid, *Setterday Nicht Symphony*, pp. 4–5.
34. Ibid., pp. 6–8.
35. Kincaid, et al., *Fowrsom Reel*, p. 4. See Hubbard, 'Reintegrated Scots: The Post-MacDiarmid Makars'.
36. Kincaid, et al., *Fowrsom Reel*, pp. 4–6.
37. Neat, *Making of the Poet*, p. 230.
38. See MacDiarmid's leader, 'Knoydary Land Seizures' (1948).
39. MacLean, *From Wood to Ridge*, p. 47.
40. See Maclean, *In the Rapids of Revolution*, pp. 217–18, 224–6.
41. MacDiarmid was expelled from the CPGB after the publication of his poem 'John Maclean (1879–1923)'. See Gallacher, *Revolt on the Clyde*, and Young, *John Maclean: Clydeside Socialist*.
42. Lyall, *Hugh MacDiarmid's Poetry and Politics of Place*, pp. 123–8.
43. See Hart, 'Nationalist Internationalism'.

44. Hamish Henderson Papers, NLS Acc. 10327 (i)
45. Maclean, *In the Rapids of Revolution*, p. 217.
46. Ibid., pp. 218–19.
47. Henderson, 'Resurgimento!', p. 12.
48. Maclean, *In the Rapids of Revolution*, p. 77.
49. MacDiarmid, 'No "Belcherising" For John Maclean', p. 1.
50. Ibid., p. 1.
51. Maclean famously stated, in his 'Speech from the Dock' on 9 May 1918 in Edinburgh: 'I am not here, then, as the accused; I am here as the accuser of Capitalism dripping with blood from head to foot', as cited in Broom, *John Maclean*, p. 178.
52. Kincaid, et al., *Fowrsom Reel*, pp. 73–4.
53. Law and Berwick, *Homage*, p. 11.
54. Ibid., p. 7.
55. Ibid., pp. 18, 20.
56. MacDiarmid, *Company I've Kept*, p. 127.
57. Henderson, 'Scotland at the World Peace Congress'.
58. In his autobiography, *Revolt on the Clyde*, Gallacher expunges almost all reference to Maclean's nationalist convictions and to the formation of the Scottish Workers' Republican Party (pp. 212–16).
59. Law and Berwick, *Homage*, p. 3.
60. Ibid., pp. 45, 19. Berwick's song is to the tune of 'The Wark o the Weavers', which evokes another connection to the radical tradition – the celebrated insurrection of 1820.
61. Law and Berwick, *Homage*, p. 3.
62. Young, *The Very Bastards of Creation*, p. 204.
63. Ibid., pp. 52, 240.
64. Henderson, 'Freedom Becomes People', p. 1.
65. MacDiarmid, 'John Maclean, Scotland, and the Communist Party', p. 4. Henderson recognises this aspect of Maclean's legacy in his 'The John Maclean March', with Highlanders, Scots-Irish, and those wearing the 'red' and the 'green' all turning out side-by-side (*CPS*, pp. 126–7).
66. Neat, *Poetry Becomes People*, p. 317.
67. 'The Kind of Poetry I Want' is the title of a long poem of MacDiarmid's, and a poetic sequence that appears in *Lucky Poet* (*Complete Poems*, pp. 1001–35, 607–27).
68. This particular instance of audacious plagiarism was the subject of some controversy in the correspondence pages of the *Times Literary Supplement* in 1964 (*Letters of Hugh MacDiarmid*, pp. 828–33). There are countless examples in MacDiarmid's corpus: 'The Little White Rose of Scotland' drew heavily on Compton Mackenzie (Bold, *MacDiarmid*, pp. 429–30), and in *In Memoriam James Joyce*, MacDiarmid lifted a considerable portion of an unsigned essay by Erich Heller on Karl Kraus from the *Times Literary Supplement*. Henderson

was in contact with Heller and MacDiarmid about getting the original source acknowledged in subsequent publications (*TAN*, pp. 174–81, 189–93).

69. Henderson evokes James Hogg's *Memoirs and Confessions of a Justified Sinner* (1824), whereby the assurances of Robert Wringhim's 'elect' status permits any digression in his worldly life.
70. 'Chthonic' is defined in the *OED* as 'dwelling in or beneath the surface of the earth'. It is a term principally used to describe aspects of classical religion.
71. MacDiarmid, *Complete Poems*, p. 351.
72. Henderson, 'Freedom Becomes People', p. 1.
73. Neat, 'The Unknown Soldier'.
74. Neat, *Poetry Becomes People*, p. 324.
75. Henderson, 'Freedom Becomes People', p. 1.
76. Ibid., p. 1.
77. The depth of Craig's allegiance with Henderson's is demonstrated in *Scottish Literature and the Scottish People 1680–1830*: 'Always the aim has been to find in the particular . . . passages of poetry or fiction in which the life of the people seems to reveal itself most genuinely' (p. 11).
78. Robinson, 'Back to the Future'.
79. In the introduction to his *Minstrelsy of the Scottish Border*, Scott made a similar point with regard to Barbour, who thinks it unnecessary to rehearse the account of a victory in Eskdale over the English, because: 'Qhasa lik, thai may her / Youngwemen, quhen thai will play, / Syng it among thaim ilk day.' (p. 220)
80. Henderson, 'Freedom Becomes People', p. 1.
81. McGinn, *McGinn of the Calton*, pp. 156–7.
82. Ibid., p. 117.
83. Alongside McGinn, Henderson wrote of Bob Bertram, an Edinburgh folk poet whose work demonstrates similar qualities (*AM*, pp. 41–2). See *Selected Songs and Poems of Bob Bertram*.
84. See Cox, *Set Into Song*.
85. Parker, et al., *The Ballad of John Axon*, pp. 1–2.
86. Henderson, 'Resurgimento!', p. 13.
87. Wesker, *Fears of Fragmentation*, p. 46.
88. Ibid., pp. 107–8.
89. Wesker, 'Vision! Vision! Mr Woodcock!'
90. MacDiarmid, *Complete Poems*, p. 1039.
91. Henderson, 'Edinburgh People's Festival, 1951–54', p. 165.
92. Neat, *Poetry Becomes People*, p. 317.
93. Ibid., p. 317.
94. Henderson, 'Postscript: Glasclune and Drumlochy', p. 206.
95. Ibid., p. 207.
96. Ibid., p. 210.
97. Ibid., p. 209.
98. Ibid., p. 210.

99. Scott, 'Hamish Henderson's Torch of Freedom'; Dick Gaughan, 'Song Notes: 'Freedom Come Aa Ye''.
100. *Ding Dong Dollar*, p. 3.
101. McNaughtan, 'Hamish Henderson – Folk Hero', p. 25.
102. Mitchell, 'An Analysis', pp. 17, 23.
103. Relich, 'Apollyon's Chasm', p. 135.
104. Brown, *The Red Paper on Scotland*, p. 8.
105. MacDiarmid, *Complete Poems*, p. 407.

CHAPTER

5

THE REVIVALIST AND THE FOLKLORIST

> *'But what on earth are you going to do with all this stuff once you've collected it?' comes a parting shot from the opposite camp. The answer is: give it back to the Scottish people who made it.*
>
> (Henderson, extract from 'Enemies of Folk-song', 1955) (*AM*, p. 50)

In Henderson's response to his imagined detractors, the work of the folksong collector is justified by the work of the folk revivalist. The processes of 'collection' and 'giving back' are bound together. The folklorist, who collects, catalogues and studies songs and tales, works in an isolated, academic sphere. The revivalist, who creates circumstances whereby such songs and tales might be reintegrated into popular culture, works as a public campaigner and a cultural-political strategist. While Henderson was both a folklorist and a folk revivalist, and refused to draw a clear distinction between the two roles, his writings on folk culture can be easily separated into those he wrote principally as a folklorist and those principally as a revivalist. In an essay such as 'Enemies of Folk-song' (1955), Henderson describes the obstacles that need to be overcome if the folk revival is to take root. In an article like 'The Green Man of Knowledge' (1958) he transcribes a recently collected folk tale, and traces its tropes and motifs back through literary and folk traditions. In the quotation above Henderson concedes that his critics might reasonably ask why this 'stuff' is worth collecting at all. He does not explain that the study of folk culture gleans insights into social history, linguistics, literature, popular culture and the processes of cultural transmission, which might have vindicated the work in scholarly terms. Instead, Henderson declares his intention to 'give it back [to] the Scottish people' who, collectively, and over many generations, '*made* it'.

Though these dual roles – revivalist and folklorist – are inextricably linked, the distinction that can be traced in Henderson's writings provides a convenient structural framework through which to analyse his approaches to folk culture. First, there is Henderson's vision for the modern revival, which can be drawn both from his early writings, during the formative years of the movement, and from his attempts to provide a retrospective account of the whole movement, with all its mutations and permutations. The difficulties that Henderson experienced as one working *within* and speaking *for* an established cultural tradition and trying to articulate its place in modern Scotland, are of particular importance here. Second, Henderson's conception of the work of the folklorist should be examined: in this capacity, his mindfulness of the history of his field and the cultural sphere his subject inhabits, are of particular interest. Third, drawing from examples of Henderson's folk scholarship, the *scope* of his notion of folk culture ought to be understood. Even in his most narrowly defined academic study, the timeless elements of folk culture are set against the transformational 'process' of transmission, to interesting effect. Finally, Henderson's conception of folk culture cannot be fully explored without acknowledging the great shift in perspective brought about by his discovery of the huge torrent of *living* oral culture still extant among Scotland's travelling people. While this event gave Henderson confidence in the possibility of a revived folk culture across the country and crystallised his ideas about the mechanics of what he called the 'folk process', it also showed him the extraordinary circumstances required for a vigorous folk culture to exist in modern Scotland. In Federico García Lorca (1898–1936), he found another poet who appreciated the inexpressible qualities of ancient folk culture – such as the song culture of his native Andalusia – and who reverted to metaphor and opaque imagistic prose in an effort to convey its depth and its significance.

Henderson set out to excavate and redistribute the arts of the oral tradition. He is often heralded as the father of the modern Scottish folk revival – every obituary in the national newspapers acknowledged him as its principal figure – and his various writings are a testament to his prominence as a theorist, promoter and practitioner in this cultural movement. As a song collector and a ballad scholar Henderson was, however, conscious of the long tradition that preceded him. The most obvious critical context within which to approach Henderson's work as a folk revivalist and a folk-song collector is in the long line of scholars who have documented Scottish song culture. We might look to David Herd (1732–1810) and his *Ancient and Modern Scottish Songs* (1776); to Francis James Child (1825–96) and his definitive work, *The English and Scottish Popular Ballads* (1882–98); and to Gavin Greig (1856–1914) and the Revd James Duncan (1848–1917) and their posthumously published *Last Leaves of Traditional Ballads and Ballad Airs* (1925). Henderson would also qualify for that parallel tradition of folk scholars who were also poets and song-collectors: Allan Ramsay (1713–84), Robert Burns (1759–96), James Hogg (1770–1835) and Walter Scott (1771–1832). In the twentieth century, figures like A. L. Lloyd (1908–92), Alan Lomax (1915–2002) and Ewan MacColl (1915–89) – all contemporaries of Henderson's – were engaged quite consciously in revivalist programmes, and all were committed to a political vision that might be advanced by a return to the traditional arts. With his peers, Henderson stood at the juncture between previous generations of collectors and antiquarians, and the professional, scholarly pursuits that were to develop, later in the twentieth century, into folkloristics, ethnomusicology and branches of literary history, cultural studies and cultural anthropology. As detailed later in this chapter, Henderson did respond directly to David Buchan's influential thesis in *The Ballad and the Folk* (1972) but for the most part his writings are not so much engaged with scholarly debate. Rather, Henderson relates to the works of others in his field only when it is convenient for his own, ulterior purposes. Since the 1950s, when Henderson first started working for the School of Scottish Studies, new generations of scholars have come to address the subjects of his multifarious writings. In terms of scholarly development we might project Henderson forward into the company of Margaret Bennett (a friend and colleague of Henderson's at the School of Scottish Studies), Mary Ellen Brown, John Miles Foley, Carl Lindahl and Maureen N. McLane, who have all produced important work on balladry, folk-song, orality and literature.

Henderson's creative responses to the War, the influence of Gramsci's rendering of 'folklore' and his own analyses of contemporary literary landscapes in Scotland, all point to a long and complex relationship with the folk arts that adapts to changing circumstances and responds to new information. The culture of the 'people' – that which has some claim to having risen up out of the collective, rather than from the individual creative artist – is a conceptual cornerstone in Henderson's work. In his capacity as a folk revivalist, the deep-seated, instinctual and sometimes inexpressible values that he attributed to the folk arts had to be explained and transformed into a practicable cultural-political agenda. Attempts to implement these principles inevitably exposed the lacuna that is liable to appear between theory and practice. Henderson was steadfast and emphatic in his support for the revival and in his high regard for the cultural importance, and artistic quality, of Scotland's folk-song traditions. Nevertheless, his own theories of folk culture had to be constantly rearticulated in an effort to validate the work of the revivalists and to protect folk-song, not only from its public detractors but from the inconsistencies and ambiguities that threatened to undermine the project from within.

In his final contribution to the 'Folksong Flyting' (1964), Henderson began: 'This folksong correspondence is like Finnegan's Wake; no sooner is the stiff decently laid out for burial than someone spills a drop of the cratur on him, and – lo and behold, see how he rises!' (*TAN*, p. 139). Henderson refers to the volatility of the debates. However, his comment also alludes to the notion that any discourse on the place of folk culture in society is ultimately irresolvable.

The issues at stake are timeless in the sense that they relate to fundamental connections between concepts of art, authorship, cultural transmission and the politics of artistic production and consumption. As such, the debate is, like Finnegan, deathless: a resolution or consensus, which might be imagined as the *death* of the argument, is unattainable. The image not only invokes the great modernist expression of this framework of perpetuity: *Finnegans Wake* (1939), opening with the conclusion of its final sentence; it also speaks to the music hall comic-ballad inspiration for Joyce's novel. In this feigned comic aside, Henderson evokes perhaps the most famous instance of that long-standing entanglement between the so-called high-literary and popular folk ballad modes. In his *Elegies for the Dead in Cyrenaica* (1948), Henderson explored the relationship between the living and the dead, and the impulse to reconcile the one with the other. His writings on folk culture provide a less explicit but no less considered understanding of the significance of mortality, in this case its usefulness in explaining the 'folk process' and, indeed, the nature of any so-called 'tradition' that is thought to outlive those individual agents who sustain it. The resurrection of Finnegan is then a fitting image with which to begin an analysis of Henderson's conception of folk culture.

Folk Revival in Theory and Practice

The modern folk revival in Scotland was not a concerted or homogeneous movement; it had no governing manifesto and no definitive beginning or end. In one sense the 'revival' simply describes the popularisation of folk music in the immediate post-war era, particularly in the 1960s and, arguably, through to the present day. In another sense the revival can be interpreted as the work of a vast network of organisations, events and institutions, such as the Workers' Music Association (WMA), the Traditional Music and Song Association of Scotland (TMSA) (est. 1965), the School of Scottish Studies (University of Edinburgh, est. 1951), Topic Records (est. 1939) and the Edinburgh People's Festival (1951–4). Beneath the level of these groups and gatherings there were also a great number of individuals who sang, performed, attended folk clubs, concerts, ceilidhs and festivals, and bought records, all of whom had stakes in this expansive project. Contemporary commercial forces, technological advances in recording and broadcasting, and general developments in the cultivation of 'mass culture' distinguished the modern revival from its historical antecedents. The folklorist Neil V. Rosenberg refers to this phenomenon in its American context as 'the great boom', and it is in a similarly crowded environment of accelerating commercialisation that Henderson charted his own vision of a national folk revival.[2] As a strategist, Henderson tried to direct the efforts of this fragmented movement. He set out to define the role of 'folk' in society, to explain its relationship with literary culture, with the study of social history and with the tradition it represented. As an adherent of an on-going movement, Henderson described the revival in the terms in which he wished it to be understood. Indeed, the greater part of his corpus can be read as an endless elaboration on the cause set out in the 1952 Edinburgh People's Festival Programme: '[to restore] Scottish folksong to the ordinary people in Scotland, not merely as a bobbysoxer vogue, but deeply and integrally' (*AM*, p. xxiv).

To understand Henderson's conception of the folk revival we must also understand his notion of the 'revivalist'. The theoretical constructions that informed Henderson's practice are not exclusive to his early, propagandising articles, or to his later, academic reflections on the folk tradition. His approach is evident in contextual and interpretative notes, in his choices about which journals and magazines to publish with, and even in the conversational tone and discursive style of his prose. It is commonly recognised among folklore scholars that the ideological framework employed by a folklorist or song-collector is rarely overt. Instead, it is inferred at the level of prefaces, introductions, footnotes and editorial decisions. Henderson was a scholar, a lecturer, a public commentator, a songwriter, a poet, a translator, a fieldworker, an organiser of cultural and political events, and a social historian; and in all of these capacities he was also a folk revivalist. To describe the shape and scale of his particular model of revivalism is, therefore, not simply a matter of accounting for his academic stance, it demands an exploration of his world view and the prominence of folk culture within it. Henderson is, as Dave Harker called it, a 'mediator' through whom our understanding of 'folk' is developed.[3] The term describes the work of the folklorist well: he or she ought to aim for dispassionate arbitration but in reality it is impossible not to shape the way folk arts are interpreted if you have a role in transmitting them. This position is even more pronounced when the folklorist is openly engaged in a broader movement to 'revive' the popular tradition.

In an interview in 1973 Henderson said that, 'in many ways', the programme for the Edinburgh People's Festival of 1952 was his 'finest work of art'.[4] The festival was first established in response to the perceived elitism of the International Festival (est. 1947) and in 1952 it ran under the slogan: 'That the People's Voice May Be Heard and the Needs of the People Met'.[5] Though Henderson was perhaps only emphasising the cultural importance of the Festival, his choice of words reveals something of his conception of artistic value. His greatest artistic achievement was a programme of events: a cultural-political agenda that saw folk-song, alongside poetry, public lectures, theatre productions and art exhibitions, at once inciting and enacting a revival of the arts and the intellectual life of 'the people'. In this sense, Henderson's own mediation becomes successful art in itself. Henderson hoped to help bring about a 'genuine people's culture' where the artist would not be isolated from society but fully integrated in it. The folk tradition provided a working model for this enterprise, but it also compelled Henderson to define the terms of his 'mediation' and to reconcile it with this ultimate aim: integration. In her recent work on minstrelsy and Romantic poetry, Maureen N. McLane has drawn on Friedrich Kittler's conception of 'mediality', and Jay David Bolter and Richard Grusin's 'remediation', to explore this 'transhistorical . . . condition of existing *in media*' (added emphasis). McLane proposes that balladeers and song-collectors in the Romantic era became 'media theorists in their own right'.[6] Henderson serves as an example of this dynamic in the twentieth century, where ideas about cultural transmission, authorship and mediation are still contested, though perhaps even more explicitly, in response to new technologies like the portable tape-recorder and the extended length LP, and the advent of 'mass culture'.

Henderson was well aware of the political implications in collecting and redistributing folk material. Of his fieldwork with Calum Maclean (1915–60) in the early years of the School of Scottish Studies, he recalled: 'we rapidly came to realise that by embarking on the study of folk material we were engaged willy-nilly in a political act'.[7] However, as a 'mediator' of folk culture, Henderson was not as complacent about the political dimension of this work as this comment suggests. His realisation, that the study of folk material was itself a political act, is akin to the realisation that the folklorist is endowed with great responsibility in representing a vast and complex tradition that can never be accurately portrayed in its entirety. In the same article, Henderson refers to an aphorism accredited to Andrew Fletcher of Saltoun (1655–1716) now inscribed on the Canongate Wall of the Scottish Parliament building: '(I knew a very wise man who believed that) if a man were permitted to make all the ballads, he need not care who should make the laws of a nation'.[8] Similarly, if a folklorist were permitted to 'mediate' all of the folk material, he or she need not care who made it. The powers of the ballad maker *and* the mediating folklorist rely on the capacity of folksongs to speak with the authority of a vast and indomitable tradition. This latent authority is central to Henderson's earliest and most pronouncedly political statements on folk-song.

In 'Enemies of Folk-song' (1955) and 'The Underground of Song' (1963), Henderson describes the scale of the task the revivalists set themselves, not least, in overcoming the insidious assumption that folk-song 'all died out years ago'. Henderson apportioned some blame for this problem of perception to the faulty conceptions of folk-song promoted by past generations of collectors and scholars, and in doing so he set apart his own position and that of the modern revival. This bleak vision of the folk arts was reinforced by the notion that if it were any good 'someone would have put it on the radio'. This presumption – that artistic quality would be recognised by radio programmers – provoked Henderson to attack the BBC for their neglect of 'ethnic song' in favour of cultivating and sustaining so-called 'popular taste' (*AM*, p. 31). The central thesis of these essays is that the folk tradition represents an indomitable historical force that will always persevere 'on the lips of the people' (*AM*, p. 45). The tradition survives 'underground', out of reach of those who would corrupt and undermine it. In this context, the view of folk-song as a moribund form was, according to Henderson, not merely the result of a disengaged public but the conceit of its 'enemies'.

Henderson describes these 'enemies' as an 'élite' who, in countries with a pronouncedly stratified class structure, 'invariably have their work cut out when trying to come to terms with their own folk-culture'. In Scotland the problem is exacerbated by the fact that 'the élite are to a big extent also the elect, and consequently have a vested interest in keeping the songs of the damned well battened down under hatches'. Conflating the terms of class politics and Scotland's Calvinist inheritance (the 'elect' and the 'damned'), Henderson imagines folk-song's enemies dwelling in every sphere of cultural, social, political and spiritual influence:

> Firmly entrenched in all key positions of administration, religion and the organisation of culture, the elect deny just as long as they are able that anything so vulgar as popular culture exists . . . Almost worse, however, than the studied ignoring of popular culture has been the attempt of the elect – once the existence of folk-song and folk-art could no longer be denied – to take possession of them, at the same time bowdlerising them and emasculating them. (*AM*, pp. 45–6)

In this construction, the cultural elitist scoffing at folk-song as a base and artless form, and the commercial forces sanitising it for popular consumption, belong to the same despised 'élite'. Folk-song is sustained only through perpetual struggle with obscurity, that space outside of sanctioned culture; and the dilution or expurgation that comes with co-option. The élite, a privileged group wielding power and influence over their field, is antithetical to Henderson's thinking. The 'folk process' he promotes, that sees songs adopted or discarded according to the preferences of accumulated generations of anonymous masses, has a levelling effect, subsuming song-makers and song-carriers alike into its collective momentum. It is this quality that awards the process with the tenacity to survive despite concerted efforts to either deny its existence or take possession of it.

Henderson turns to the folklorist John Francis Campbell (1821–85) in explaining the psychological dimension of the assumption that 'folksong is dead':

> In the Highlands, as elsewhere, society is arranged in layers, like the climates of the world. The dweller on an Indian plain little dreams that there is a region of perpetual frost in the air above him; the Eskimo does not suspect the slumbering volcano under his feet; and the dwellers in the upper and lower strata of society, everywhere, know as little of each other's ways of life, as the men of the plain know of the mountaineers of the snow. (*AM*, p. 32)[9]

This vision of societal and cultural strata embellishes the class framework that Henderson had evoked with the 'élite'. However, the imagery of habitat and atmosphere suggests that the disjuncture between these 'strata' is incumbent on environmental factors. It occurs only as organically as that between the populations of different continents and climates. It is human insularity, and the constraints of the familiar on the imagination, that are to blame for the popular ignorance of living folk-song. Still, just as folk-song endures because of the adaptability of the oral tradition, it is surely able to transcend class and geography, and even pass between those who dwell in the mountains and those in plains. All that is required for these divisions to be overcome is that the respective strata encounter one another and prove themselves capable of empathy. Henderson's proposal for the revivalists seems to be that an investment in the kind of encounters that sustain the oral tradition – in 'collecting' folksongs and 'giving them back to the people' – would not only overcome the kind of divisions we have come to understand through modern economics, or natural science, but it would do so in a way that does not presume to 'take possession' of folk-song but be possessed by it (*AM*, p. 46). A considered intervention simply provides these songs with further opportunity for proliferation on the 'carrying stream', transcending autochthony and social hierarchy. The folk revivalist is conceived as another vessel for the tradition, providing 'mediation' without contamination.

In these early works, Henderson debunked received notions of folk-song and, in doing so, inched towards a working definition of the mode. In response to the assumption that folk is archaic, he insisted on its prevalence in contemporary society, attested by the '3,000 odd records made from living singers in the archives of the School of Scottish Studies' (*AM*, p. 48). Another of these uncritical assumptions states that if a song has an identifiable author it cannot qualify as a 'folksong'. Henderson describes 'The Hairst o' Rettie', a popular corn-kister with a known author, and a long publishing and broadcast history – in short, all of the hallmarks of what he imagines his 'enemies' regard as a 'clear case of "contamination"' (*AM*, pp. 49–50). Though this song could not technically be attributed to 'Anon.', and despite the fact that it had been subject to broadsheet publication and radio broadcasts, in Henderson's view it remains a folksong 'because the people have taken it, possessed themselves of it, gloried in it, recreated it, loved it. That is the only test worth a docken' (*AM*, p. 50).

Folk-song therefore inhabits a contradictory space: it is at once alive on the 'lips of the people' and driven 'underground' by its enemies. Though it is indomitable, it must hide in plain sight. The 'underground' is not a euphemism for a vigorous counter-culture; it is a description of the diminished territory of the oral culture of 'the people'. There is a stasis that comes from the balance between the indefatigable fact of folk culture, and the magnitude and sophistication of those forces that Henderson sees as its enemies. Folk-song is the cultural expression of a political potential – a genuinely popular, indigenous movement grown and sustained among the collective. It is also a stark reminder of the limited space allowed for communal self-expression in both the cultural and political spheres. Its contestability confirms that 'folk-song is an elusive thing, and [that] captivity is hateful to it' (*AM*, p. 46). Folksongs are awarded agency despite their reliance on the people who create and sustain them. Looking back on the achievements of the modern revival in 1980, particularly in aiding the passage of folk material from the 'tradition-bearers' to a broader segment of the Scottish public, Henderson reflected on this interface between folk-song and the people:

> When I say they [the songs] have moved from the traditional singers, I do not mean of course that these singers have in any sense lost them, or relinquished their hold on them, for folksong is one of those agreeable zones of human experience in which it is possible to give all, and retain more – hence the folly of attaching to it any form of copyright symbol.[10]

Concepts of intellectual or creative property have no jurisdiction over folk culture because its defining characteristics are antithetical to notions of private property. Henderson concluded: 'the revival will sink or swim by its capacity to throw up new and constantly fresh thinkers and writers who will be open and free to take and adapt anything. The health of the whole set-up depends on the maximum freedom of movement'.[11] The potential success of the revival was therefore entirely dependent on revivalists staying faithful to the principles of the 'folk process', even in their efforts to promote it.

According to Henderson's framework, individual folksongs always evoke a sense of the vast and complex oral tradition on which they depend. In line with Fletcher of Saltoun's dictum, the revivalists recognised the significance of their own work collating and publishing folksongs. The *Rebels' Ceilidh Song Book*, produced by the Bo'ness Rebels' Literary Society throughout the 1950s and 1960s, opens with a preface by William Kellock describing the types of songs in the collection:

> songs of the Popular Hero . . . of the drama of resistance against impossible odds, Songs of Land-hungry Scots and Alien land-owners, Songs of revulsion against the hypocrites and rogues in our midst, Songs for the Glasgow Irish – both Orange and Green –, Songs of World War II, Songs echoing the heart-cry of farm and city workers for better conditions, Songs of joy, of sorrow, of Scotland's pride . . . Sangs o' the Stane that's awa, and Songs on the popular reaction to the fact that London Officialdom just can't count . . . Songs of defiance and rebellion, of heilans and Lallans all with a beauty of their own. Through it all runs the magic of the Gaeltacht.[12]

Though Kellock's appeal is to 'all the varieties of Scottish Rebels', there is an implied unity to these songs that relies on the idea that they are consistent with the 'song tradition' that precedes them. Some songs are attributed to their writers while others are transcribed from individual singers' versions. Some are left unattributed, thereby adding depth to the portrayal of a vast anonymous radical tradition – to the eponymous 'rebels'. The collection makes it clear that the 'rebels' of previous generations have inheritors in contemporary Scotland. McLane describes seven types of poetic authority. Second in her list is 'the authority of anonymity', and it is this prerogative that is often pursued by compilers of protest songs and political folksongs in the modern revival.[13]

Melodies and lyrics are manipulated and reoriented to reconcile modern political agendas with the historical validity of the 'folk' aesthetic. The humour in the collection is deployed to ridicule political enemies and to underline the absurdity of those positions opposed by the implied 'rebel' consensus. 'Coronation Coronach' by Thurso Berwick envisages a republican Scotland to the tune of the unionist song 'The Sash': 'Nae Liz will ever dae, / We'll mak oor land republican / In a Scottish breakaway'. The 'White Cockade', a romantic song of the Jacobite cause, has its tune recast in a disillusioned political satire, 'The Labour Provost', whose eponymous councillor sings: 'the principles of socialism are a' very well / Bit ye mustnae forget tae look after yersel'.[14] *Sangs o' the Stane* (1952) gathered some of the songs and folk-poems of the Scottish republican cause and featured sardonic responses to the 'reiving' of the Stone of Scone in 1950 and the 1953 coronation of Elizabeth II (despite there never having been an Elizabeth I of Scotland).[15]

The LP *Ding Dong Dollar: Anti-Polaris and Scottish Republican Songs* (Folkways 1962) combined the popular discontent directed at the docking of American *Polaris* nuclear submarines at Holy Loch with the cause of the independence movement. The songs present different levels of political discourse, from the very localised, through the national, to the international. We can infer, from the variety of the album, that Scotland suffers from a lack of political representation that, combined with the greed and corruption of officials at all levels, allows unpopular policies like the docking of American nuclear submarines to go ahead without a popular mandate.[16] The liner notes, which Neat has ascribed to Henderson, read like a manifesto on behalf of the folk poets whose work is presented.[17] The songs and their political contexts are set out and a long tradition of Scottish satire is outlined, culminating in the contemporary 'metropolitan', 'folk-rebel corpus'. In the notes for both the *Rebels' Ceilidh Song Book* and *Ding Dong Dollar*, a peculiar vein of satire able to puncture the pretentions and hypocrisy of those who exercise power is traced through Scottish literary and folk-song traditions. Kinnock states that humour is the 'only bloodless weapon against Authority', while *Ding Dong Dollar* explores the early Celtic bard's *aoir* (satire) as a 'political corrective'; the fifteenth and sixteenth-century literary practice of 'flyting'; and the '"sub-literary" tradition of partisan and often scurrilous satirical verse and song'. The 'literary' and 'sub-literary' traditions are said to have met in the work of

Burns and Hugh MacDiarmid, and the contemporary 'line of advance' that emanates from these figures' legacies is identified as the 'Scottish folk-song renaissance'. The songs of the people represent an unrefined, unreconstructed democratic impulse that goes unfulfilled in the realpolitik.

Henderson's vision of folk culture found its harshest critic in MacDiarmid. In Gramsci it found its political-philosophical grounding and its most troubling contradictions. It was tested in practice through the cultural strategies of the folk revival. Perhaps because of these wranglings, Henderson had enough confidence in his idea of folk culture to embrace it as a forum for his politics. To produce songs and attach them to a radical 'underground' tradition is to publicly assume the authority of this tradition. Despite his assertions on the capacity of folk-song to constantly adapt to changing circumstances (*AM*, pp. 19–20), it is not the inherent flux in the tradition that is emphasised in a record like *Ding Dong Dollar*; it is a sense of continuity. Folk culture survives because of its adaptability, but there must be a point at which the transformations that are required go so far as to jeopardise the legitimacy of a term such as 'tradition'. The songs in these collections are detached from their original contexts and planted in the historical continuum of this amorphous 'radical' agenda. As a result, specific political claims are rendered homologous with one another. They become generic representations of a transhistorical 'rebel' position. The revivalists' relationship with conceptions of 'tradition' and 'history' is, therefore, complicated. For these terms to be meaningful, they need to be reconciled with one another: the 'rebel' song needs to be timeless in that it belongs to this enduring tradition, yet it must also be tied fast to the particular historical context that demanded its inception.

In a newspaper article titled 'The Voice of the People' (*Sunday Mail* 1989), Henderson wrote of artists on the frontier, where the 'lines between tradition and revival, and between "art" and "folk", become steadily more blurred'. To explain the prevalence of this process in Scotland's cultural history he draws from Thomas Crawford: 'Each resurgence of the creative spirit in Scotland since 1707 has been associated with renewed interest in popular culture, and with something of a folk revival: each has felt the need to tap the popular tradition, which is, perhaps, the most abidingly *national* part of our culture' (*AM*, pp. 3–4). Crawford suggests that the modern revival was inevitable: the folk tradition is as ineluctable as the nation. Since the 1707 Union of the Parliaments, these re-engagements with the 'popular tradition' are the result of an historical determinism borne out of the absence of political autonomy. The same argument was deployed to explain the 'literary revival' of the 1980s and 1990s. At that time Christopher Whyte argued: 'in the absence of elected political authority, the task of representing the nation has been repeatedly devolved to its writers'.[18] The notion borders with Shelley's grand claim, that 'Poets are the unacknowledged legislators of the world'; and reprises Fletcher of Saltoun's dictum: 'if a man were permitted to make all the ballads, he need not care who should make the laws of a nation'. The dominant forms of cultural expression in a given historical period are, according to this view, interchangeable, or at least commensurable, with the political or legal structures of society. The folk tradition is, perhaps, exactly as ineluctable as the nation but, like the nation, it is perpetually lost and forgotten, forever consigned to the past. Henderson's conclusion leaves these implications unexplored. It is difficult to imagine how parts of 'our culture' might be measured in terms of how '*national*' they are, but a relation to the 'popular' (as distinct from the esoteric), is surely the minimum required. A degree of collaboration, of popular commitment to the idea of the 'nation' is, according to Benedict Anderson's famous thesis, perhaps all that constitutes the 'nation'.[19] It stands that the 'folk-song tradition' may be willed into existence just like the 'imagined community' of the nation. In his use of Crawford, Henderson – perhaps inadvertently – exposes the contestability of his model for national folk revivalism.

The national framework is not the only aspect of Henderson's revivalism that appears inconsistent with his conception of folk culture. Though he identified a kind of immortality in folk-song through focusing on the resilience of the 'process', this degree of abstraction served to undermine the practice of revivalism. The 'collecting' and the 'giving back' can be dismissed as insignificant acts in the greater context of the folk tradition, which is indifferent to the work of the individual, and is always, and by definition, 'underground' and evasive. The folk tradition extends, historically, back to the beginnings of human language, and geographically, all over the populated world. It is both embattled and perennial. In his early defensive tracts Henderson defined 'folk-song' as that which is suppressed by the 'elect' who 'deny just so long as they are able that anything so vulgar as *popular culture* exists' (emphasis added) (*AM*, p. 46). Elsewhere, he asserted that folk-song had survived among the industrialised urban working class just as it had in the rural settings with which it is ordinarily associated (*AM*, pp. 21–2). In the Edinburgh People's Festival, folk culture and working-class culture were elided in the promotion of a movement 'toward a people's culture'.[20] The conflation of these terms is common in Henderson's work. The national framework, along with ideas of 'popular culture', 'working-class culture' and 'the people's culture', provides ways of approaching folk culture that lie somewhere between the transience of a song living through its performance in any given moment, and the broad conception of an indomitable 'folk tradition' that is not defined by its constituent songs or singers but by the adaptability afforded by its oral transmission. In this way, Henderson's reflections on the radical tradition in Scottish folk-song provide a perspective that is more substantial than that which can be gleaned from following an isolated song passing from one individual to another. At the same time, his approach is not as intractable as one that centres on the transhistorical reach of the 'folk process' and its extension beyond any conceivable critical boundaries. 'Folk' is national, it belongs to a class and to a political cause, and it is 'popular' in that it relates to the common people, rather than the 'elite', but these categorisations are at best unstable and at worst opportunistic.

Henderson's 'folk' becomes functional; it is a culture for which a revival can be staged. The idea of the 'underground' of song might mitigate these misleading and somewhat limiting associations with a 'national' culture or a 'class' culture by defining 'folk' by its opposition to hegemonic forces. However, the terms on which Henderson worked as a strategist for the revival were ultimately irreconcilable with the conclusions he was to come to in his work as a folklorist. By setting the agenda of the theorist of folk-song next to that of the revivalist, we can see the tension that arises between the model of the 'folk process' as anti-political and transcendent, and the attempt to articulate a popular politics based on this model. This tension between theory and practice is tempered to some degree by Henderson's reflexivity. His writings are distinguished by their use of anecdotes, 'personal reminiscences' (as he often refers to them) and autobiographical fragments. Henderson's signature prose style might be attributed to the fact that he was anxious about the subjectivity of his experience and, therefore, about the legitimacy of his views. It might simply be a reflection of his methodology: his personal experiences are as good a foundation as any on which to build broader theoretical structures.

Writing in 1993, Rosenberg reflected on the modern folk revivals of the mid-twentieth century, identifying the need for 'revival ethnography', and for sensitivity to the complexities of these kinds of movements: the relationship between 'preservation' and 'promotion', the shifting criteria of 'authenticity', the agency of the revivalists and the 'discovered' performers.[21] In short, Rosenberg wanted to subject the most recent series of revivals to the kind of scrutiny generally applied by folklorists and ethnomusicologists to other historical periods of popular engagement with the folk arts. Though Henderson was not so forthright, his later writings demonstrate the care he took not to overstate his case or jeopardise his conclusions with sweeping claims. In his contribution to *Scotland: A Concise Cultural History* (1993), Henderson wrote of 'The Oral Tradition'. Rather than emphasising its indomitable nature and its resilience in the face of an 'elite' who would like to see it destroyed, Henderson explored the territory of the oral tradition in great detail. He offered precise accounts of the movement of ballads, bawdy songs and folk tales among Gaelic speaking communities, the travelling people of the north-east and the agricultural labourers of the Lowlands.[22] Plotting these materials wherever they arise, in print culture and in field recordings, Henderson accounts for the specifics in a song's relationship with the oral tradition and thereby invokes the immense intricacies of the tradition as a whole. By providing parameters within which his ideas could be substantiated, Henderson tried to reconcile his more abstract conceptions of folk culture with their practical application through the revival. His insistence on the 'living' tradition implied that only the passage of time and the lives of countless 'tradition-bearers' could decide the fate of any given song. Though this approach emphasises the limitations of the individual observer, it champions the work of the folklorist as seeking out the mechanics of the oral tradition and revealing small working parts of the inconceivable whole.

The Work of the Folklorist

Henderson collected songs and put them into circulation as part of a 'definite cultural strategy' (*TAN*, pp. 158–9) and having observed the relative success of this aspect of his revivalism, his understanding of the processes by which folk material is disseminated was tested in real terms. In his later work, Henderson absorbed the revivalism of the recent past into the field of folklore studies and thereby afforded himself and his peers a place in the tradition of collectors and folklore scholars, alongside figures like David Herd and Gavin Greig. In 'The Voice of the People' (1989), which details the explosion of creative investment in folk culture associated with the modern revival, Henderson begins by plotting the history of folk revivalism through the publication of landmark song collections. He notes that through Herd's work the eighteenth century witnessed 'an exceedingly lively and creative popular culture, which crossed class boundaries, and which displayed a muscular capacity for dealing poetically with the most diverse human moods and conditions'. This 'golden age of Scottish culture' during the years up to and including Burns' lifetime was, according to Henderson's historical trajectory, followed by a period of relative stagnation in the nineteenth century. The Kirk suppressed the vital energies of folk culture and Britain's 'empire-building' fostered an environment whereby those songs that were published were refined, 'cleaned-up' versions, often 'mawkishly sentimental and . . . braggadocio-patriotic'. Henderson suggested that it was not until the twentieth century that the enormity of the 'underground culture' of folk-song became apparent, with the work of Gavin Greig and the Revd James Duncan in Aberdeenshire (*AM*, p. 1). The next significant juncture in this history is Alan Lomax's arrival in Britain in 1950, an event that Henderson later identified as the inception of the modern folk revival in Scotland.[23] This potted history of revivalism renders the modern movement as, on one level, simply the most recent revolution in favour of an often-maligned cultural form. Indeed, Henderson had previously written that 'the [folk] tradition as it exists today is in large part the heritage of many similar revivals in the past' (*AM*, p. 74). This conception of a series of revivals and remissions appears frequently in his writings, and provides a framework through which the folklorist can retrospectively interpret his achievements as a revivalist, as part of an historical continuum between folk culture and the popular tradition.

The modern Scottish revival faced similar obstacles to those encountered by its antecedents. In Henderson's view, there were always 'enemies'. Writing in 1965, he charged the singer and composer Marjory Kennedy Fraser

(1857–1930) with 'the distortion of an entire folk-tradition' and cast her as an embodiment of those forces that conspire to misrepresent the folk tradition through the production of kitsch (*AM*, pp. 8–9). The BBC of the 1930s, which employed 'art-singers' to 'slum it' in folk-song performances, and the young singers on the contemporary folk circuit who 'aped Yanks', were seen as similarly corruptive influences in the modern era (*TAN*, p. 134). Henderson recognised the threat of the 'fatty degeneration' of commercialism and agreed with Maurice Fleming, a Perthshire collector, that the folk clubs had shown a regrettable preference for the 'Tin Pan Alley standards of Television Light Entertainment' (*AM*, p. 15). Rather than claiming that the cultural threats of the mid and late twentieth century were unprecedented in their pervasiveness and ingenuity, Henderson acknowledged that folk-song is in constant dialogue with the cultural contexts in which it seeks a space. This was as true for advocates of folk culture in the 1960s as it was for those of the 1790s.

Revivalists seem to have employed common creative practices, as well as having faced common 'enemies'. When Henderson writes of Burns and Scott's work 'improving' the material they collected, for example, the parallels with his own position are very clear. Writing at the height of the modern folk revival, in 1965, Henderson delineated successful attempts to 'improve' songs as those that, like the majority of the Burns' efforts, demonstrate an ability to 'counterfeit the anonymous folk voice' (*AM*, p. 46). Burns' version of 'MacPherson's Rant', titled 'MacPherson's Farewell', provides Henderson with an exception that diverges from traditional forms to such a degree that it belies its individual author. Where the 'old Rant' transcends the time and place to which it belongs, speaking 'proudly with a universal tongue for the outlaws and dispossessed of the world'; by exaggerating the sentiment of the song, Burns' rendering appears as mere 'operatic braggadocio' (*AM*, p. 48). In Henderson's estimation, if the fingerprints of the 'improver' are evident, they have failed to create a work commensurate with the folk tradition. The 'individual author' has to reproduce the effects of the 'communal reshaping' of oral transmission if their works are ever to be collected as 'real folk-songs' in the future (*AM*, pp. 47–8).

According to Henderson's historical gloss, from the middle of the eighteenth century, 'once the religious fanaticism that had stultified so much of Scottish life' had subsided, intellectuals were 'liberated from the theocratic tyranny, and free to investigate our folk culture, which had been driven underground' (*AM*, p. 44).[24] Henderson envisaged an equivalent break with the ideological precepts of the recent past, as a precursor to his modern revival:

> To a certain extent the revival is an aspect of anti-fascism, a rejection of what was already being planned for Europe – a kind of 'high heid yin's paradise' – the revival is 'a man's a man for a' that' and no wonder therefore that Scotland played a part in it. There is this wonderful democratic tradition. You could say that Burns was the Ewan MacColl of the 18th century.[25]

The folk revival is portrayed as a movement in opposition to projected historical trajectories. While it breaks with the plans of Europe's 'high heid yins', it relies on an inherited 'democratic' folk tradition. Henderson's ambitions for the contemporary revival extended to a full reconciliation between the artist and society through the cultivation of a 'genuine people's culture'. This was to be achieved by drawing folk culture from the margins to the centre and extending its own processes to apply to the whole cultural sphere. By recognising that a capacity for democratic radicalism is characteristic of Scotland's folk tradition, Henderson legitimises his aims, but he also inadvertently concedes that folk culture has only ever been able to provide a voice in perpetual opposition to dominant ideologies. Again, in his efforts to delineate the modern revival, Henderson only reinforces common perceptions of folk culture as a passive force that inhabits the same social and political territory it has for hundreds of years. While its unbounded, chaotic and disparate character might make it anathema to fascism, it is hardly the basis for anything more substantial than resistance.

Where the printing press and the publishing industry had contributed to the 'liberation' of Scotland's intellectuals in the eighteenth century, and to the popularisation of folk culture that followed it, the arrival of Lomax and his tape recorder in 1950 had a comparable effect upon the modern revival.[26] Song-collectors could demonstrate that their subject was indeed a 'living tradition', as material was 'discovered' among the people, alive in inherited forms, not dredged from library archives or dusty ballad collections. The portable tape recorder allowed folklorists to record songs on site and in the context of the lives of their 'carriers' and 'tradition-bearers'. Song-collectors working in print had had almost total control over the presentation of 'discovered' material and became in effect folklorists-as-editors. Those wielding tape recorders captured the songs as they were performed and this meant that the potential for distortion or amendment in the 'mediation' of the folklorist was drastically diminished. From Henderson's perspective the relationship between a song and the singer who sustains it became as important as the song-version itself. He conceived of the role of the collector as a 'deeply humanistic one', and as such, the social, geographical, historical and, above all, personal contexts of song were explored through conversation in the recording sessions.[27]

In one instance, interviewing a Stirlingshire horseman, Jock Ainslie, Henderson gently steers the conversation from Ainslie's first hearing of a particular song towards his personal experiences as a ploughman in the Stirlingshire area: the impromptu ceilidhs and singing sessions, the demographic of the work force on the farms, the living conditions and even the secret society of 'The Horseman's Word', which was once active all over Scotland.[28] Henderson's questions and comments ensure that the folklorist's role as a 'mediator' is not lost. His presence means that the recording sessions can be approached as dialogues, conversations whereby folklore is shared with an individual, as well as with the reel-to-reel recorder. Henderson's reflexive practice is exemplified by the fact that he also appears as a 'contributor' (rather than as a 'reporter') in various recordings for the School's archives. In some he is even listed as both the 'reporter' and the 'contributor'. Henderson's belief in the primacy of the 'folk process', and its dependence on the personal narratives of those who sustain it, was founded in part on the methodological developments that arose from the use of the portable tape-recorder.

The first traditional singer to record his entire repertoire with the School was Willie Matheson, a retired farm servant who had collected songs since childhood. An itinerant labourer, Matheson kept a great kist of songs collected from fellow ploughmen or else tracked down through correspondence. Matheson provided Henderson with a living example of the 'underground' aspect: as a child he had concealed his passion for song from his father and the dominie for fear of a 'thrashing' (*AM*, p. 32). Matheson and his kist, therefore, represented an unofficial model of collection functioning within the folk process.[29] It was an ever-growing personal archive tied closely to the life of its compiler: an autobiography in song. The project to digitise the archives of the School of Scottish Studies, BBC Scotland and the National Trust for Scotland's Canna Collection, has been titled *Tobar an Dualchais* or 'Kist o Riches'.[30] The 'kist', the receptacle for a personal folklore collection with Matheson, becomes an image for the public folklore inheritance as catalogued by these bodies. It is a treasure chest but also a sarcophagus, and both of these renderings – a vessel for treasure or a tomb – capture something of the contradiction of folk collection, whilst falling short of the living dynamic of the process that Henderson and his colleagues were so eager to emphasise. While this contemporary project is undoubtedly faithful to the legacy of collectors like Henderson in that it makes recordings publicly accessible, the act of preservation still relies on an image of something buried, something belonging to the past that must be revived. Again, an insistence on the 'living' nature of a cultural tradition is contingent on the revival, or exhumation, of that tradition.

In 1950 Lomax set out his view on the position of the folklorist in society: 'we have become . . . the champions of the ordinary people of the world who aren't backed up by printing presses, radio chains and B29's. We believe in the oral tradition, we believe in the small cultural situation [. . .] we have to work [on] behalf of the folk, the people'.[31] Adapting Bronisław Malinowski's assertion that 'the role of the ethnologist is that of the advocate of primitive man', Lomax surmised that 'the role of the folklorists [sic] is that of the advocate of the folk'.[32] Like Henderson, Lomax recognised that folklore can be understood as 'the voice of the people': the communal self-expression of those who cannot rely on official discourse. As such, folklorists must engage in the kind of advocacy that Lomax wants and with the kind of 'deeply humanistic' role that Henderson imagines, if they are to represent their material faithfully. By the late seventies, Lomax was making his 'Appeal for Cultural Equity', an ambitious vision which had been formulated out of a long career as a folklorist, cataloguing and theorising upon traditions that seemed to struggle for survival in the face of hostile hegemonic cultural forces. He regrets that 'cultural variety lies under threat of extinction' due to the centralisation of culture and the dominance of those 'standardised, mass-produced and cheapened cultures' that are so pervasive.[33] Like Henderson, Lomax rejects the 'false Darwinism' that sees subaltern cultures consigned to an early death. In fact, Lomax celebrated cultural difference by dismissing the national paradigm for music-culture in favour of a more regionalist approach.[34] He envisaged the commitment to 'cultural equity' as a natural extension of the pursuit of political, social and economic justice. While these principles are organised in service of a broader argument about the validity of local cultures, their rootedness in folk culture and in the work of the revivalist is clear. Ailie Munro draws from the same cultural-political line for the title of her history of the modern Scottish folk revival, *The Democratic Muse*. It opens with a passage from Tom Leonard's *Radical Renfrew*:

> Once you accept that the model of literature is based on universal equality of human existence, past and present, then you can travel in literature, as a writer or a reader, wherever you like . . . No caste has the right to possess, or even imagine it has the right to possess, bills of exchange on the dialogue between one human being and another. And such a dialogue is all that literature is.

The 'truly democratic, all-embracing approach to the arts' that Munro finds in Leonard is built on the same 'cultural equity' proposed by Lomax.[35] According to this model, no form of cultural expression should be privileged over any other. Just as a classless society is the political aim, its cultural counterpart will not allow the elevation of any form of artistic self-expression over any other. For Henderson, Munro and Lomax, this is an important precept in the study of folklore as well as the intended outcome of such study. When Henderson spoke of Scotland's 'wonderful democratic tradition' reviving itself in opposition to the planned fascist Europe (the 'high heid yin's paradise'), he also set out a larger political context in which folk culture could serve as a symbol of democracy.[36] The corruptive threat of modern commercialism undoubtedly contributed to this emphasis on the validity of all cultural modes no matter how localised or provincial, but it is the intrinsic aspect of human dialogue – the moment of communication and cultural transmission – that is its foundation.

Henderson admired those in his field who became utterly absorbed in the object of their study. He celebrated the career of his former colleague at the School of Scottish Studies, Calum Maclean, by insisting that his temperament would not have been suited to the 'mechanistic structuralist analysis of folk literature' that took hold after his death (*AM*, p. 206). Maclean, wrote

Henderson, would have been in agreement with A. N. Whitehead's dictum: 'The self-confidence of learned people is the comic tragedy of civilisation'. For Maclean 'any trace of condescension towards the "folk" was anathema to him, and he took pride in sharing the beliefs and mental attitudes – and even maybe, at times, some of the wilful prejudices – of the ordinary folk among whom he worked' (*AM*, p. 203). Henderson was confident that this approach was not only commensurate with the nature of the artefacts they were collecting, it also allowed for insights that would otherwise be impossible. In the early 1980s, for example, Henderson tried to explain the prominence of women's resistance during the Highland Clearances. Accepted explanations, which relied on notions of expediency – women were less likely to be assaulted – were not sufficient, and Henderson felt that the folklorist was better placed than the historian to access the deeper running societal structures in these communities (*AM*, pp. 247–56). The 'hidden "matriarchal" women's world' was a 'relic from the mental world of the shattered tribal system' and Henderson provided evidence for this from sources as diverse as Hector Boece, G. K. Chesterton and the Highland folk singer, Mary MacPherson (or *Màiri Mhór nan Oran*, 'Big Mary of the Songs') (*AM*, pp. 252–5).

In his introductory essay to Gramsci's *Prison Letters*, Henderson points to both Bruce Chatwin, author of *The Songlines* (1987) and Joseph Gould, the homeless bohemian of New York City who claimed to be writing *An Oral History of Our Time* throughout the 1940s, as figures who reflect something of the Sardinian philosopher's interest in 'all that concerns people' (*PL*, pp. 12–13, 15–16). Chatwin's book, which is part fact, part fiction, records his conversations with Australian Aborigines and the song traditions they use to map the landscape and describe their personal heritage. Gould, informally known as 'Professor Seagull', did not produce his great work, but he did broach the idea of a vast subaltern history of the people, not of leaders but of 'the shirt-sleeved multitude – what they had to say about their jobs, love affairs, vittles, sprees, scrapes, and sorrows' (*PL*, p. 12).[37] Chatwin's relationship with the Australian Aborigines, Gould's with New Yorkers and Henderson's with the 'tradition-bearers' he recorded, can be compared to the anthropologist's 'participant observation'; though they are less deliberate and go further, dispelling with the critical distance that is retained in this phrase. The depth of their involvement means that they assume an unstable critical position whereby analyses are made mutable, even in the moment they are expressed.

This problem has been vital in the modern era of Anthropology, where specialists of all corners of the field must negotiate with the provisional quality of ethnographic knowledge, which is always in the process of becoming and is never absolute or totalising. In *Time and the Other* (1983), for example, Johannes Fabian insisted that the anthropologist must pursue a radical formulation of humankind's universal contemporaneity, rejecting those interpretative frameworks that keep the subject (the scholar and his or her theories) and the object (the 'Other') temporally distant.[38] James Clifford and George E. Marcus also addressed related issues in their influential volume, *Writing Culture* (1986). Here, Clifford, Marcus and the other contributors examine the 'poetics and politics of ethnography' and seek to redress the literary dimension of ethnographic research. They recognise that though the textual agency of the ethnographer is liable to undermine the scientific value of his or her findings, if it is acknowledged and assimilated into their methodology, it can allow for more penetrative and responsible scholarship. Clifford describes the inherent partiality of ethnographic truth and explains why it ought to be embraced in the post-colonial twentieth century, proclaiming that 'there is no longer any place of over-view . . . from which to map human ways of life . . . one cannot occupy, unambiguously, a bounded cultural world from which to journey out and analyse other cultures'.[39] Clifford developed these ideas further in *The Predicament of Culture* (1988), in which he describes his 'topic' (the book's subtitle is 'Twentieth-Century Ethnography, Literature, and Art') as 'a pervasive condition of off-centeredness in a world of distinct meaning systems, a state of being in culture while looking at culture, a form of personal and collective self-fashioning'.[40] Clifford expands his conception of ethnography to include the work of people like Henderson, Chatwin and Gould, and to artists, scholars and social scientists of all kinds. In this framework the fundamental difficulty in trying to reconcile the impressions of the individual with the idea that a collective can be accurately represented in writing, or in any other medium, is brought to the fore.[41] In *The Songlines*, Chatwin blurs fact and fiction so that the cultures described are always refracted through the questioning mind of the reader. Gould's *An Oral History of Our Time* never transpired, nor did any hard evidence of his efforts to compile the work in earnest. However, in both cases, the writer, or observer, stands at the centre and destabilises their study by dealing openly with the fact of their own agency. Henderson's admiration for these figures was in response to their reflexive practice and their willingness to assimilate with the landscapes and communities they hoped to understand.

Henderson wrote of folksongs in context, as materials shared and maintained on the 'carrying stream' of the oral tradition, which is, in turn, an accumulation of millions of these moments of transmission. He insisted that 'folk-song has, as its natural habitat, almost every imaginable set-up of human loneliness or togetherness *except* the concert-hall – or, indeed, the regular planned entertainment'. When a friend suggested that 'the only justification of a public ceilidh was the private ceilidh (or ceilidhs) which it spawned', he was reminded of Auden: 'Private faces in public places / Are wiser and nicer / Than public faces in private places' (*AM*, p. 10).[42] It is this personal dynamic – or in Leonard's construction, this 'dialogue' – that is of particular importance in the 'folk process'. Ceilidhs provide a public forum for the private relationship that a singer has with their songs. Field recordings capture this tradition in motion and in this sense they are both synchronic and diachronic representations of the 'folk process'. A recording arrests the tradition and isolates a moment within it but it is also a representation of the countless transitions and adaptations that are accreted in and embodied by any individual performance. A recorded song version therefore presupposes the potential for its own descendent versions. Introducing a selection of ballad recordings from the School of Scottish Studies archives Henderson writes:

> One cannot forget . . . when one listens to the singers on these discs, that their art is in some sense the culmination of the reshaping and re-singing which has gone on over the centuries by countless singer ancestors: a whole hierarchy of shades, unknown and now unknowable, who in their time 'bore the gree' ['won through', or 'were victorious']. (*AM*, p. 429)

Though he insisted that the concert hall was not the 'natural habitat' of folk-song and that its preferred climate was more intimate, Henderson was confident that the folk-song tradition could absorb non-traditional, non-oral mediums, and even assimilate more commercial modes of transmission with what Lomax termed the 'small cultural situation'. In an early article titled 'Rock and Reel', Henderson states:

> Almost invariably the same singers [those who have inherited their songs from family members] have 'collected' folk-songs from the wireless and gramophone records too, but the versions taken from these sources begin to get modified and transformed in exactly the same way as many of the old broadsheet ballads did which entered folk currency from printed copies hawked at fairs or feeing markets. (*AM*, p. 20)

He goes on to stress that the broadsheet did not jeopardise folk-song, it simply introduced a 'less assimilable strain' to the process, leaving 'gobbets of material which might take decades and even centuries to dissolve'. Even radio and TV are identified as 'fluent media' more flexible than the cold black text of the broadsheet, that might become powerful allies of oral culture (*AM*, p. 22). Indeed, Ewan MacColl, Charles Parker and Peggy Seeger's 'Radio Ballads' and the films Henderson went on to make with Timothy Neat can be understood as attempts to put this alliance into practice.[43]

Forms of Folk Scholarship

In a series of articles written for *Scottish Studies* – the periodical of the School of Scottish Studies – in the 1960s, Henderson traced song fragments and song types through the expansive networks of the anonymous folk tradition. Beginning with recently discovered threads, Henderson tracked songs back as far as he was able, even to their composition. He searched for related song-versions from distant regions and from distant generations, all the while gesturing towards the vastness of the tradition by documenting in detail the sporadic and often scant evidence on which the folklorist must rely. In 'Folk-song from a Tile' (1961) he describes the discovery of an old clay culvert tile with the verse of a song etched on its surface. His subsequent search for information about the song also involves research on the material history of the tile itself. This song fragment, from 'The Bonny Green Tree', leads Henderson to his conclusion: that this song had many variants still in existence and that it had therefore 'developed along more than one line' in its history (*AM*, p. 108).

In 'An Aberdeen "White Paternoster"' (1962) Henderson follows the trail of a children's rhyme collected from Jeannie Robertson in 1957. The song, which bears a strong resemblance to one collected in Cornwall, and to skipping-songs found in Edinburgh and London, is a direct descendant of the medieval 'White Paternoster', to which Chaucer refers in 'The Miller's Tale' (*AM*, p. 112).[44] Besides this historical reach, Henderson also acknowledges that the 'White Paternoster' is a 'widely diffused international charm', with versions in French, Provençal, German, Spanish, various Italian dialects and Irish Gaelic (*AM*, p. 113). In all of the incarnations that Henderson lists, the song's speaker describes the angels who, in the sleep of death, will carry their soul to heaven. Henderson concludes:

> this elemental folk-poetry is more than a 'cry in the street' – it is a joyful assertion of youth and life which names the bogey and (with the vigorous thwack of the rope on the pavement) jumps over him, and lays him. The laughter of Norman Douglas's school children [Douglas had included a version in his *London Street Games* (1916)] is like the Mexican *fiesta* of the dead; it is the exultation of a momentary triumph over the 'auld enemy'. (*AM*, p. 114)

Though he recognises the historical ubiquity of the 'paternoster' throughout Christendom, Henderson dedicates the closing lines of his brief study to an interpretation in context, drawn from the school playground of the early twentieth century. He recognises hundreds of years of folklore accretion in the skipping songs of contemporary Edinburgh school children, and brings the weight of the folk process, complete with medieval prayers on death and ascent to heaven, into the modern urban landscape, finally reaffirming the life that is sustained in these old oral artefacts.

In 'A Colliery Disaster Ballad' (1962) Henderson takes the 'rough-hewn ballad stanzas' of 'Starlaw Disaster', collected from a Midlothian miner, as a document of social-historical relevance. He reproduces contemporary articles from *The Scotsman* on the details of the disaster – a fire in a shale pit near Bathgate, 9 April 1870 – and notes the historical accuracy of the song's lyrics. Henderson describes it as a chronicle as well as an elegy. He considers its composition: the choice of tune, a variation on 'The Bonny Boy is Young But He's Growing', is identified as a tribute to the youngest fatality who was only seventeen, and the song-maker is imagined as a 'miner-balladeer' writing soon after the disaster itself (*AM*, p. 122). Henderson draws from A. L. Lloyd's *Come All Ye Bold Miners* (1952) to picture the scene:

> It goes to the heart, the thought of the pitman stirred by the drama of some strike or disaster, who sits by candle-light with a blunt pen in his fist . . . and who wrestles by scratch and score with his rough, stubborn muse, till day dawns and the pit buzzer blows, and another ballad has come bawling or timorous into the world. (Ibid.)

Though the vastness of the tradition is ever-present in these articles, manifested in the fact that the precise history of a song is essentially unknowable, Henderson demonstrates a sensitive approach to the lives of folksongs, emphasising their social-historical relevance and tying them imaginatively to individual 'tradition-bearers' wherever possible.[45]

Henderson also applied his methods for tracing folk-song fragments to the interpretation of literature. His essay 'The Laverock i' the Caller Lift' (*Cencrastus* 1994), is a study of MacDiarmid's short lyric 'The Watergaw'. It is shot through with Henderson's personal encounters with the poem and focuses on possible interpretations of the lines 'There was nae reek i' the laverock's hoose / That nicht – an' nane i' mine'.[46] Isolating this passage, Henderson considers its potential etymological roots. First, he acknowledges the source and meaning that MacDiarmid provides: in James Wilson's *Lowland Scotch as spoken in the Lower Strathearn District of Perthshire* (1915) the phrase is described as one used 'when the night is cold and stormy', and in two of his letters MacDiarmid echoes this reading, explaining that the lines evoke 'a dark and stormy night' (*AM*, p. 295). However, on his first reading, Henderson thought of Alexander Nicholson's edited volume, *Gaelic Proverbs and Familiar Phrases* (1881), in which the Gaelic version of this aphorism is printed with the translation: 'The bird of most aspiring and happy song has untainted air in its lowly home' (*AM*, p. 297). Henderson suspects that the Scots saying was a descendant of its Gaelic equivalent, and while he qualifies his argument by stating that the question of the accuracy of MacDiarmid's usage cannot jeopardise the power of the poem, he approaches the expression as a folklore fragment by disregarding authorial intention and tracing it back through various appropriations and transformations. In this context Henderson proposes that the speaker in 'The Watergaw' might not refer to a bleak and stormy outlook but to a clarity of vision, one unobscured and unfettered by the 'smoke' that thickened in the blackhouses once common to Scotland's Gaelic-speaking regions. This interpretation, as well as the gradual elucidation of the phrase through the essay itself, is alluded to in Henderson's title, which transfers the Laverock to the 'Caller Lift': the cool, fresh skies (*Concise Scots Dictionary*).

Henderson considers the journey this phrase has taken to appear in MacDiarmid's lyric. And if this method is extended, poetic analysis becomes, like the task of the folklorist and Clifford's ethnologist, inherently partial. The full complex of etymological histories, of cultural, social, political associations that lie latent in any given phrase, can never be fully comprehended. To do so would be to see what a given poem means to every conceivable reader. Nevertheless, the fact that Henderson applies the techniques of the folklorist to the work of literary analysis is in itself an acknowledgement of the unknowable elements of any literary work. By unpacking one alternative reading of the 'reek' in the laverock's house, Henderson gestures toward the infinite contestability of this poem, and all poetry.

Henderson also produced a number of longer discursive essays on folksong, balladry and the oral tradition and, though they are usually given a broader remit than those tracing particular song fragments, they emphasise the same characteristics of the folk tradition. In his essay 'The Green Man of Knowledge' (*Scottish Studies* 1958), on a tale of the same name, Henderson arrives at broader conclusions about the transgressive nature of folk culture. Beginning with an unabridged transcription of the tale as delivered in one of his field recordings, the bulk of the essay traces the tale type, 'The Girl as Helper in the Hero's Flight' (number 313 in the Aarne-Thompson classification), from the Greek myth of Jason and Medea through its international variants. The nomenclature, motifs and plot devices of the transcribed version are then compared to related sources in Scottish story-telling traditions (both Lowland Scots and Gaelic); to literary relatives like *Sir Gawayne and the Grene Knight*; and to Welsh Romany tales, Hindu Myths and Sanskrit lore. The breadth and depth of the genealogy of this folk tale leads Henderson to conclude that 'where folk-culture is concerned, the erection of boundary marks, either geographical or temporal, is at best only a convenience'. The diffusion of this tale type, and the 'extraordinary unity in diversity' that it displays, suggests that it is 'one of the basic *Märchen* of the human race', one 'submerged deep in time and [reaching] out to the ends of the earth'.[47] Henderson uses the Aarne-Thompson tale type index to formulate his thoughts, and his comments on the 'basic *Märchen* of the human race' are also in keeping with emergent scholarship in his field. Vladimir Propp's *Morphology of the Folktale* was published in its first English translation in the same year that this essay appeared, introducing folklore scholars to a formalist approach that was to become dominant in the field. Henderson's framework might also be seen in a wider context, as a reflection of the contemporary vogue in literary criticism for Northrop Frye's model of 'archetypal criticism' – *Anatomy of Criticism* had been published in 1957. Henderson singles out 'The Green Man of Knowledge' in a later interview as one of both literary and academic value, and characteristic of the kind of writing he wanted to produce (*AM*, p. 451). While it seems to draw from the intellectual climate in which he was working during this period, it also promotes ideas that were to be developed in his folk scholarship for at least the next thirty years. As an exercise in demonstrating the universality and simultaneous localism of the folk tradition, this essay reconciles the meticulousness of Henderson's research with a conclusion that reaches further than the particularities of the tale in question, out towards an abstracted view of the deeper structures represented in cultural artefacts.

In 'The Ballad and the Popular Tradition to 1660', a survey piece written for the first volume of *The History of Scottish Literature* (1988), Henderson again made use of 'The Green Man of Knowledge'. Here, the folk tale takes its place among other examples of Scottish songs, tales and literary works that conceal within their lines evidence of the vast networks of oral tradition on which they depend. Henderson begins by emphasising that Scotland is, and always has been, a 'multi-ethnic' country and that 'the various strands of its popular tradition necessarily reflect this chequered linguistic past' (*AM*, p. 78). From Barbour's *Bruce*, through the writings of religious reformers in the sixteenth century, to the balladry associated with the seventeenth and eighteenth centuries, Henderson explores the reach of the oral tradition. Though most of the oldest surviving records of the ballads belong to the period after 1660, Henderson claims that he can confidently assume a much longer history if a ballad story appears in the traditions of a number of other countries (*AM*, p. 83). He provides examples of folk tales and songs that have 'surmounted the barriers of language, geography and culture' (*AM*, pp. 81–9). For example, the fifth book of Blind Harry's *Wallace* is identified as a source for the ballad 'Gud Wallace' (Child 157); Henderson surmises that 'it is by no means unlikely that an earlier ballad or ballads on the same subject may have entered the epic poem, and then (so to speak) found an oral outlet from its confines' (*AM*, p. 84). In his speculation, Henderson will not allow for an original literary source. He returns to the pervasiveness of the oral tradition and signals towards its still uncharted territories throughout Scotland's literary history.

Towards the conclusion of this survey, Henderson reminds the reader that many of Scotland's ballads arrived from England, and that this too is an element of the hybrid strength of Scottish balladry, further illuminating the phenomenon documented by the works of William Dunbar and Robert Henryson, that 'Scottish Literature is both "Inglis" and "Scottis"'. He cites the folklorist Gavin Greig:

> As we pursue the subject we are carried beyond the bounds of Scotland and quite away from the present time; for the field of folk-song admits of no delimitation either in a geographical or a secular way, reaching forth ultimately to the ends of the earth through countless affinities, and back to primeval times through an unbroken chain of derivation.[48]

Having emphasised the reach of the oral tradition Henderson concludes: 'The Border (English-Scottish) . . . was – and remains to this day – a cultural and linguistic watershed. Anonymous Scottish ballad-composers and ballad-singers have given these great songs "a local habitation and a name"' (*AM*, p. 93). The phrase is borrowed from *A Midsummer Night's Dream*, and belongs to Theseus:

> The poet's eye, in fine frenzy rolling,
> Doth glance from heaven to earth, from earth to heaven;
> And as imagination bodies forth
> The forms of things unknown, the poet's pen
> Turns them to shapes and gives to airy nothing
> A local habitation and a name.
> (V, i, 12–18)

Henderson shores up the 'cultural and linguistic watershed' between Scotland and England, and, at the same time, undermines it. At a fundamental level, the *Scottish* folk tradition appears to be just that. It is simply 'a local habitation and a name' for a far more expansive, and infinitely more complex historical process. Given that Henderson explores these ideas in relation to folk culture, we might infer that his views on literary culture were equivalent. He was uncomfortable with strict distinctions between folk and literary culture, and though much of his writings on poetry in particular assume a national framework, this may be explained away as simply the conceit of a 'Scottish folk-song tradition': it is a convenient framework for thinking about cultural production, though it is less than satisfactory in describing the variety and fluidity of cultural practices in any given territory. This is not to say that Henderson set out a model for the comparative study of literature, or a 'transnational' framework that might be assumed. He was merely aware of the limitations of a 'local habitation and a name' – that is, a national framework – especially when too much meaning is awarded to the designation.

In 'The Ballad, the Folk and the Oral Tradition', Henderson critiques David Buchan's influential monograph *The Ballad and the Folk* (1972), identifying three problems with the thesis. First, Henderson's own experience recording the repertoires of singers and 'tradition bearers', like Jeanne Robertson, leads him to reject Buchan's suggestion that songs are 'recreated' or improvised in every performance through a kind of formulaic oral composition. Second, he finds fault with Buchan's assertion that rising literacy condemned ballads to extinction and third, he regrets the omission of bawdy songs from the study.[49] The first of these criticisms is speculative, though it comes from extensive experience in the field of song-collection. Henderson submits that, although singers often have a fluid relationship with their songs, frequently adjusting lyrics and melodies, it is extending this flexible approach too far to suggest that song texts are not memorised at all, that they are instead 'recreated' around a narrative structure or theme.[50] Henderson promotes the *song* in his account of the oral tradition; while individual creative agents can influence its passage, it is maintained by the accumulation and not by isolated individual performances.

Henderson's second and third criticisms of Buchan's thesis are made as premises to his own theories on the nature of the Scottish folk-song tradition. Henderson recounts Buchan's explanation for the 'slack', 'inchoate' and 'vulgar' style of the songs gathered by the collector Peter Buchan (1790–1854), stating that they represent the 'first fruits of a fumbling and imperfect literacy among the "folk"'.[51] Buchan's argument is that collectors of the 1820s could not possibly capture quality works of oral composition uncorrupted by literacy as had been possible for Anna Brown of Falkland (1747–1810). Brown learned her songs in the late eighteenth century and it was her repertoire that convinced Buchan of the validity of oral composition theory. Henderson disregards Buchan's view of literacy as a corruptive force, dismissing it as another version of the old familiar fatalistic approach to ballad scholarship. Henderson celebrated Peter Buchan's bawdy songs as sources that could provide insights into the workings of a largely anonymous tradition, particularly in relation to the language of Scottish folk-song, and the influence of literacy on song-making.[52] Henderson exposes the limitations of Buchan's study by holding to an idea of the oral tradition that is perhaps not so fluid and formless as the concept of 'oral composition' but that is certainly flexible enough to withstand the rise of literacy, and even benefit from it. According to Henderson's conception of the oral tradition, it could even survive in *living forms* in contemporary Scotland, encouraged and facilitated by the work of the revivalists.[53]

Henderson concludes this essay with observations on the 'fruitful cross-fertilisation in the fields of literary and "folk" poetry in the Scottish cultural tradition'. He notes that ballads, in their countless variants, still evoke the existence of original 'craftsman-balladeers' who developed their art with the care of a literary poet; while there are also 'art-poets' who function like 'folk-poets', 'appropriating opening lines or even whole stanzas from earlier or contemporary authors . . . and using them as a basis for their own productions'. In this context, Henderson reminds us that within the oral tradition the techniques of both non-literate and lettered composers coexist.[54] In his later essay, '"At the Foot o' yon Excellin' Brae": The Language of Scots Folk-song' (*Scotland and the Lowland Tongue* 1983), Henderson develops these ideas further, demonstrating that 'a curious "bilingualism in one language" has been characteristic of Scots folk-song at least since the beginning of the seventeenth century'. Scotland is, like Switzerland, a 'multi-lingual community', and Henderson insists on the prevalence of this dynamic in both the literary and folk traditions. He identifies 'Ballad-Scots' as 'a flexible formulaic language which grazes ballad-English along the whole of its length, and yet remains clearly identifiable'. And he goes on to state that 'in the folk field, as well as in the less agile literary Lallans, Scots may be said to include English and go beyond it' (*AM*, pp. 52–3).[55]

Addressing Scotland's linguistic history, Henderson is careful to note that the King James Bible did much to cultivate this 'bilingualism in one language', particularly in the idiom of 'ballad-Scots'. It was not simply a force in the 'galloping anglicisation of the seventeenth and later centuries', indeed, the picture of an English register corrupting and diluting Scots (or civilising it, depending on the perspective), is a reductive one that ignores evidence of assimilation and symbiosis (*AM*, p. 52). Henderson distinguishes the language of folk-song from the 'colloquial', or 'punterspeak': it is a formal and highly stylised form, as far from the speech of the singer as the language of Augustan art-poetry is from the everyday speech of its poets (*AM*, pp. 54, 59). Henderson explains that the language of older folk-song in particular has been 'licked into shape like pebbles by the waves of countless tongues' (*AM*, p. 54). Describing the ways in which the 'bilingualism' of Scottish folk-song can be traced, Henderson then points to a song collected from an 'old illiterate tinker woman' whose natural speech consisted of a mixture of Deeside and Perthshire Scots, fragmentary Gaelic and traveller's cant. The song itself is in perfect ballad-English but for one 'Scots locution': 'nae'. Henderson asserts that as a result, the whole piece must be read and pronounced '*more Boreali*', and certainly not in 'refined Suddroun'. Henderson also refers to the fact that Scots speakers might unconsciously choose to pronounce 'dead' rather than 'deid' in their songs, according to 'deep instinctive aesthetic patterns' rather than the tendencies of everyday speech (*AM*, p. 56). In Henderson's view, accounts of Scotland's gradual linguistic 'anglicisation' do not allow for these oscillations between Scots and English.

Towards the end of this essay Henderson turns his attention to the '"crambo-clink" poets – the local bards who aspired to appear in print' (*AM*, p. 71). After some examples of the work of such poets, he suggests that 'one cannot fail to be struck by the extraordinary contrast between the slack, insipid and nerveless lucubrations of the poetasters who wrote with an eye to print, and the verve, spunk and genuine poetry of the anonyms' (*AM*, p. 72). Henderson returns to the terms of the 'Folksong Flyting', insisting that the oral dimension of folk poetry allows for a freedom of expression that is frustrated by any ambition towards publication. Having described the linguistic profile of Scottish folk culture and its relationship with the English of the King James Bible, and of published poetry and broadsheet ballads, Henderson returns to the place of literacy in Scotland's folk-song tradition. He suggests that it might be possible

> to postulate the existence, at more than one level of society, and at many if not most periods of our history, of makars who foreswore print, and consciously embraced the aesthetic prejudices and the prosodic and musical techniques of an essentially non-literate song poetry. (*AM*, p. 73)

Though Henderson does remark, like Lomax before him, on the 'bookishness' of the folk tradition in Scotland, he proposes that the excellence of Scottish balladry is due, at least in part, to 'the literate Scot's wilful and purposive suspension of literacy' (Ibid.). Folk culture becomes a framework for tracing the interrelatedness of Scotland's languages and its literature and folk-arts: Scots language is only as distinguishable from English, as folk poetry is from art-poetry. That is to say that each belongs to the other. Scots contains English and goes beyond it. The 'folk process' extends so far as to *preclude*, and *include*, all literary production.

Henderson finishes this essay by citing Lorca as a poet who assimilated and subsequently re-created Andalusian folksongs in his own lyrics (*AM*, p. 74). The closing lines are from Lorca's 'Balada de la Placeta' (Ballad of the Little Square):

> *The Children*: What do you feel in your mouth scarlet and thirsting?
> *Myself*: The taste of the bones of my big skull!
> *The Children*: Drink the tranquil water of the antique song. Clear stream, serene fountain! Why do you go so far from the little square?
> *Myself*: I go in search of magicians and princesses!
> *The Children*: Who showed you the path of the poets?
> *Myself*: The fountain and the stream of the antique song.
> (*AM*, pp. 74–5)

This passage expresses a theoretical construction remarkably similar to that Henderson pursued in his folk scholarship. In his articles and essays, folk-song is characterised by its boundlessness. Not only do songs travel across international boundaries and between historical epochs, they also pass over that border that physically delineates Scotland. In his flytings with MacDiarmid, Henderson pushed against the boundary between 'folk' and 'literature', and in his folk scholarship he constantly returns to the symbiotic relationship between the two. In many of his early articles, Henderson traced the passage of folksongs through the 'folk process', relying on fragmentary evidence and an apparently instinctual receptiveness to the accretions and exuviations that characterise this 'process'. He turned this same critical method on MacDiarmid's poetry, demonstrating that folk culture and literary art exist in a similar relationship with their constitutive influences. In his longer, more discursive pieces on the folk tradition, Henderson emphasised its vastness and its complexity, reminding his readers that any effort to track this process, or to contribute to it, is necessarily a partial and infinitesimal gesture. Henderson responded to Buchan's seminal work on the ballad by deepening and widening the scope of folk scholarship. He proposed a conception of mediation that is in line with more recent work in this area, refusing to distinguish, on a metaphysical level, between the oral and the written, and disregarding the notion that increasing levels of literacy could jeopardise the workings of the folk process. In the language of folk-song, Henderson found a repository of

Scotland's linguistic history, which provides a profile far more nuanced and complex than over-simple trajectories of gradual anglicisation. As Lorca's poem suggests, 'the fountain and the stream of the antique song' is the original source of literature; it showed Lorca 'the path of the poets'. As Greig stated, folk culture 'admits no delimitation', and as Henderson wrote in his essay on 'The Green Man of Knowledge', it is 'submerged deep in time and reaches out to the ends of the earth'.[56]

Lorca and the Travelling People

Lorca appears throughout Henderson's work. In the above example, he expresses Henderson's appreciation for 'antique song' as the fountainhead of literary poetry. In another passage he exemplifies the poet who, like Henderson, is mistrustful of print and purports that 'poetry requires as interpreter a living body' (*AM*, p. 288). Lorca validated Henderson's theories on the relationship between folk culture and literary culture and his prioritisation of the oral tradition over print. However, Henderson does not simply use 'Lorca' as shorthand for the figure of the celebrated poet who practised his art according to principles commensurate with Henderson's own. Alongside Burns, Henderson identified Lorca as a poet who 'learned much from a lively and virile folk-culture' and who wrote songs which were to be 'absorbed into local folk-traditions' (*AM*, p. 281). However, the poet's most prominent role in Henderson's thought is as a figure able to articulate those qualities of folk culture that he struggled to express.

The only article Henderson wrote directly concerned with Lorca is a review of *Deep Song and Other Prose* (1986), edited and translated by Christopher Maurer. Writing for *Cencrastus*, Henderson explored a series of implicit and explicit affinities between his own work and that of the Andalusian poet. Describing Lorca's creative outlook, Henderson cited his explanation for the title of the collection *Romancero Gitano* ('Gypsy Ballads' 1928): 'I called it Gypsy because the Gypsy is the loftiest, most profound and aristocratic element of my country, the most deeply representative of its mode, the very keeper of the glowing embers, blood, and alphabet of Andalusian and universal truth' (*AM*, p. 288). This attitude chimed with Henderson's view of Scotland's indigenous travelling people as the custodians of a venerable folk tradition of local, national and international significance. In the sleeve notes for an LP of folksongs recorded among the travellers during the berry-picking season in Blair, Henderson describes the seasonal community of migrants as 'a little traveller principality of its own, a joyful snook cocked at orthodox law and order, like Garcia Lorca's "City of the Gypsies"' (*AM*, p. 101). In a later article for *The Scotsman* on the storyteller and traveller, Betsy Whyte, Henderson proposes that a 'fitting epigraph' for her new book might be Lorca's lines:

O city of the gypsies, who
that saw you could forget you soon?
Let them seek you in my forehead
The playground of the sands and moon.
(*AM*, pp. 243–4)

Henderson thereby frames his own understanding of the travellers' communal folk culture through Lorca's 'city of gypsies'; a phrase from the poem 'Romance de la Guardia Civil Española' ('Ballad of the Spanish Civil Guard'). Here, the 'city of gypsies' is a community of great spiritual worth razed and slaughtered by the fascists, the 'Spanish Civil Guard'; but despite its desolation it survives in the mind of the poet ('let them seek you in my forehead . . .'). The 'city of gypsies' will endure through Lorca's creative engagement with it. The profundity of Henderson's appreciation for the culture of the travelling people of Scotland is no less pronounced.

Henderson's 'discovery' of the folk culture of Scotland's travelling people was perhaps the most important of his career.[57] The so-called 'Tinker Project' of the 1950s led to Henderson meeting Jeannie Robertson, the most celebrated traditional ballad singer of the early revival, and an exemplar of the kind of 'tradition bearer' carrying a rich and varied repertoire, he had long been searching for.[58] In *The Ballad and the Folk*, Buchan imagines the insights that might be gleaned from tape-recorded texts of the songs of illiterate ballad composers but regrets that such a resource would be impossible to obtain in the twentieth century; that would be to 'rax fur the meen' ('reach for the moon').[59] In his critique, Henderson assures Buchan that 'this particular moon-landing' in fact came in the early 1950s with the commencement of fieldwork among the travellers (*AM*, pp. 80–1). Indeed, in conjunction with the introduction of transportable reel-to-reel tape recorders, the riches garnered from the travellers did more to influence Henderson's conception of folk culture and its living processes than any amount of archival research. The sheer scale of the find, and the vitality of the oral tradition that Henderson witnessed, led him to refer to his recording work among the travellers, particularly in the berry fields of Blair, as 'like holding a tin-can under Niagara Falls' (*AM*, p. 102). In terms of the historiography of folk scholarship, this was '[the] third great zone of Scottish folk culture', after the balladry of the borders and the northeast, and the folklore of Scottish Gaeldom:

> at that particular moment in the early nineteen-fifties, the oral literature and song of the Travelling People was, probably, not only the most substantially ancient but also the most vital of all Scotland's various, towering folk traditions – traditions which are of crucial national importance here at home, and matchless gems in the crown of international folk music.[60]

This most 'ancient' and 'vital' of Scottish folk cultures gave Henderson grounds for testing and refining his idea of the 'folk process'. It exposed those most successful elements of the 'process' that bore out their connections with the oldest traceable sources. It also offered a 'vital' living source, a song culture still thriving and relevant to the lives of the people. In 'The Oral Tradition', Henderson set out a history of this defining aspect of folk culture drawn almost entirely from anecdotal accounts of songs and tales gathered among the travellers.[61] The folk culture of the travellers became a living historical database that not only sustained materials of considerable age, but also described their lineage.

The fact that Henderson found the cultures of the travellers so valuable to the study of the oral tradition more generally can also be explained in terms of its appeal to his sense of the 'underground' of Scottish folk, of a tradition in perpetual opposition to the cultures of officialdom (*AM*, p. 34). Henderson wrote of the lore that survived in those nomadic communities, particularly tales for children, describing the threat posed by non-migratory peoples. For example, there were the 'burkers' (doctors), who might capture children wandering too far from camp, and who represented an equivalent of the tinker-as-child-stealer in the lore of settled populations (*AM*, pp. 223–4, 230, 242). In Henderson's estimation their 'persecution complex' was more than justified by their history: he notes that in the seventeenth century 'it was a capital crime in Scotland to be an "Egyptian" . . . not merely gypsy, any kind of wanderer or vagabond minstrel or travelling tinsmith' (*AM*, p. 230). The travellers represent a genuinely alternative cultural, political and social framework. In Henderson's analyses, these exceptional circumstances go some way toward an explanation for the relative health and richness of their inherited oral culture.

Having asked a 'tinker youth' about the difference between the travellers, or 'tinkers', and other kinds of itinerant or migratory people in Scotland, Henderson got the response: 'That sort of lad [an "Irish tramp" known to the "tinker youth"] just lives from day to day, but we (tinkers) live entirely in the past' (*AM*, p. 229). The presence of the past in the everyday lives of the travellers, and their awareness of this distinctive quality, come through in Henderson's descriptions of the travellers' lives. As opposed to other, more solitary migrants, the travellers made up a 'kind of "underground" clan system of their own', whereby 'individuals are intensely conscious of kinship and family ties' (Ibid.). Although they travelled, extended family networks were tied to particular regions. They returned to the same camps and to the same seasonal work, year after year. As descriptors of the folk culture of the travellers, 'ancient' and 'vital' capture something of this living, breathing, presence of history. While Henderson recognised that these qualities were particular to these communities, he was convinced that recording and studying this material could have broader implications for our understanding of the nation and its historical narratives: 'the Travellers through their history, their cultural heritage, their unpropertied lifestyle have crafted themselves to become, as it were, the unframed mirror within which Scotland can view and be herself – backwards and forwards in time'.[62] Henderson wrote of one particular family – the Stewarts – that although they were a 'tiny band', 'their lifestyle and their culture were affirmation of a major strand in Scotland's history, what Scotland was, is, and will be'. He concluded: 'they're in the archive now . . . death hath no dominion!'[63] The folk traditions of the travellers provide a vehicle for time travel: Scotland's past can be explored without restriction and without having to address the problems incurred by historians when they try to speak for the dead. In this case, the dead speak for themselves through those inherited songs and tales still living among the contemporary 'tradition bearers'.

In his review of Lorca, Henderson prioritises the concept of *cante jondo*, or 'deep song'. Comparing the 'Andalusian gypsies' with Scotland's 'travelling folk', he points to their common roles as custodians of this valuable song culture. Lorca distinguishes *cante jondo* from flamenco by its origins in 'the very first manifestations of song', and its evocation of the 'mysterious colour of primordial ages'. Through further quotations from Lorca, Henderson writes of the threat of commercialism, of the emotional intensity of folk poetry and of its power to endure: 'The passionate wind of poetry will throw fuel on the dying fire, livening its flames and the people will continue to sing' (*AM*, p. 290). Lorca's observations apply as well to Henderson's conception of the Scottish folk tradition as they do to their original Andalusian subject. In both instances the 'depth' of the song culture refers not only to profundity or emotional quality but also to the 'depth' of their historical connections. 'Deep song' is song that has endured and remained valuable for countless generations of singers and audiences. Lorca's lecture on 'deep song' helps Henderson to address the tensions that pervade in his own approach to the 'ancient' and 'vital' folk culture of the travellers.

The travellers represent the exception rather than the rule: they confirm that the oral tradition thrives in isolation, when protected from commercial forces and separated from concentrated urban populations. However, Henderson sought to prove that folk culture was an indomitable and permanent aspect of human society that could absorb the transformations of modern Scotland and prosper under any circumstances. The songs and tales of the travellers had, however, not been reconciled with modernity. Instead, they had survived by circumventing the potentially corruptive or degenerative influences of twentieth-century Scotland. More recently, poststructuralist thinkers like Pierre Clastres, Gilles Deleuze and Félix Guattari, and Rosi Braidotti, have drawn on the ideas of 'nomadism' to challenge the logic of the nation and the state.[64] Travellers, or nomads, present an opposition to the settled community and to received notions of identity and history. Deleuze and Guattari assert that 'the nomads have no history; they have only a geography'; that 'the defeat of the nomads was such, so complete, that history is one with the triumph of States'.[65] Braidotti later set out her conception of the 'nomadic subject':

> Nomadic consciousness . . . consists in not taking any kind of identity as permanent: the nomad is only passing through; he makes those necessarily situated connections that can help him to survive, but he never takes on fully the limits of one national, fixed identity. The nomad has no passport or has too many of them.[66]

Nomads therefore unsettle our notions of *national* tradition. Henderson's informant's feeling that, as 'tinkers', they live 'entirely in the past', can perhaps be understood not as a 'past' Scotland – as part of the accepted national 'history' – but as an archaic past prior to the national framework. The travellers can never be part of 'national' or state-related notions of identity or history. In this sense, their folk culture is an example of the pure 'folk process': it is unchallenged by 'officialdom' and by the 'enemies of folk-song'. By existing outside these frameworks, the struggle, the periods of popularisation and banishment 'underground', are circumvented.

Henderson's other great anthropological 'discovery' was the secret society of 'The Horseman's Word', which was active across Scotland, particularly in the northeast, throughout the nineteenth century and into the early twentieth century. It was a diabolic cult for ploughmen that, through pacts with the devil, enabled its members to tame and control horses with great skill. In their initiation rites – including reciting passages from the bible backwards, shaking the hoof of the devil (a goat or a sheep) and giving the correct responses to a staged interrogation: 'Who cometh? In the name of the Word speak your name' – Henderson saw the Horseman's Word as an organisation of the 'Damned'.[67] Calvinist dogma divided society into the 'Elect' and the 'Damned' and, echoing his writings on folk-song and the 'Elect' or the 'élite' who conspired to suppress or else sanitise it, Henderson describes this secret society as part of the struggle of folk culture to gain hold in a society that cannot sanction such modes of collective self-expression without delegitimising its own establishment. The distinction between the ploughmen and the travellers is very clear: the former seek out clandestine organisations in an effort to practise a folk culture of their own, whereas the latter are free from any need to resist as they live (and therefore sing) outside these structures.[68]

Recounting Lorca's passionate and poetic defence of *cante jondo*, Henderson concedes that, as Gavin Greig noted, 'the project [of collecting folksongs] is in the first instance a patriotic one' (*AM*, p. 290). It is based on a kind of faith in the work as (in Lorca's words) 'a labour of salvation, friendship, and love', and in the material itself, as constituting 'the musical soul of our people' (Ibid.). This is the central conceit of the folklorist: in recognising the 'patriotism' inherent in song-collection, Henderson makes allowances for the hopefulness that informs his view of folk culture and its potential in modern Scotland. Like Lorca, he is steadfast in his belief that 'the passionate wind of poetry will throw fuel on the dying fire . . . and the people will continue to sing' (Ibid.). He chooses to remain 'patriotic' in his work as a folklorist, despite the possible connection between the vitality of the folk culture of the travellers and their exclusion from the nation and the state. According to Henderson's analysis, the travellers' culture represents a living reflection of Scotland's history, but to connect this with the concerns of modern Scotland requires a degree of 'patriotism', that is, an elision of the disjuncture between the reality of the lives of the travelling people, and the political and cultural potential Henderson invested in the folk arts that they exemplified.

Lorca's lecture 'On Lullabies' begins with a statement of intent: 'I am not trying, as in former ones [lectures], to define, but to emphasise. I want to suggest, not to delineate. To animate, in the exact sense of the word'.[69] In his introduction, Maurer remarks that Lorca 'thought by metaphor': he approached meaning indirectly and from multiple directions, honing his emphasis but not presuming to define his terms precisely.[70] This evasive heuristic technique appealed to Henderson. Indeed, in his repeated description of song-collecting among the travellers as 'like holding a tin-can under Niagara Falls', Henderson seems to have 'thought by simile' in accounting for the work of the folklorist.[71] The tin can bears the same relation to the waterfall as the folklorist does to the oral tradition. The best that can be hoped for is to capture a small sample from the enormous torrent that was flowing long before the collector's arrival and that will continue to flow long after their departure. The tin can quickly overflows and the folklorist must recognise the limitations of his or her work. The collector has no choice but to remain humble before the vastness of the folk tradition. Only so much can be inferred about the whole from a single tin can-sized sample.

The most elusive concept addressed by Lorca in this collection of lectures, and the most reliant on his practice of 'thinking by metaphor', is the *duende*. Henderson describes it as 'the mysterious indefinable power in a singer or artist without which even the greatest technical prowess is of no avail' (*AM*, p. 289). Concluding what Henderson regarded as the 'most revealing and suggestive' of the lectures in the volume, 'Play and Theory of the Duende', the poet depicts this phenomenon as 'a mental wind blowing restlessly over the heads of the dead, in search of new landscapes and unknown accents; a wind that smells of baby's spittle, crushed grass, and jellyfish veil, announcing the constant baptism of newly created things'.[72] This astonishing prose conceals and reveals simultaneously. The unlikely series of images is part of the hypothetical search of the *duende* for new ways to articulate itself. It is as much about the contents of the world as it is about the lenses through which we observe them. Henderson focuses on some of Lorca's less opaque statements on the *duende*, in particular he notes that 'the duende is a power, not a work: it is a struggle, not a thought . . . it is not a question of ability, but of true, living style, of blood, of the most ancient culture, of spontaneous creation' (*AM*, p. 289). The *duende* appealed to Henderson as it stood to contain all that he found difficult to express about the essential qualities of folk-song: its relationship with the individual, with society and with human history. In the citation above, for example, Lorca manages to express the fact that, with *duende*, the spontaneity of the performance is wholly reconciled with the most enduring forms of human culture, stretching back into pre-history. Where Lorca writes, 'the real fight is with the duende', Henderson agrees with Maurer in his assertions on the dialectical nature of this construction. He cites Lorca: 'the artist must fight the *duende* hand to hand – i.e., he must fight his own irrationality, his own demonism, and his own death. Inspired art is born of that struggle' (Ibid.).

On the domain of the *duende*, Lorca states: 'All arts are capable of duende, but where it finds greatest range, naturally, is in music, dance, and spoken poetry, for these arts require a living body to interpret them, being forms that are born, die, and open their contours against an exact present'.[73] He addresses Henderson's field directly. Indeed, Henderson offers his own thoughts on the *duende* in reference to the folk cultures with which he was most familiar: 'It is not without interest that the Scots travelling people have an expression the "conyach", which exactly corresponds to the *duende*'. The 'conyach', writes Henderson, is most likely related to the Gaelic *caoineadh*, or 'weeping' which is also the root of 'keening', and relates to wailing or lamenting bitterly (*AM*, p. 290). This quality is taken to reflect the delivery of songs as well as their subject matter and Henderson calls upon Lorca to show the prominence of weeping in his conception of 'deep song' and in his creative work more generally. Turning this interest in the etymological back to '*duende*' itself, Henderson writes of the 'prosaic' and even 'faintly comic' root of the term: *duen de casa*, or 'lord of the house' – a character in Spanish folklore who causes mischief around the home, 'a sort of cross between a poltergeist and a brownie' (Ibid.).

In his statements on the Gaelic equivalent of *duende*, and its relationship with the process of mourning, he elaborates on Lorca's conception. Here, death resonates in the *duende*, and is in keeping with the cultural currency of death in Spain. Henderson notes the tragedy of the poet's murder at the hands of the fascists, before addressing 'the black and baleful Spanish obsession with death' that pervades his work and characterises his conception of the *duende*. He cites Lorca: 'Everywhere else, death is an end. Death comes, and they draw the curtains. Not in Spain. In Spain they open them . . . A dead man in Spain is more alive as a dead man than in any place in the world' (*AM*, p. 291). In his lecture 'On Lullabies', Lorca seems to claim precisely the opposite, that 'a dead man is deader in Spain than in any other part of the world'.[74] Both statements in fact explore the same truth. In his analysis of lullabies, Lorca writes: 'there are no smudgy limits one can cross to flee to the other world. Everything is delineated and bounded very exactly'.[75] The dead are thereby more thoroughly dead in Spain than they are elsewhere but they also have far more presence in the lives of the living.

The article ends with an extended passage from Lorca's tender 'Elegy for Maria Blanchard', written for the hunchback Spanish painter who fled to Paris to escape maltreatment. Here, Lorca emerges as a political martyr, a towering symbol of solidarity with the marginalised and disregarded. However, Henderson addresses the death of this individual poet in the same breath as that death that must be faced if the *duende* is to appear in the work of the artist. In Lorca's words: 'The *duende* does not come at all unless he sees that death is possible. The *duende* must know beforehand that he can serenade death's house and rock those branches we all wear, branches that do not have, will never have, any consolation' (*AM*, p. 291). For this indescribable quality of the *duende* to be present, the fact of mortality must be engaged with, deeply and profoundly. It must cut through our pretensions, our intellectual or imaginative constructions ('the branches we all wear'), and bring us closer to the presence of death, even in life. This struggle is explored in Henderson's own song-poem 'The Flyting o' Life and Daith', which, like Lorca's *duende*, is an expression of the dialectics of living with mortality:

Quo daith, the warld is mine.
I hae dug a grave, I have dug it deep,
For war an' the pest will gar ye sleep.
Quo daith, the warld is mine.
Quo life, the warld is mine.
An open grave is a furrow syne.
Ye'll no keep my seed frae fa'in in.
Quo life the warld is mine.
(*CPS*, p. 145)[76]

In a letter to the folksinger Jimmy MacGregor in 1967, Henderson wrote to explain that the song was for a single singer: 'Life and Daith are present in the one man. If it were done by two singers as a dialogue, it would be an empty dualism' (*TAN*, p. 156). Henderson's concern is with the dialectical relationship between life and death. Death is a certainty but if it is to carry any meaning it depends on life. Henderson's imagined performer is an observer who sees both speakers lay out their claims on the world and, at the same time, he or she is an embodiment of both of these speakers. Life and death are each present in the individual. Henderson's piece is therefore a literal re-enactment of Lorca's conditions for *duende*: 'the artist must fight . . . his own death. Inspired art is born of that struggle' (*AM*, p. 289).

It is against this backdrop that Henderson seeks to understand the folk tradition. As a revivalist he hoped to resurrect songs that had been relegated to the past and foster the creation of new ones according to the same enduring 'folk process'. As a folklorist, Henderson sought to understand this 'folk process', and in an effort to do so he traced songs back through their respective histories according to the fragmentary evidence available to him. Out of this method Henderson found that the 'process' he tried to analyse was impossible to appreciate in its entirety. It cannot be approached comprehensively because it is an abstract conception only made real by the cultural transactions of people. It transcends nation, historical epoch, language and even death. When Henderson proposed to reconnect the artist with society, this was to be achieved by reinvesting in the idea of the anonymous collective of the folk tradition. This not only prioritises the collective over the individual, it asks that we submit to a process that extends far into the past and the future, which is made up of the entire history of society. The work of the individual artist is to be subsumed into a vast anonymous tradition, just as the contribution of any individual is overwhelmed and succeeded by the processes of the oral tradition. Henderson's consciousness of this framework meant that any work that described or contributed to the Scottish folk-song tradition was also a submission, and an accession, to the boundless processes of cultural transmission. It is an acknowledgement that the shared imaginary life, though ever changing, endures beyond the lives of individuals. Henderson's 'The Flyting o' Life and Daith' demonstrates this metaphorical transfer between the life and death of the individual, and that of the folk process. The competition in which Life and Death are engaged is eternal. They each depend on the other. The song, and song more generally, is made up of this timeless exchange, just as folk culture is replenished and sustained by passing generations of the anonymous collective. Henderson was part of the process he sought to understand and while he promoted a popular revival of Scottish folk culture, and studied the machinery of the tradition that he championed, his work also asks that we consider the limits of our agency and our knowledge, as individuals, and as mortals.

Notes

1. Some of these issues have been explored more generally in my previous work: 'The Politics of the Modern Scottish Folk Revival'; and 'Tomorrow, songs / Will flow free again, and new voices / Be born on the carrying stream'.
2. Rosenberg, *Transforming Tradition*, p. 27.
3. Harker, *Fakesong*, p. 2.
4. Henderson, 'Resurgimento!', p. 12.
5. Henderson, 'The Edinburgh People's Festival, 1951–54', p. 168.
6. McLane, *Balladeering, Minstrelsy, and the Making of British Romantic Poetry*, pp. 6, 45.
7. Henderson, 'It Was In You That It A' Began', p. 11.
8. Ibid., p. 6.
9. From *Popular Tales of the West Highlands* (1860).
10. Henderson, 'The Ballad, the Folk and the Oral Tradition', p. 81.
11. Henderson, 'Resurgimento!', p. 12.
12. Bo'ness Rebels' Literary Society, *Rebels' Ceilidh Song Book*, pp. 1–2.
13. McLane also writes of the authority of 'inspiration', of 'imitative authorship',

of 'authoritative translation', 'editorial authority', 'ethnographic authority', and 'experiential authority' (pp. 181–211).

14. Bo'ness Rebels' Literary Society, *Rebels' Ceilidh Song Book*, pp. 16, 15.
15. The poems and songs in *Sangs o' The Stane* are not attributed to authors, however, Ewan McVicar has noted that half the songs were written by Morris Blythman. Other contributors included Goodsir Smith, MacCaig, MacDiarmid, John McEvoy and T. S. Law (*The Eskimo Republic*, pp. 21–2).
16. In the title song, 'Ding Dong Dollar' (sung to the tune of 'Ye canny shove yer Granny aff a bus'), the chorus is 'O ye canny spend a dollar when ye're deid, / O ye canny spend a dollar when ye're deid: / Singin Ding . . . Dong . . . Dollar; Everybody holler / Ye canny spend a dollar when ye're deid' (p. 3).
17. Neat, *Poetry Becomes People*, p. 97.
18. Whyte, 'Masculinities in Contemporary Scottish Fiction', p. 284.
19. Anderson, *Imagined Communities*, p. 6.
20. Henderson, 'The Edinburgh People's Festival, 1951–54', p. 165.
21. Rosenberg, *Transforming Tradition*, pp. 2–14.
22. Henderson, 'The Oral Tradition', pp. 159–71.
23. Henderson, 'Foreword', *Democratic Muse*, p. ix.
24. Like Edwin Muir, Fionn MacColla and many other literary figures in Scotland, Henderson regretted the cultural legacy of the Scottish Reformation. Folk culture in particular was, he claimed, threatened and driven underground by the 'religious fanaticism' of Calvinist Scotland (*AM*, p. 35). See Cowan, 'Calvinism and the Survival of Folk' (pp. 30–53).
25. Henderson, 'Resurgimento!', p. 12.
26. See Cowan and Paterson, *Folk in Print*.
27. Goldstein, *A Guide for Field Workers*, p. x.
28. Henderson, 'Jock Ainslie: A Stirlingshire Horseman', pp. 51–8.
29. Henderson frequently refers to Matheson, the secretive singer and song-collector, who became an exemplar of the 'tradition bearer' in 'The Underground of Song', 'The Ballads' and 'Zeus as Curly Snake: The Chthonian Image' (*AM*, pp. 32, 25, 428).
30. The *Tobar an Dualchais – Kist o' Riches* project is accessible online: www.tobarandualchais.co.uk/en/.
31. Alan Lomax, *Selected Writings*, pp. 115–16.
32. Ibid., p. 155.
33. Ibid., p. 285.
34. Ibid., pp. 286–7, 290–3.
35. Munro, *The Democratic Muse*, p. 1.
36. Henderson, 'Resurgimento!', p. 12.
37. In *Joe Gould's Secret*, Mitchell explores Gould's life, *An Oral History of Our Time*, and uncovers the 'secret', that this magnum opus did not in fact exist except as an idea.
38. Fabian, *Time and the Other*, pp. 143–65.

39. Clifford and Marcus, *Writing Culture*, pp. 7, 22.
40. Clifford, *Predicament of Culture*, p. 9.
41. Clifford's study poses a series of questions pertinent to Henderson: 'Who has the authority to speak for a group's identity or authenticity? What are the essential elements and boundaries of a culture? How do self and other clash and converse in the encounters of ethnography [?]' (p. 8).
42. See prefatory verses to Auden's *The Orators* (1932).
43. Henderson contributed to many of Neat's films including *The Tree of Liberty* (1987) (on Burns), *Play Me Something* (1989) (based on a short story by John Berger) and *Journey to a Kingdom* (1991) (on Henderson and the folk-song of the North-East). See Neat, *Poetry Becomes People*, pp. 278–96.
44. 'Jhesu Crist, and seinte Benedight / Blesse this hous from every wikked wight / For nyghtes verye, the White Paternoster . . .' Chaucer, as cited by Henderson (*AM*, p. 112).
45. See 'How a Bothy Song Came into Being', 'The Buckie Wife' and "The Lassies in the Coogate" for further examples (*AM*, pp. 115–18, 125–6, 127–8).
46. MacDiarmid, *Complete Poems*, p. 17.
47. Henderson, 'The Green Man of Knowledge', pp. 47–85.
48. See Greig, *Folk-Song in Buchan and Folk-Song of the North-East.*
49. Henderson, 'The Ballad, the Folk . . .', pp. 69, 72–3, 4.
50. Ibid., pp. 69–70.
51. Ibid., p. 72.
52. Ibid., pp. 74–7.
53. Ibid., p. 81.
54. Ibid., pp. 99–100.
55. Sweeny-Turner considers Henderson's contention in a 'poststucturalist context'. Where Scots is said to include English and yet remain distinct from it, Sweeny-Turner finds resonances with Deleuze and Guattari's notion of 'minor literature', and with the 'problem of economy and strategy' envisaged by Derrida ('Borderlines: Bilingual Terrain in Scottish Song', p. 155).
56. Henderson, 'The Green Man of Knowledge', p. 82.
57. In 'The Tinkers', Henderson's piece for Daiches' *A Companion to Scottish Culture* (1981), he describes the 'tinkers' as a group distinct from Romany gypsies, likely 'the descendants of a very ancient cast of itinerant metal-workers whose status in tribal society was probably high' (*AM*, p. 229).
58. Henderson once stated that his 'discovery' of Jeannie Robertson was the single most important achievement of his life. Neat goes so far as to say that Henderson 'liked to see her as having 'come to him', almost mystically, to fulfil what he saw as his life's purpose' (Neat, *Poetry Becomes People*, pp. 16, 23).
59. Buchan, *The Ballad and the Folk*, p. 173.
60. Henderson, 'The Man with the Big Box', p. 65.
61. Henderson, 'The Oral Tradition', pp. 159–71.
62. Henderson as cited by Neat, *The Summer Walkers*, p. 195.

63. Henderson, 'The Man with the Big Box', p. 73.
64. See Clastres, *Society against the State*; Deleuze and Guattari, *A Thousand Plateaus* and *Nomadology: The War Machine*; and Braidotti, *Nomadic Subjects*.
65. Deleuze and Guattari, *A Thousand Plateaus*, pp. 393–4.
66. Braidotti, *Nomadic Subjects*, p. 33.
67. Henderson, 'The Horseman's Word', pp. 118–20.
68. The Horseman's Word had some influence in post-war Scottish writing. A version of the cult appears in George Mackay Brown's *Greenvoe*, and, in 1970, Edwin Morgan published a series of concrete poems under the title *The Horseman's Word*.
69. Lorca, *Deep Song and Other Prose*, p. 7.
70. Lorca, *Deep Song*, p. xii.
71. Henderson used this image repeatedly: see, 'The Voice of the People' (*AM*, p. 2), 'Folk-songs and Music from the Berryfields of Blair' (*AM*, p. 102), and in his contribution to Neat's *The Summer Walkers*, 'The Man with the Big Box' (p. 67).
72. Lorca, *Deep Song*, p. 53.
73. Ibid., p. 47.
74. Ibid., pp. 9–10.
75. Ibid., p. 9.
76. The song-poem is based on an anonymous medieval German piece that Henderson had discovered in the library at the University of Göttingen in 1939 (*TAN*, p. 115n).

EPILOGUE

O remorseless spirit that guides me
The way seems infinite;
What endless distance divides me
From the people yet!
(MacDiarmid, 'Etika Preobrazhennavo Erosa')[1]

Henderson was familiar with the frustration MacDiarmid expresses in this poem. Lamenting the isolation of the artist in modern society, he sought to overcome this 'distance' between the poet and 'the people', and he felt that much could be learned from the folk tradition in achieving this end. These few lines of MacDiarmid's speak to the scale and the difficulty of the task that Henderson set himself: to represent the voices (and lives) of the soldiers of the Second World War; to achieve that confluence of theory and practice that he so admired in Gramsci; to relinquish his own poetic agency to *Anon.*; to represent and extend a radical national tradition; and to reconcile the perspectives of the folklorist and the revivalist with the unbounded folk tradition. The fact that no fixed, or final position is reached in Henderson's lifelong engagement with these ideas is testament to his intellectual rigour. Even where it suits Henderson's agenda to treat complex notions of orality or the folk tradition as though they were simple and uncontested, he leaves ample room for these doubts.

MacDiarmid is the victor in their flytings because his terms are unequivocal. The base desire for, and vulgar pleasures of folk culture sit in sharp contrast to the cool disinterestedness of philosophic inquiry and poetic truth. This debate raged during the eighteenth-century ballad revival and the same opposition is played out between the intellectual vanguard of the Scottish Literary Renaissance and the central theorist and strategist behind the modern folk revival. Where MacDiarmid claims the rhetorical high ground of critical distance, Henderson writes of dissolving himself in the process he champions. MacDiarmid rejects his opponent's criticisms outright based on this vaunted revelation, that the ideal they have in common can never, has never and will never, be met. Henderson's work always allows for the possibility, though it also seeks out the fissures and gaps in the theories it posits. He shores up his commitment to a *democratic* model of poetry and song that connects with the lives of the people, whilst never addressing the fact that this requires him to submit to the inherent threat posed by a democratic model: the tyranny of the majority. Henderson does not have a satisfactory response to MacDiarmid's accusation that he represents a 'parasitical "interpreting class"' which patronises 'the people' by insisting that 'the level of utterance should be that of popular understanding' (*TAN*, p. 127). Nor does he have a rejoinder to Gramsci's vision of a revolutionary future where folk culture will have no positive contribution. The expansive folk tradition that he unearths in his writings, unbridled by national boundaries, by political partisanship and by the constraints of human mortality, sits in stark contrast to the purview of the folklorist with his tape-recorder, or the revivalist and his Edinburgh ceilidh. However, these contested territories are mapped in Henderson's writings, these tensions are uncovered and gradually defined. Unfortunately for Henderson, his patience with these problems did not make them easier to overcome. He could not have avoided such difficulties and impasses without adopting MacDiarmid's sure-headedness. Perhaps Henderson was right, that the isolation of the artist in modern society could be remedied by looking at the processes of the folk tradition. That he was never able to explain precisely what this meant, or how it might be realised, was his greatest achievement. By resisting both *Anon.* and MacDiarmid, he serves to articulate this space between the artist and 'the people', with all its contradictions.

In the introduction, I referred to Henderson's ill-defined 'legacy'. Because of the range of Henderson's interests, and his largely anecdotal reputation, there is a risk that this 'legacy' may simply be that of a folk hero on whom a range of political and cultural views can be projected. Existing work on Henderson has recognised the breadth of his 'cultural force' in modern Scotland through his war poetry, his folk-song, his many 'discoveries' and recordings, and his cultural and political commentary. Some, including Alec Finlay and Timothy Neat, have presented detailed accounts of his work in context, relating his ideas to contemporary intellectual climates and placing them in a biographical narrative. Henderson's place as a nexus for different political and cultural communities is well documented, from his close ties to the editorial boards of the *New Edinburgh Review* (1969–84) and *Cencrastus* (est. 1979), to his 'discovery' of Jeannie Robertson and the song culture of the travelling people of the North-East; from his programmes for the Edinburgh People's Festivals, to his translations of some of the greatest Italian poets of the twentieth century.

On the basis of this detailed critical analysis of Henderson's writings, I think he might be still more accurately and more usefully located.

Writing of Henderson's long essays on the nature of the 'folk process', the methodology of the folklorist and the song cultures of the travelling people, Alec Finlay notes that they might constitute

> a Scottish companion to the radical experimental anthologies and archaeologies of Michel Foucault; the American poets Jerome Rothenberg and George Quasha, who anthologised ancient poetry in *Technicians of the Sacred* and *Shaking the Pumpkin*; John Berger, a friend and admirer, author of the peasant novel trilogy, *Into Their Labours*; and the Friuliano poet and film-maker, Pier Paolo Pasolini, who identified with archaic society in films such as *Medea*a and *The Arabian Nights*. (*AM*, p. xxx)

To the list of figures who have made significant contributions to, or have symbolised, the importance of ethnopoetics and oral history, we might add those evident connections with Alan Lomax, Bruce Chatwin and Joseph Gould. In the mould of the poet-as-folklorist, we might draw parallels with Carl Sandburg or Langston Hughes. While Henderson's conscious project certainly aligned him with many of these writers, the difficulties he encountered – in trying to reconcile his romantic nationalism with his socialist internationalism, or his conception of the role of the artist with his notion of the folk process – exemplify the anxieties about history, identity and tradition that he felt but never expressed overtly. These issues only become apparent in a careful examination of the whole of his corpus and, in this way, though his work shows signs of the scepticism that informed post-structuralist and postmodernist thinkers in the post-war era, it does not belong on the same shelf. It is my hope that this project has, however, laid the foundations for these kinds of comparisons.

Henderson can be readily aligned with the New Left. During the 'Flytings', faced with MacDiarmid's particular strain of Communism, he expressed his admiration for the 'new School of Socialist thinking [that] has grown up around *Universities and Left Review*, *The New Reasoner*, Hoggart's *The Uses of Literacy* and Raymond William's *Culture and Society*' emerging from the ideological fallout of 1956.[2] Here, he found a school of thought 'which is not afraid of sociological revaluations, and goes out into the streets to hear not only the "gamin cry", but the voice and song of the people' (*TAN*, p. 93). He might also be more precisely located in modern Scottish literary history, which is the context in which he himself most frequently set his work. As an innovator hoping to extend MacDiarmid's 'Renaissance' to include the modern folk revival and a conscious reinvestment in the 'cross-fertilisation' of the literary and folk traditions, Henderson challenges the view that has been allowed to emerge of this post-war period as a mere stop-gap between the interwar Renaissance and the experimentation of the 1960s. Ian Brown and

Colin Nicholson have written of the 'transformational strands' that characterised the 1960s and 1970s: 'affront to established *genii loci*, new performative modes, more cosmopolitanism and domestic revitalisation'.[3] Henderson challenged the Renaissance 'establishment', promoted the oral tradition as a form of cultural transmission and called for a conscious 'revival' of traditional literary modes. He was allied with experimental writers like Edwin Morgan, Ian Hamilton Finlay and Alexander Trocchi, at least in his opposition to MacDiarmid's attacks on this younger generation of writers. Though cosmopolitanism might seem far from the remit of the folk revivalist, Henderson emphasised the arbitrariness of national boundaries when faced with a fluid and transgressive folk tradition.

Apart from these broader narratives of Scottish literary history, we can also see Henderson as a significant critic of MacDiarmid; as a theorist of folk culture, authorship and 'mediation'; and as a writer who recognised the arbitrariness of the 'nation' yet chose to work within a national framework. In all the potential insights Henderson affords in the intellectual history of the Left in Britain, or in the study of Scottish literary history, his negotiation with ideas of art and its relationship with society are always present. Indeed, it would be absurd to restrict Henderson's relevance to either the history of the intellectual Left in Britain, or to the history of debates among Scottish poets of the twentieth century. As this book argues, Henderson's career was marked by a constant flyting. In this sense Henderson's corpus is invaluable; it has the potential to impact Scottish literary studies in more than unearthing half-forgotten disputes, rarely published radical poets, or unrecorded ploughmen balladeers; Henderson's work connects the modern period, its wars, its ideological conflicts and its isolated artists, with the language of the Romantic period, the birth of the nation-state and its claims on historical memory, fuelled and validated by folk culture. Henderson was beholden to inherited notions of Scotland, its people and its culture, but his insights and experience led him to undermine these principles, while he tried to reformulate them for a generation who had 'grown for war' and who now found the cultures they might otherwise have inherited laid low by the alienating force of modernity.

In preparation for the 700th anniversary of the Battle of Bannockburn, the National Trust for Scotland, in collaboration with the Scottish Poetry Library, commissioned ten Scottish poets to propose inscriptions for the rotunda marking the site. The chosen piece, by Kathleen Jamie, was selected by public vote. Naturally, the commission came with a challenging remit:

> The weight of history, the sobriety of the monuments, the weather and the light, the slaughter, resistance, the subsequent union, devolution, turns of fate, a refusal to submit, 'freedom', whatever that means – the whole Bannockburn thing was ours in a small way to redirect.[4]

The pressure applied by these cultural, historical and political contexts is increased and concentrated by the long-established claims of cultural critics, binding Scotland's literary cultures to its political and constitutional history. Since the failed referendum of 1979, the notion that writers exercise a kind of cultural autonomy in lieu of, and in advance of, its political manifestation, has become commonplace.[5] This task of commemoration comes burdened with the past, present and future. It must take what is valuable from the legacy of the Wars of Independence and leave the rest. Unveiled in the year of Scotland's independence referendum, it had to speak to a common historical trajectory that would not alienate either side. And it had to address a future that could not be anticipated.

It seems fitting, therefore, that in their submissions, both Alec Finlay and Jamie invoked Henderson. Finlay's title is 'Freedom Becomes People', after Henderson's translation of Heine. The poem is derived from the *Declaration of Arbroath* (1320) and addresses Bruce directly. It ends: 'SHOULD MYTH BECOME TYRANNY WE SHALL EXERT OURSELVES / TO DRIVE OUT YOUR MEMORY FOR FREEDOM BECOMES PEOPLE'. Jamie's piece, 'Here lies our land', adopts a different phrase and feeling from Henderson's work to achieve the same resistance to 'myth', romantic nationalism, and the historical memory it fosters:

> We are mere transients, who sing
> [. . .]
> Small folk playing our part.
> '*Come all ye*', the country says
> *You win me, who take me most to heart.*[6]

Just as Henderson's 'folk process' invites us to submit to its collective force, Jamie's poem encourages us to embrace the same sense of scale, circumventing the nation by appealing to both the small, individual, evanescent life, and the cumulative and enduring impulse of the 'Come-All-Ye'. Henderson, like MacDiarmid, committed to the long and difficult task of diagnosing Scotland's modern political and cultural malaise, and proposing appropriate cures and salves. Finlay and Jamie seek to resolve the same tension: that between the political sphere, the pursuit of 'liberty', the real struggle, and an instinctive faith in the overwhelming and anonymising process of folk culture.

Notes

1. MacDiarmid, *Complete Poems*, p. 407.
2. See my previous work, 'Recoiling the Springs of Action: *The Uses of Literacy* and the Conceptualisation of Scottish Folk-Song Revivalism'.
3. *Edinburgh Companion to Twentieth-Century Scottish Literature*, p. 133.

4. Jamie, 'The spirit of Bannockburn'.
5. See Thomson, '"You can't get there from here": Devolution and Scottish literary history', and Hames, *Unstated: Writers on Scottish Independence.*
6. The full set of submissions were first published on the website of the Battle of Bannockburn visitor's centre: www.battleofbannockburn.com, last accessed 20 April 2014. Both Jamie and Finlay's poems can be found on Finlay's blog: http://alecfinlayblog.blogspot.co.uk/2013/02/bannockburn-rotunda.html, last accessed 25 November 2014.

WORKS CITED

Aarne, Antti, and Stith Thompson, *The Types of the Folktale* (1928), 2nd edn (Helsinki: Helsinki Suomalainen Tiedeakatemia, 1964).

Anderson, Benedict, *Imagined Communities: Reflections on the Origin and Spread of Nationalism* (1983), 3rd edn (London: Verso, 2006).

Anderson, Perry, 'The Origins of the Present Crisis', *New Left Review* I/23 1964, pp. 26–53.

Auden, W. H., *Selected Poems*, Edward Mendelson (ed.) (London: Faber, 2009).

Auden, W. H., *The Orators: An English Study* (London: Faber, 1932).

Barbour, John., *The Bruce*, A. A. M. Duncan (ed.) (Edinburgh: Canongate, 1997).

Bawcutt, Priscilla, *Dunbar the Makar* (Oxford: Clarendon, 1992).

Behan, Brendan, *The Letters of Brendan Behan*, E. H. Mikhail (ed.) (Basingstoke: Macmillan, 1992).

Bell, Eleanor, 'Old Country, New Dreams: Scottish Poetry since the 1970s', in Ian Brown (gen. ed.), Thomas Owen Clancy, et al. (eds) (Edinburgh: Edinburgh University Press, 2007), pp. 185–97.

Benda, Julien, *The Treason of the Intellectuals (La Trahison des Clercs)* (1928), Richard Aldington (trans.) (New York: Norton, 1969).

Bertram, Bob, *Selected Songs and Poems of Bob Bertram: Folksinger and Edinburgh Character* (Edinburgh: Norma I. M. Allan, 2008).

Berwick, Thurso, *'Aa Breenge In!': Rebel Scottish Songs* (Glasgow: Gallus, 1990).

Berwick, Thurso, *Ballad of the Four 'Conspirators'* (Edinburgh: M. MacDonald, 1962).

Berwick, Thurso, *Coronach for the Dean of Westminster* (Edinburgh: Scottish National Congress Committee, 1950).

Blind Harry, *The Wallace*, Anne McKim (ed.) (Edinburgh: Canongate, 2003).

Bold, Alan, *MacDiarmid: Christopher Murray Grieve: A Critical Biography* (London: John Murray, 1998).

Bolter, Jay David, and Richard Grusin, *Remediation: Understanding New Media* (London: Massachusetts Institute of Technology Press, 1999).

Bo'ness Rebels' Literary Society, *The Rebels Ceilidh Song Book* (Bo'ness: Bo'ness Rebels' Literary Society, 1953–1969).

Bort, Eberhard (ed.), *Borne on the Carrying Stream: The Legacy of Hamish Henderson* (Ochtertyre: Grace Note, 2010).

Bort, Eberhard (ed.), *'Tis Sixty Years Since: The 1951 Edinburgh Peoples Festival Ceilidh and the Scottish Folk Revival* (Ochtertyre: Grace Note, 2011).

Bort, Eberhard (ed.), *At Hame Wi' Freedom: Essays on Hamish Henderson and the Scottish Folk Revival* (Ochtertyre: Grace Note, 2012).

Bower, Walter, *A History Book for Scots: Selections from Scotichronicon*, D. E. R. Watt (ed.) (Edinburgh: Mercat, 1998).

Braidotti, Rosi, *Nomadic Subjects: Embodiment and Sexual Difference in Contemporary Feminist Theory* (New York: Columbia University Press, 1994).

Broom, John, *John MacLean* (Loanhead: Macdonald, 1973).

Brown, George Mackay, *Greenvoe* (1972) (Harmondsworth: Penguin, 1986).

Brown, Gordon (ed.), *The Red Paper on Scotland* (Edinburgh: EUSPB, 1975).

Brown, Ian, and Alan Riach (eds), *The Edinburgh Companion to Twentieth-Century Scottish Literature* (Edinburgh: Edinburgh University Press, 2009).

Brown, Mary Ellen, *Burns and Tradition* (London: Macmillan, 1984).

Brown, Mary Ellen, 'The Forgotten Makars: The Scottish Local Poet Tradition', in Simon J. Bronner (ed.), *Creativity and Tradition in Folklore: New Directions* (Logan: Utah State University Press, 1992), pp. 239–54.

Bruce, George (ed.), *The Scottish Literary Revival: An Anthology of Twentieth-Century Poetry* (London: Collier-Macmillan, 1968).

Bruford, Alan (ed.), *Tocher: Tales, Songs, Tradition* 43, 1991.

Buchan, David, *The Ballad and the Folk* (1972) (East Linton: Tuckwell, 1997).

Buchan, John, *Memory Hold-the-Door* (1940) (London: Dent, 1984).

Buchan, Norman (ed.), *101 Scottish Songs* (Glasgow: Collins, 1963).

Buchan, Peter, *Secret Songs of Silence*, Ian Spring (ed.) (Edinburgh: Hog's Back, 2010).

Büdel, Oscar, *Pirandello*, 2nd edn (London: Bowes, 1969).

Bullen, Keith and John Corner (eds), *Salamander: A Miscellany of Poetry* (London: G. Allen and Unwin, 1947).

Burnett, Ray, 'Scotland and Antonio Gramsci', *Scottish International* 9, 1972, p. 12.

Burns, Robert, *Burns: Complete Poems and Songs*. James Kinsley (ed.). (Oxford: Oxford University Press, 1969).

Buthlay, Kenneth, *Hugh MacDiarmid* (Edinburgh: Oliver and Boyd, 1964).

Byrne, Moira, 'Antonio Gramsci's Contribution to Italian Folklore Studies', *International Folklore Review* 2, 1982, pp. 70–5.

Byrne, Steve (ed.), *The Hamish Henderson Papers: A Commemorative Collection of Essays* (Edinburgh: Hamish Henderson Archives Trust, 2013).

Calder, Angus, *Revolving Culture: Notes from the Scottish Republic* (London: Tauris, 1994).

Calder, Angus, 'Scottish Language in Transition: Some thoughts arising from Hamish Henderson's essay '"Flower and Iron of the Truth"', *Chapman* 82, 1995, pp. 63–70.

Calder, Angus, 'Scottish Poets in the Desert', *Southfields* 6.1, 1999, pp. 64–82.

Cammett, John M., *Antonio Gramsci and the Origins of Italian Communism* (Stanford: Stanford University Press, 1967).

Campbell, John Francis (ed.), *Popular Tales of the West Highlands*, 4 vols (Edinburgh: Edmonston and Douglas, 1860–2).

Campbell, Roy, *The Flowering Rifle: A Poem from the Battlefield of Spain* (London: Longmans, 1939).

Casement, Roger, 'The Language of the Outlaw', in Herbert O. Mackey (ed.), *The Crime Against Europe: The Writings and Poetry of Roger Casement* (Dublin: C. J. Fallon, 1958), pp. 112–16.

Chambers, Bob (ed.), *The Carrying Stream Flows On: Celebrating the Diamond Jubilee of the School of Scottish Studies* (Kershader: Islands Book Trust, 2013).

Chatwin, Bruce, *The Songlines* (London: Jonathan Cape, 1987).

Child, Francis James (ed.), *The English and Scottish Popular Ballads*, 5 vols (Boston and New York: Houghton Mifflin, 1882–98).

Chun, Lin, *The British New Left* (Edinburgh: Edinburgh University Press, 1993).

Clastres, Pierre, *Society against the State* (Oxford: Basil Blackwell, 1977).

Clifford, James, *The Predicament of Culture: Twentieth-Century Ethnography, Literature, and Art* (London: Harvard University Press, 1988).

Clifford, James and George E. Marcus (eds), *Writing Culture: The Poetics and Politics of Ethnography* (Berkeley: University of California, 1986).

Clyde Group, 'The Working Class And The Arts: Clyde Group Festival and Exhibition', *National Weekly* 1.1, 11 September 1948, p. 5.

Concise Scots Dictionary (1985) (Edinburgh: Edinburgh University Press, 2005).

Corbett, John, *Written in the Language of the Scottish Nation: A History of Literary Translation into Scots* (Clevedon: Multilingual Matters, 1999).

Corrie, Joe, *In Time o' Strife: A Play in Three Acts* (Edinburgh: 7:84 Theatre Company, 1984).

Cowan, Edward J., 'Calvinism and the Survival of Folk', in Edward J. Cowan (ed.), *The People's Past: Scottish Folk, Scottish History* (Edinburgh: Polygon, 1980), pp. 30–53.

Cowan, Edward J. (ed.), *The People's Past: Scottish Folk, Scottish History* (Edinburgh: Polygon, 1980).

Cowan, Edward J., and Michael Paterson (eds), *Folk in Print: Scotland's Chapbook Heritage, 1750–1850* (Edinburgh: John Donald, 2007).

Cox, Peter, *Set Into Song: Ewan MacColl, Charles Parker, Peggy Seeger and the Radio Ballads* (London: Labatie, 2008).

Craig, David, 'A National Literature?: Recent Scottish Writing', *Studies in Scottish Literature* 1.3, 1963–1964, pp. 151–69.

Craig, David, *Scottish Literature and the Scottish People, 1680–1830* (London: Chatto and Windus, 1961).

Daiches, David (ed.), *A Companion to Scottish Culture* (London: Edward Arnold, 1981).

Davidson, Neil, 'Gramsci's Reception in Scotland', *Scottish Labour History* 45, 2010, pp. 37–58.

Davie, George Elder, *The Crisis of the Democratic Intellect* (Edinburgh: Polygon, 1986).

The Dead, The Innocent, Keith Alexander (dir.), Hamish Henderson (writ.) (BBC Scotland, 1990).

Deleuze, Gilles and Félix Guattari, *Nomadology: The War Machine* (New York: Semiotext(e), 1986).

Deleuze, Gilles and Félix Guattari, *A Thousand Plateaus: Capitalism and Schizophrenia* (London: Athlone, 1988).

Dictionary of Greek and Roman Biography and Mythology, 3 vols, William Smith (ed.) (London: Taylor, Walton, and Mayberly, and John Murray, 1849).

Ding Dong Dollar: Anti-Polaris Songs (Glasgow: Glasgow Song Guild, 1962).

Ding Dong Dollar: Anti-Polaris and Scottish Republican Songs (Folkways, 1962).

Douglas, Norman, *London Street Games*, 2nd edn (London: Chatto and Windus, 1931).

Dunbar, William, *William Dunbar: Selected Poems* (Manchester: Fyfield Books, 2003).

Duval, K. D. and Sydney Goodsir Smith (eds), *Hugh MacDiarmid: A Festschrift* (Edinburgh: K. D. Duval, 1962).

Eagleton, Terry, 'Nationalism and the Case of Ireland', *New Left Review* I-234, March/April 1999.

Edinburgh University Library, *Hugh MacDiarmid and Company: An exhibition to mark the centenary of the birth of Christopher Murray Grieve ('Hugh MacDiarmid')* (Edinburgh: Edinburgh University Library, 1992).

'An Editorial Diary: Short Course in Plastic Scots', *Glasgow Herald*, 9 November 1946, p. 4.

Eliot, T. S., 'Was There a Scottish Literature?', *Athenaeum*, 1 August 1919, pp. 680–1.

Featherstone, David, '"Gramsci in Action": Space, Politics, and the Making of Solidarities', in Michael Ekers, et al. (eds), *Gramsci: Space, Nature, Politics* (Oxford: Wiley-Blackwell, 2013), pp. 65–82.

Featherstone, Simon, *War Poetry: An Introductory Reader* (London: Routledge, 1995).

Femia, Joseph V., *Gramsci's Political Thought: Hegemony, Consciousness and the Revolutionary Process* (Oxford: Clarendon, 1987).

Findlay, Bill (ed.), *Frae Ither Tongues: Essays on Modern Translations into Scots* (Clevedon: Multilingual Matters, 2004).

Finlay, Alec, 'A River That Flows On', *Alias MacAlias: Writings on Songs, Folk and Literature*, 2nd edn (Edinburgh: Polygon, 2004), pp. xvii–xxxiii.

Finlay, Alec, 'Bannockburn Rotunda', *Alec Finlay Blog*, 11 February 2013, http://alecfinlayblog.blogspot.co.uk/2013/02/bannockburn-rotunda.html (last accessed 30 May 2014).

Finlay, Alec, 'A River That Flows On: A Critical Overview of Hamish Henderson's Life and Work', in Alec Finlay (ed.), *The Armstrong Nose: Selected Letters of Hamish Henderson* (Edinburgh: Polygon, 1996), pp. 299–356.

Finlay, Alec, 'A River That Flows On: The Folk Revival and the Literary Tradition in Scotland', *Chapman* 82, 1995, pp. 37–48.

Fiori, Giuseppe, *Antonio Gramsci: Life of a Revolutionary*, Tom Nairn (trans.) (London: New Left Books, 1970).

Foley, John Miles (ed.), *Theory of Oral Composition: History and Methodology* (Bloomington: Indiana University Press, 1988).

Folksongs and Music from the Berryfields of Blair (Prestige / International, 1962).

Forgacs, David, 'Gramsci and Marxism in Britain', *New Left Review* I/176, 1989, pp. 70–88.

Forgacs, David, 'National-Popular: Genealogy of a Concept', in Tony Bennett (ed.), *Formations of Nation and People* (London: Routledge and Kegan Paul, 1984), pp. 83–97.

Frye, Northrop, *Anatomy of Criticism: Four Essays* (1957) (Princeton: Princeton University Press, 2000).

Fürnberg, Louis, Poetry, Hamish Henderson (trans.), *Our Time* 4:3, October 1944, p. 8

Gallacher, William, *Revolt on the Clyde: An Autobiography*, 4th edn (London: Lawrence and Wishart, 1978).

Garioch, Robert, *Collected Poems* (Loanhead: Macdonald, 1977).

Gatherer, W. A., 'The Flyting Scotsman', *Lines Review* 14, 1958, pp. 4–11.

Gaughan, Dick, 'Song Notes: "Freedom Come Aa Ye"', in *Dick Gaughan's Song Archive*, 2008, http://www.dickgaughan.co.uk/songs/texts/freecaye.html (last accessed 2 May 2012).

Gencarella, Stephen Olbrys, 'Gramsci, Good Sense, and Critical Folklore Studies', *Journal of Folklore Research*, 47.3, 2010, pp. 221–52.

Gencarella, Stephen Olbrys, 'Gramsci, Good Sense, and Critical Folklore Studies: A Critical Reintroduction', *Journal of Folklore Research*, 47.3, 2010, pp. 259–64.

Gibbon, Lewis Grassic, *Scots Quair*, Tom Crawford (ed.) (Edinburgh: Canongate, 1995).

Gibson, Corey, 'The Folkniks in the Kailyard: Hamish Henderson and the "Folk-song Flyting"', in Eleanor Bell and Linda Gunn (eds), *The Scottish Sixties: Reading, Rebellion, Revolution?* (Amsterdam: Rodopi, 2013), pp. 209–26.

Gibson, Corey, '"Gramsci in Action": Antonio Gramsci and Hamish Henderson's Folk Revivalism', in Eberhard Bort (ed), *Borne on the Carrying Stream: The Legacy of Hamish Henderson* (Ochtertyre: Grace Note, 2010), pp. 239–56.

Gibson, Corey, 'The Politics of the Modern Scottish Folk Revival', in Sarah Dunnigan and Suzanne Gilbert (eds), *The Edinburgh Companion to Scottish Traditional Literatures* (Edinburgh: Edinburgh University Press, 2013), pp. 134–43.

Gibson, Corey, 'Recoiling the Springs of Action: *The Uses of Literacy* and the Conceptualisation of Scottish Folk-Song Revivalism', in Michael Bailey and Mary

Eagleton (eds), *Richard Hoggart: Culture and Critique* (Nottingham: Critical, Cultural and Communications Press, 2011), pp. 167–80.

Gibson, Corey, '"Tomorrow, songs / Will flow free again, and new voices / Be born on the carrying stream"': Hamish Henderson's Conception of the Scottish Folk-Song Revival and its Place in Literary Scotland', *The Drouth* 32, 2009, pp. 48–59.

Gifford, Douglas, 'Literature and World War Two', in Ian Brown and Alan Riach (eds), *The Edinburgh Companion to Twentieth-Century Scottish Literature* (Edinburgh: Edinburgh University Press, 2009), pp. 88–102.

Glen, Duncan, 'Hamish Henderson: Poetry Becomes People', in *Selected Scottish and Other Essays* (Kirkcaldy: Akros, 1999), pp. 60–8.

Glen, Duncan, *Hugh MacDiarmid and the Scottish Renaissance* (Edinburgh: W. and R. Chambers, 1964).

Glen, Duncan (ed.), *Poems Addressed to Hugh MacDiarmid and Presented to him on his Seventy-Fifth Birthday* (Preston: Akros, 1967).

Gobetti, Piero. 'A 1924 Profile of Antonio Gramsci', Draft Manuscript, Hamish Henderson and Tom Nairn (trans.), Hamish Henderson Papers, National Library of Scotland, Edinburgh. Acc. 10616.

Goldstein, Kenneth S., *A Guide for Field Workers in Folklore* (London: Herbert Jenkins, 1964).

Gramsci, Antonio, *Lettere dal Carcere* (Turin: Eindaui, 1948) with notes and marginalia by Hamish Henderson, Hamish Henderson Papers, National Library of Scotland, Edinburgh. Acc. 10327 (ii).

Gramsci, Antonio, *Letters from Prison*, Lynne Lawner (trans.) (London: Cape, 1975).

Gramsci, Antonio, *Letters from Prison*, 2 vols, Raymond Rosenthal (trans.) (New York: Columbia University Press, 1994).

Gramsci, Antonio, *Modern Prince and Other Writings* (1957), Louis Marks (trans.) (New York: International, 1967).

Gramsci, Antonio, *Prison Letters* (1988), Hamish Henderson (trans.) (London: Pluto, 1996).

Gramsci, Antonio, *Prison Notebooks*, 3 vols, Joseph A. Buttigieg (ed. and trans.) (New York: Columbia University Press, 1992–2007).

Gramsci, Antonio, *Selections from Cultural Writings*, David Forgacs and Geoffrey Nowell-Smith (eds), William Boelhower (trans.) (London: Lawrence and Wishart, 1985).

Gramsci, Antonio, *Selections from the Prison Notebooks,* Quintin Hoare and Geoffrey Nowell Smith (ed. and trans.) (New York: International, 1971).

Gramsci: Everything that Concerns People, Brian Cox (narr.), Douglas Eade (writ.), Michael Alexander (dir.), John Sessions (perf.) (Pelicula Films and Channel Four, 1987).

Gramsci: Here and Now, Les Wilson (dir.), Hamish Henderson, Lidia Curti, Stuart Hall, and John Reid (part.) (Scottish TV and Channel Four, 1987).

Green, Marcus E., *Rethinking Gramsci* (New York: Routledge, 2011).

Greig, Gavin, *Folk-Song in Buchan and Folk-Song of the North-East*, 2 vols (Hatboro: Folklore Associates, 1963).

Greig, Gavin, and Alexander Keith (eds), *Last Leaves of Traditional Ballads and Ballad Airs* (Aberdeen: Aberdeen University Press, 1925).

Hall, Stuart, 'Gramsci and Us', *Marxism Today*, June 1987, pp. 16–21.

Hames, Scott (ed.), *Unstated: Writers on Scottish Independence* (Edinburgh: Word Power, 2012).

Harker, Ben, *Class Act: The Cultural and Political Life of Ewan MacColl* (London: Pluto, 2007).

Harker, Dave, *Fakesong: The Manufacture of British 'Folksong', 1700 to the Present Day* (Milton Keynes: Open University Press, 1985).

Harrison, Jane Ellen, *Prolegomena to the Study of Greek Religion* (1903) (Chichester: Princeton University Press, 1992).

Hart, Matthew, 'Nationalist Internationalism: A Diptych in Modernism and Revolution', *Journal of Modern Literature*, 31. 1, 2007, pp. 21–46.

Harvie, Christopher, *Scotland and Nationalism: Scottish Society and Politics, 1707 to the Present*, 4th edn (London: Routledge, 2004).

Heine, Heinrich, *Selected Verse*, Peter Branscombe (ed. and trans.) (London: Penguin, 1986).

Henderson, Hamish, *Alias MacAlias: Writing on Songs, Folk and Literature*, 2nd edn, Alec Finlay (ed.) (Edinburgh: Polygon, 2004).

Henderson, Hamish [Polonius], 'America', *The Alleynian*, 66.466, 1938, pp. 206–7.

Henderson, Hamish, *The Armstrong Nose: Selected Letters of Hamish Henderson*, in Alec Finlay (ed.) (Edinburgh: Polygon, 1996).

Henderson, Hamish [Z. Marcas], 'As Burns Might Have Translated Catullus's Ode', *The Alleynian*, 64.453, 1936, n. pag.

Henderson, Hamish, 'The Ballad, the Folk and the Oral Tradition', in Edward J. Cowan (ed.), *The People's Past: Scottish Folk, Scottish History* (Edinburgh: Polygon, 1980), pp. 65–101.

Henderson, Hamish, 'Ballade des Noms de Plume', *The Alleynian*, 66.407, 1938, p. 302.

Henderson, Hamish (ed.), *Ballads of World War II* (Glasgow: Lili Marleen Club of Glasgow, 1947).

Henderson, Hamish, *Collected Poems and Songs*, Raymond Ross (ed.) (Edinburgh: Curly Snake, 2000).

Henderson, Hamish, Draft of letter to John Lehman, Publisher, c. 1949. Hamish Henderson Papers, National Library of Scotland, Edinburgh. Acc. 10788.

Henderson, Hamish (trans.), Drafts of translations of *Prison Letters*, Hamish Henderson Papers, National Library of Scotland, Edinburgh. Acc. 10157.

Henderson, Hamish, 'The Edinburgh People's Festival, 1951–1954', in Andy Croft (ed.), *A Weapon in the Struggle: The Cultural History of the Communist Party of Great Britain* (London: Pluto, 1998), pp. 163–70.

Henderson, Hamish, Editorial 'A Scottish Issue', *Our Time*, 7.12, 1948, p. 303.

Henderson, Hamish, *Elegies for the Dead in Cyrenaica* (London: J. Lehman, 1948).

Henderson, Hamish, *Elegies for the Dead in Cyrenaica* (Edinburgh: EUSPB, 1977).

Henderson, Hamish, *Elegies for the Dead in Cyrenaica* (Edinburgh: Polygon, 2008).

Henderson, Hamish [Agrippa], 'Essays at Translating Christian Morgenstern', *The Alleynian*, 65.459, 1937, pp. 182–3.

Henderson, Hamish, 'Foreword', in Ailie Munro, *The Democratic Muse* (Aberdeen: Scottish Cultural Press, 1996), pp. ix–xi.

Henderson, Hamish, 'Freedom Becomes People', *Chapman* 42, 1985, pp. 1–7.

Henderson, Hamish (trans.), 'Further Letters of Gramsci', in Peter Worsley (ed.), *The New Reasoner* 10, 1959, pp. 123–7.

Henderson, Hamish (trans.), 'Gramsci on the Jews', Valerie Gribbin (ed.), *The New Reasoner* 9, 1959, pp. 141–4.

Henderson, Hamish, 'The Green Man of Knowledge', *Scottish Studies* 2.1, 1958, pp. 47–85.

Henderson, Hamish, 'The Horseman's Word', *Scots Magazine* 87.2, 1967, pp. 118–24.

Henderson, Hamish, 'Hugh MacDiarmid: The Langholm Byspale', *Edinburgh City Lynx* 35, 21 September–4 October 1978, pp. 21–2.

Henderson, Hamish, '"It Was in You That It A' Began": Some Thoughts on the Folk Conference', in Edward J. Cowan (ed.), *The People's Past: Scottish Folk, Scottish History* (Edinburgh: Polygon, 1980), pp. 4–15.

Henderson, Hamish, 'Jock Ainslie: A Stirlingshire Horseman', *Tocher* 43, 1991, pp. 51–8.

Henderson, Hamish, Handwritten draft of Introduction to *Prison Letters* by Antonio Gramsci, Hamish Henderson Papers, National Library of Scotland, Edinburgh. Acc. 10327 (i).

Henderson, Hamish, 'The Man with the Big Box', in Timothy Neat (ed.), *The Summer Walkers: Travelling People and Pearl-fishers in the Highlands of Scotland* (Edinburgh: Canongate, 2002), pp. 65–86.

Henderson, Hamish (trans.), *The Obscure Voice: Translations from Italian Poetry* (Edinburgh: Morning Star, 1994).

Henderson, Hamish, 'The Oral Tradition', in P. H. Scott (ed.), *Scotland: A Concise Cultural History* (Edinburgh: Mainstream, 1993), pp. 159–71.

Henderson, Hamish, *Pipes, Goatskins and Bones: The Songs and Poems of Hamish Henderson* (Audiocassette) (Grampian Television, 1992).

Henderson, Hamish, 'Postscript: Glasclune and Drumlochy', Edward J. Cowan (ed.), *The People's Past: Scottish Folk, Scottish History* (Edinburgh: Polygon, 1980), pp. 206–10.

Henderson, Hamish (trans.), *Prison Letters*, Antonio Gramsci (London: Pluto, 1996).

Henderson, Hamish, 'Problacht na H-Eireann: Irish Republic Proclaimed', *National Weekly* 1.32, 23 April 1949, p. 5.

Henderson, Hamish, 'Resurgimento!' Interview with Geordie McIntyre, *Folk Song and the Song Tradition*. Spec. issue of *New Edinburgh Review*, August 1973, pp. 11–12.

Henderson, Hamish, 'Scotland at the World Peace Congress', *National Weekly* 1.34, 7 May 1949, p. 2.

Henderson, Hamish, 'Scotland's Alamein', *Voice of Scotland* 3.4, June 1947, pp. 3–4.

Henderson, Hamish (trans.), Typescript of *Prison Letters* by Antonio Gramsci as translated by Hamish Henderson, Hamish Henderson Papers, National Library of Scotland, Edinburgh. Acc. 10528 (iv).

Hendry, Joy. 'The Scottish Accent of the Mind: Introduction to the Sympathetic Imagination: Scottish Poets of the Second World War', *Borne on the Carrying Stream: The Legacy of Hamish Henderson* (Ochtertyre: Grace Note, 2010), pp. 195–203.

Hendry, Joy, 'Sorley MacLean: The Man and his Work', Raymond J. Ross and Joy Hendry (eds), *Sorley Maclean: Critical Essays* (Edinburgh: Scottish Academic Press, 1986), pp. 9–38.

Henryson, Robert, *Testament of Cresseid and Other Poems* (London: Penguin, 1988).

Herd, David, *Ancient and Modern Scottish Songs, Heroic Ballads, etc.* (1769) (Edinburgh: Scottish Academic Press, 1973).

Hieble, Jacob, 'Lili Marlene – A Study of a Modern Song', *The Modern Language Journal* 31.1, 1947, pp. 30–4.

Hobsbawm, E. J., 'Gramsci and Political Theory', *Marxism Today*, July 1977, pp. 205–13.

Hobsbawm, E. J., *Primitive Rebels: Studies in Archaic Forms of Social Movement in the 19th and 20th Centuries* (1959) (London: Norton, 1965).

Hogg, James, *The Private Memoirs and Confessions of a Justified Sinner* (1824), Karl Miller (ed.) (London: Penguin, 2006).

Hoggart, Richard, *The Uses of Literacy* (London: Chatto and Windus, 1957).

Horne, Marc, 'Highbrow v "Highlander": the feud', *The Sunday Times (Scotland)*, 8 November 2009.

How To Be Celtic: Scotland – All Quiet on the Northern Front. Michael Alexander (dir.), Hamish Henderson and Jean Redpath (pref.) (Pelicula Films and Channel Four, 1983).

Hubbard, Tom, 'Reintegrated Scots: The Post-MacDiarmid Makars', *The History of Scottish Literature* Vol. 4. Cairns Craig (ed.) (Aberdeen: Aberdeen University Press, 1988), pp. 179–94.

Hubble, Nick, *Mass Observation and Everyday Life* (London: Palgrave Macmillan, 2005).

Hunter, Andrew J., 'Hamish Henderson: The Odyssey of a Wandering King', *Aberdeen University Review* 178, 1987, pp. 117–26.

Ives, Peter, *Gramsci's Politics of Language: Engaging the Bakhtin Circle and the Frankfurt School* (London: University of Toronto, 2004).

Ives, Peter, and Rocco Lacorte (eds), *Gramsci, Language, and Translation* (Plymouth: Lexington, 2010).

Jackson, Alan, *Salutations: Collected Poetry, 1960–1989* (Edinburgh: Polygon, 1990).

Jamie, Kathleen, 'Here lies our land', in Alec Finlay, 'Bannockburn Rotunda', *Alec*

Finlay Blog, 11 February 2013, http://alecfinlayblog.blogspot.co.uk/2013/02/bannockburn-rotunda.html (last accessed 30 May 2014).

Jamie, Kathleen, 'The spirit of Bannockburn', *New Statesman*, 7 February 2013 http://www.newstatesman.com/politics/politics/2013/02/spirit-bannockburn (last accessed 30 May 2014).

Jamieson, John, *Jamieson's Dictionary of the Scottish Language* (Paisley: A. Gardner, 1912).

Jewell, Derek (ed.), *Alamein and the Desert War* (London: Times, 1967).

Johnson, James, and Robert Burns (eds), *The Scots Musical Museum, 1787–1803*, 2 vols (Aldershot: Scholar, 1991).

Jones, David, *In Parenthesis* (1937) (London: Faber, 2010).

Joyce, James, *Finnegan's Wake* (1939) (London: Penguin, 1992).

Kay, George, et al. *Four Part Song* (Edinburgh: Serif, 1950).

Kemp-Ashraf, P. M., and Jack Mitchell (eds), *Essays in Honour of William Gallacher* (Berlin: Humboldt University, 1966).

Kennedy, David, *Elegy* (Abingdon: Routledge, 2007).

Kennedy, Walter, *The Poems of Walter Kennedy*, Nicole Meier (ed.) (Edinburgh: Scottish Text Society, 2008).

Kincaid, John, et al. *Fowrsom Reel: A Collection of New Poetry* (Glasgow: Caledonian, 1949).

Kincaid, John, *Setterday Nicht Symphonie* (Glasgow: Caledonian, 1946).

Laclau, Ernesto, and Chantal Mouffe, *Hegemony and Socialist Strategy: Towards a Radical Democratic Politics* (1985), 2nd edn (London: Verso, 2001).

Law, T. S., *Whit Tyme in the Day and Ither Poems* (Glasgow: Caledonian, 1948).

Law, T. S., and Thurso Berwick (eds), *Homage to John Maclean* (Larkhall: John Maclean Society, 1973).

Lehman, John, Letter to Hamish Henderson, 4 Oct. 1949, Hamish Henderson Papers, National Library of Scotland, Edinburgh. Acc. 10788.

Leibovitz, Liel and Matthew Miller, *Lili Marlene: The Soldiers' Song of World War II* (New York: Norton, 2009).

Leonard, Tom (ed.), *Radical Renfrew: Poetry from the French Revolution to the First World War by Poets Born, or Sometimes Resident in, the County of Renfrewshire* (Edinburgh: Polygon, 1990).

'Letters to the Editor', *Glasgow Herald*, 11, 16, 18–19, 21, 22 and 25–6 November 1946, p. 4.

Lewis, Wyndham, *Hitler* (London: Chatto and Windus, 1931).

Limón, José E., 'Breaking with Gramsci: Gencarella on Good Sense and Critical Folklore Studies', *Journal of Folklore Research* 47.3, 2010, pp. 253–7.

Lindsay, Maurice (ed.), *Modern Scottish Poetry: An Anthology of the Scottish Renaissance: 1925–1975* (Manchester: Carcanet, 1976).

Lindsay, Maurice, *The Scottish Renaissance* (Edinburgh: Serif, 1948).

Littlewood, Joan, *Joan's Book: The Autobiography of Joan Littlewood* (1994) (London: Methuen, 2003).

Lloyd, A. L. (ed.), *Come All Ye Bold Miners: Ballads and Songs of the Coalfields* (London: Lawrence and Wishart, 1952).

Lloyd, A. L., *Folk Song in England* (London: Workers' Music Association, 1967).

Lloyd, A. L., 'The Guerrilla Songs of Greece', *Our Time* 4.5, 1944, n. pag.

Lloyd, A. L., *The Singing Englishman: An Introduction to Folksong* (London: Workers' Music Association, 1944).

Lloyd, A. L., 'Songs of Musso's Army', *Our Time* 2.11, 1943, pp. 17–21.

Lloyd, A. L., 'The Songs of Tito's Partisans', *Our Time* 3.9, 1944, pp. 10–12.

Lomax, Alan, *1951 Edinburgh People's Festival Ceilidh*, Hamish Henderson (perf.), John Strachan, Jessie Murray, Jimmy MacBeath, Calum Johnston and others (perf.) (Rounder Records, 2005).

Lomax, Alan, *Selected Writings: 1934–1997*, Ronald D. Cohen (ed.) (London: Routledge, 2005).

Lorca, Federico García, *Deep Song and Other Prose*, Christopher Maurer (ed. and trans.) (London: Boyars, 1980).

Lorca, Federico García, *Gypsy Ballads*, Jane Duran and Gloria García Lorca (eds) (London: Enitharmon, 2011).

Lorca, Federico García, *In Search of Duende*, Christopher Maurer (ed.) (New York: New Directions Bibelot, 1998).

Lyall, Scott, *Hugh MacDiarmid's Poetry and Politics of Place: Imagining a Scottish Republic* (Edinburgh: Edinburgh University Press, 2006).

Lyndsay, David, *Sir David Lyndsay: Selected Poems*, Janet Hadley Williams (ed.) (Glasgow: Association for Scottish Literary Studies, 2000).

McArthur, Alexander, and Kingsley H. Long, *No Mean City: A Story of Glasgow Slums* (London: Longmans, 1935).

MacCaig, Norman (ed.), *The Honour'd Shade: An Anthology of New Scottish Poetry to Mark the Bicentenary of the Birth of Robert Burns* (Edinburgh: Chambers, 1959).

McClure, J. Derrick (ed.), *Scotland and the Lowland Tongue: Studies in the Language and Literature of Lowland Scotland* (Aberdeen: Aberdeen University Press, 1983).

MacColl, Ewan, 'Ewan MacColl on Hamish', *Tocher* 43, 1991, pp. 13–14.

MacColl, Ewan, *Journeyman: An Autobiography* (London: Sidgwick and Jackson, 1990).

MacColla, Fionn, *At the Sign of the Clenched Fist* (Edinburgh: M. MacDonald, 1967).

McCulloch, Margery Palmer (ed.), *Modernism and Nationalism: Literature and Society in Scotland, 1919–1939* (Glasgow: Association for Scottish Literary Studies, 2004).

MacDiarmid, Hugh, *Albyn; or, Scotland and the Future* (London: Kegan Paul, 1927).

MacDiarmid, Hugh, *Collected Poems of Hugh MacDiarmid (C. M. Grieve)* (Edinburgh: Oliver and Boyd, 1962).

MacDiarmid, Hugh, *The Company I've Kept* (London: Hutchinson, 1966).

MacDiarmid, Hugh, *The Complete Poems of Hugh MacDiarmid*, 2 vols, Michael Grieve and W. R. Aitken (eds) (Manchester: Carcanet, 1993).

MacDiarmid, Hugh, Editorial 'The Flytin' o the Makars', *Voice of Scotland* 4.3, 1948, pp. 43–8.

MacDiarmid, Hugh, 'John Maclean, Scotland, and the Communist Party', *John Maclean: Scottish Martyr and Revolutionary Socialist.* Spec. issue of *Scots Socialist* 5, November–December 1940, pp. 2–4.

MacDiarmid, Hugh, 'Knoydart Land Seizures', *National Weekly* 1.10, 20 November 1948.

MacDiarmid, Hugh, *The Kind of Poetry I Want* (Edinburgh: K. D. Duval, 1961).

MacDiarmid, Hugh, *The Letters of Hugh MacDiarmid*, Alan Bold (ed.) (London: Hamish Hamilton, 1984).

MacDiarmid, Hugh, '"Lewis Grassic Gibbon" – James Leslie Mitchell (1946)', in Kenneth Buthlay (ed.), *The Uncanny Scot: A Selection of Prose* (London: MacGibbon and Kee, 1968), pp. 154–63.

MacDiarmid, Hugh, *Lucky Poet: A Self-Study in Literature and Political Ideas* (Manchester: Carcanet, 2001).

MacDiarmid, Hugh, 'Maugham Prize for Scotland: Young Gael's Success', *National Weekly* 1.28, 26 March 1949, p. 6.

MacDiarmid, Hugh, 'No "Belcherising" For John Maclean', *National Weekly* 1.12, 4 December 1948, pp. 1–2.

MacDiarmid, Hugh, Editorial 'Scottish Arts and Letters', *National Weekly* 1.21, 5 February 1949, p. 5.

MacDiarmid, Hugh, Editorial 'Scottish Arts and Letters', *National Weekly* 1.30, 9 April 1949, p. 5.

MacDiarmid, Hugh, *Selected Prose*, Alan Riach (ed.) (Manchester: Carcanet, 1992).

MacDiarmid, Hugh, *The Socialist Poems of Hugh MacDiarmid*, T. S. Law and Thurso Berwick (eds) (London: Routledge and Kegan Paul, 1978).

MacDiarmid, Hugh, *Ugly Birds Without Wings* (Edinburgh: A. Donaldson, 1962).

MacDiarmid, Hugh, and Edwin Muir, 'For the Vernacular Circle (*The Bulletin* January 1938)', *Scottish Studies Review* 6.1, Spring 2005, pp. 59–72.

MacDougall, James D., 'John MacLean and Scotland To-day', *National Weekly* 1.11, 27 November 1948, p. 5.

MacGill-Eain, Somhairle [Sorley Maclean] and Robert Garioch, *17 Poems for 6d: In Gaelic, Lowland Scots and English* (Edinburgh: Chalmers Press, 1940).

McGinn, Matt, *McGinn of the Calton: The Life and Works of Matt McGinn, 1928–1977* (Glasgow: Glasgow District Libraries, 1987).

McGonigal, James, *Beyond the Last Dragon: A Life of Edwin Morgan* (Dingwall: Sandstone, 2010).

Mackay, Peter, 'Townland, Desert, Cave: Irish and Scottish Second World War Poetry', in Peter Mackay (ed.), *Modern Irish and Scottish Poetry* (Cambridge: Cambridge University Press, 2011), pp. 87–101.

McLachlan, Donald H., 'The Partisans of Peace', *International Affairs* 27.1, 1951, pp. 10–17.

McLane, Maureen N., *Balladeering, Minstrelsy, and the Making of British Romantic Poetry* (Cambridge: Cambridge University Press, 2008).

McLaren, Moray, 'MacAliases', *New Statesman*, 12 March 1960, p. 360.

Maclean, John, *In the Rapids of Revolution: Essays, Articles, and Letters, 1902–1923*, Nan Milton (ed.) (London: Allison and Busby, 1978).

MacLean, Sorley. *From Wood to Ridge: Collected Poems* (Manchester: Carcanet and Birlinn, 1990).

McNaughtan, Adam, 'Hamish Henderson', *Tocher* 43, 1991, pp. 2–5.

McNaughtan, Adam, 'Hamish Henderson – Folk Hero', *Chapman* 42, 1985, pp. 22–9.

MacNeill, F. Marian, *The Silver Bough*, 4 vols (Glasgow: MacLellan, 1957–68).

McVicar, Ewan, *The Eskimo Republic: Scots Political Song in Action, 1951–1999* (Linlithgow: Gallus, 2010).

Maisels, C. K. (ed.), *Antonio Gramsci: Letters from Prison, Political History, and Conference Papers*. Spec. issues of *New Edinburgh Review* 25–27, 1974.

Martin, James (ed.), *Antonio Gramsci Critical Assessments of Leading Political Philosophers*, 4 vols (London: Routledge, 2002).

Martin, Neill, *The Form and Function of Ritual Dialogue in the Marriage Traditions of Celtic-Language Cultures* (Lampeter: Edwin Mellen, 2007).

Mayakovsky, Vladimir, *Selected Works in Three Volumes*, 3 vols (Moscow: Raduga, 1985).

Mitchell, Jack [John], 'Hamish Henderson and the Folk-song Revival', *Essays in Honour of William Gallacher* (Berlin: Humboldt University, 1966), pp. 199–215.

Mitchell, John, 'An Analysis of the Poetic Elements in Hamish Henderson's Songs', *Chapbook* 3.6, 1967, pp. 7–23.

Mitchell, Joseph, *Joe Gould's Secret* (London: Jonathan Cape, 1997).

Mitchison, Naomi, '"Wild Poets Chasing Stars": A Bard Who Picks Up the Song of the Future', *Forward*, 8 January 1949, p. 2.

Morgan, Edwin, 'The Beatnik in the Kailyard', *Essays* (Cheadle: Carcanet, 1974), pp. 166–76.

Morgan, Edwin, *The Horseman's Word: A Sequence of Concrete Poems* (Preston: Akros, 1970).

Morgan, Edwin, 'MacDiarmid Embattled', *Lines Review* 15, 1959, pp. 17–25.

Morgan, Edwin, 'The Sea, the Desert, the City: Environment and Language in W. S. Graham, Hamish Henderson and Tom Leonard', *The Yearbook of English Studies* 17, 1987, pp. 31–45.

Morgan, Edwin (trans.), *Wi The Haill Voice: 25 Poems by Vladimir Mayakovsky Translated into Scots by Edwin Morgan* (Oxford: Carcanet, 1972).

Muir, Edwin, *Scott and Scotland: The Predicament of the Scottish Writer* (1936) (Edinburgh: Polygon, 1982).

Munro, Ailie, *The Democratic Muse: The Folk Music Revival in Scotland* (Aberdeen: Scottish Cultural Press, 1996).

The Muckle Sangs: Classic Scottish Ballads (Greentrax, 1975).

National Collective, 'Flytings', http://nationalcollective.com/2013/03/10/project-flytings/ (last accessed 30 May 2014).

Neat, Timothy (dir.), *Journey to a Kingdom* (Grampian Television, 1993).

Neat, Timothy, *The Making of the Poet (1919–1953)* Vol. 1, *Hamish Henderson: A Biography* (Edinburgh: Birlinn, 2007).

Neat, Timothy (dir.), *Play Me Something* (British Film Institute, 1989).

Neat, Timothy, *Poetry Becomes People (1952–2002)* Vol. 2, *Hamish Henderson: A Biography* (Edinburgh: Birlinn, 2009).

Neat, Timothy, *The Summer Walkers: Travelling People and Pearl-Fishers in the Highlands of Scotland* (Edinburgh: Canongate, 1996).

Neat, Timothy (dir.), *The Tree of Liberty* (Everallin, 1987).

Neat, Timothy, 'The Unknown Soldier', *Scotland on Sunday*, 11 November 2007, n. pag.

The New Princeton Encyclopedia of Poetry and Poetics, Alex Preminger and T. V. F. Brogan (eds) (Princeton: Princeton University Press, 1993).

Nicholson, Alexander (ed.), *A Collection of Gaelic Proverbs and Familiar Phrases, Based on Macintosh's Collection* (1881) (Edinburgh: Birlinn, 2011).

Nicholson, Colin, *Edwin Morgan: Inventions of Modernity* (Manchester: Manchester University Press, 2002).

Nicholson, Colin, *Poem, Purpose and Place: Shaping Identity in Contemporary Scottish Verse* (Edinburgh: Polygon, 1992).

'Official Report Debate Contributions at the Scottish Parliament for Wednesday 27 March 2002 (Afternoon)', http://www.scottish.parliament.uk/ParliamentaryBusiness.aspx (last accessed 2 May 2012).

Orwell, George, 'Inside the Whale', *Inside the Whale and Other Essays* (London: Penguin, 1957).

Parker, Charles, Ewan MacColl and Peggy Seeger, *The Ballad of John Axon* (1958) (Topic, 2008).

Piccone, Paul, 'Gramsci's Marxism: Beyond Lenin and Togliatti', *Theory and Society* 3.4, 1976, pp. 485–512.

Prebble, John, *Glencoe: The Story of the Massacre* (London: Secker and Warburg, 1966).

Propp, V., *Morphology of the Folktale*, Lawrence Scott (trans.), 2nd edn (Austin: University of Texas, 1968).

Ransford, Tessa, 'Encompass the Crossed-Sword Blades: Hamish Henderson's Poetry', in Eberhard Bort (ed.), *Borne on the Carrying Stream: The Legacy of Hamish Henderson* (Ochtertyre: Grace Note, 2010), pp. 137–60.

Rattenbury, Arnold, 'Flytings', *London Review of Books* 25.2, 23 January 2003, pp. 26–8.

Relich, Mario, 'Apollyon's Chasm: The Poetry of Hamish Henderson', in Eberhard Bort (ed.), *Borne on the Carrying Stream: The Legacy of Hamish Henderson* (Ochtertyre: Grace Note, 2010), pp. 123–36.

Rickword, Edgell, 'Poetry and Two Wars', *Our Time* 1.2, 1941, pp. 1–6.

Robinson, Christine, 'Back to the Future: *The Bruce* and Relevance to the 21st Century Reader', *The Bottle Imp* 4, 2008, http://www.arts.gla.ac.uk/ScotLit/ASLS/SWE/TBI/TBIIssue4/Bruce.html (last accessed 2 May 2012).

Rosenberg, Neil V. (ed.), *Transforming Tradition: Folk Music Revivals Examined* (Urbana and Chicago: University of Illinois, 1993).

Ross, Raymond J., 'Hamish Henderson: In the Midst of Things', *Chapman* 42, 1985, pp. 11–18.

Roy, Kenneth, Editorial, *Scottish Review*, 14 November 2011.

Sangs o' The Stane (Glasgow: Scottish National Congress, 1952).

Sassi, Carla, 'Hamish Henderson: Un Gramsciano a Edimburgo', *Italia & Italy* 5, 2000, pp. 36–7.

Sassi, Carla, 'Italian Songlines', in Hamish Henderson, *Obscure Voice: Translations from Italian Poetry* (Edinburgh: Morning Star, 1994).

Saurat, Denis, *Death and the Dreamer* (London: Westhouse, 1946).

Saurat, Denis, 'Le Groupe de la Renaissance Ecossaise', *Revue Anglo-Américaine*, April 1924, pp. 295–307.

Scott, Alexander, *The MacDiarmid Makars, 1923–1972* (Preston: Akros, 1972).

Scott, Bill, 'Hamish Henderson's Torch of Freedom', *Frontline* 2.11, January 2010.

Scott, P. H., *Scotland: A Concise Cultural History* (Edinburgh: Mainstream, 1993).

Scott, Tom, Somhairle MacGill-Eain [Sorley Maclean] and Hamish Henderson, *Pervigilium Scotiae = Scotland's Vigil* (Buckfastleigh: Etruscan, 1997).

Scott, Walter, *Minstrelsy of the Scottish Border* Vol. 1 (Edinburgh: Adam and Charles Black, 1807).

Selwyn, Victor (ed.), *From Oasis to Italy: War Poems and Diaries from Africa and Italy, 1940–1946* (London: Shepheard-Walwyn, 1983).

Selwyn, Victor (ed.), *Poems of the Second World War: The Oasis Selection* (London: Salamander Oasis Trust, 1985).

Selwyn, Victor (ed.), *Return to Oasis: War Poems and Recollections from the Middle East, 1940–1946* (London: Salamander Oasis Trust, 1980).

Selwyn, Victor (ed.), *The Voice of War: Poems of the Second World War* (London: Salamander Oasis Trust, 1996).

Shakespeare, William, *Troilus and Cressida* (London: Penguin, 1987).

Shakespeare, William, *A Midsummer Night's Dream* (London: Penguin, 1967).

Sharp, Alfred, Editorial, *Our Time* 2.7, 1942, p. 3.

Shepherd, Nan, 'The Poetry of Hugh MacDiarmid', *Aberdeen University Review* 26, 1938, p. 76.

Sir Gawain and the Green Knight, Bernard O'Donoghue (trans.) (London: Penguin, 2006).

Simpson, Kenneth, 'The Legacy of Flyting', *Studies in Scottish Literature* 26, 1991, pp. 503–14.

Slater, Montagu, 'Bless 'em All: A Piece About Army Songs', *Our Time* 1.1, 1941, pp. 21–5.

Smith, G. Gregory, *Scottish Literature: Character and Influence* (London: Macmillan, 1919).

Smith, Sydney Goodsir, *Collected Poems, 1915–1975* (London: John Calder, 1975).

Smith, Sydney Goodsir, *Deevil's Waltz* (Glasgow: William MacLellan, 1946).

Smith, Sydney Goodsir, 'MacDiarmid's *Three Hymns to Lenin*', in Duncan Glen (ed.), *Hugh MacDiarmid: A Critical Survey* (Edinburgh: Scottish Academic Press, 1972), pp. 141–54.

Speirs, John, *The Scots Literary Tradition: An Essay in Criticism*, Rev. 2nd edn (London: Faber, 1962).

Spivak, Gayatri Chakravorty, 'Can the Subaltern Speak?', in Cary Nelson and Lawrence Grossberg (eds), *Marxism and the Interpretation of Culture* (London: Macmillan, 1988), pp. 271–314.

Srivastava, Neelam, and Baidik Bhattacharya, *The Postcolonial Gramsci* (London: Routledge, 2012).

Stevenson, Robert Louis, *Strange Case of Dr. Jekyll and Mr. Hyde*, Katherine Linehan (ed.) (London: Norton, 2003).

Stevenson, Robert Louis, 'Thrawn Janet', in *The Complete Stories of Robert Louis Stevenson* (New York: Modern Library, 2002), pp. 410–19.

Sweeny-Turner, Steve, 'Borderlines: Bilingual Terrain in Scottish Song', *The Place of Music*, Andrew Leyshon, et al. (eds) (London: Guilford, 1998), pp. 151–75.

Thomas, Greg, 'Turning their Fey Shoulders to the Wheel: Edwin Morgan's letters to Hamish Henderson', in Steve Byrne (ed.), *The Hamish Henderson Papers: A Commemorative Collection of Essays* (Edinburgh: Hamish Henderson Archives Trust, 2013), pp. 7–14.

Thompson, E. P., 'Comments on a People's Culture', *Our Time* 7.2, 1947, pp. 34–8.

Thompson, E. P., *The Making of the English Working Class* (London: Victor Gollancz, 1963).

Thompson, E. P., 'A New Poet.' Rev. of Hamish Henderson, *Elegies for the Dead in Cyrenaica*, *Our Time* 8.6, 1949, p. 158.

Thompson, E. P., 'Patrician Society, Plebeian Culture', *Journal of Social History* 7.4, 1974, pp. 382–405.

Thompson, E. P., 'Socialist Humanism', *The New Reasoner* 1, 1957, pp. 105–43.

Thomson, Alex, '"You can't get there from here": Devolution and Scottish Literary History', *International Journal of Scottish Literature* 3, 2007.

Thwaite, Anthony, 'The Barbarous Arena', *Times Literary Supplement*, 9 September 1977.

Tobar an Dualchais / Kist o Riches, Digital Archives from the School of Scottish Studies (University of Edinburgh), BBC Scotland, and the National Trust for Scotland's Canna Collection, http://www.tobarandualchais.co.uk (last accessed 2 May 2012).

Togliatti, Palmiro, *On Gramsci and Other Writings*, Donald Sassoon (ed. and trans.) (London: Lawrence and Wishart, 1979).

Trott, F. H., et al., *Ding Doun the Waas: A Cantata* (Glasgow, 1930).

Watson, Roderick, '"Death's Proletariat": Scottish Poets of the Second World War', *The Oxford Handbook of British and Irish War Poetry*, Tim Kendall (ed.) (Oxford: Oxford University Press, 2007), pp. 315–39.

Watson, Roderick, *The Literature of Scotland: The Twentieth Century* (Basingstoke: Palgrave Macmillan, 2007).

Wesker, Arnold, *Fears of Fragmentation* (London: Jonathan Cape, 1970).

Wesker, Arnold, 'Vision! Vision! Mr Woodcock!', *New Statesman*, 30 July 1960, p. 153.

Whyte, Christopher, 'Masculinities in Contemporary Scottish Fiction', *Forum for Modern Language Studies* 34.3, 1998, pp. 274–85.

Williams, Raymond, 'Base and Superstructure in Marxist Cultural Theory', *New Left Review* I/82, 1973.

Williams, Raymond, *Culture and Society 1780–1950* (1958) (Harmondsworth: Penguin, 1963).

Williams, Raymond, *The Long Revolution* (1961) (London: Pelican, 1965).

Williams, Raymond, *Marxism and Literature* (Oxford: Oxford University Press, 1977).

Wilson, James, *Lowland Scotch as spoken in the Lower Strathearn District of Perthshire* (London: Oxford University Press, 1915).

Wittig, Kurt, *The Scottish Tradition in Literature* (Westport: Greenwood, 1958).

Wyntoun, Andrew, *The Orygynale Cronykil of Scotland* Vol. 1, David Laing (ed.) (Edinburgh: Edmonston and Douglas, 1872).

Yeats, W. B., 'The Death of Cuchulain', in David R. Clark and Rosalind E. Clark (eds), *The Complete Works of W. B. Yeats: Vol. II: The Plays* (London: Scribner, 2001), pp. 545–55.

Young, Douglas, Letters to Hamish Henderson, 30 January 1949, 30 October 1957, 26 November 1957, 20 February 1958, 25 March 1958, 9 April 1966, Hamish Henderson Papers, National Library of Scotland, Edinburgh. Acc. 10528 (ii), Acc. 10788.

Young, Douglas, *'Plastic Scots' and the Scottish Literary Tradition: An Authoritative Introduction to a Controversy* (Glasgow: Maclellan, 1946).

Young, Douglas, Postcard to Hamish Henderson, 26 October 1967, Hamish Henderson Papers, National Library of Scotland, Edinburgh. Acc. 10788.

Young, Douglas (ed.), *Scottish Verse 1851–1951* (Edinburgh: Nelson, 1952).

Young, James D., *The Rousing of the Scottish Working Class* (London: Croom Helm, 1979).

Young, James D., *The Very Bastards of Creation: Scottish-International Radicalism: A Biographical Study, 1707–1995* (Glasgow: Clydeside, 1996).

INDEX

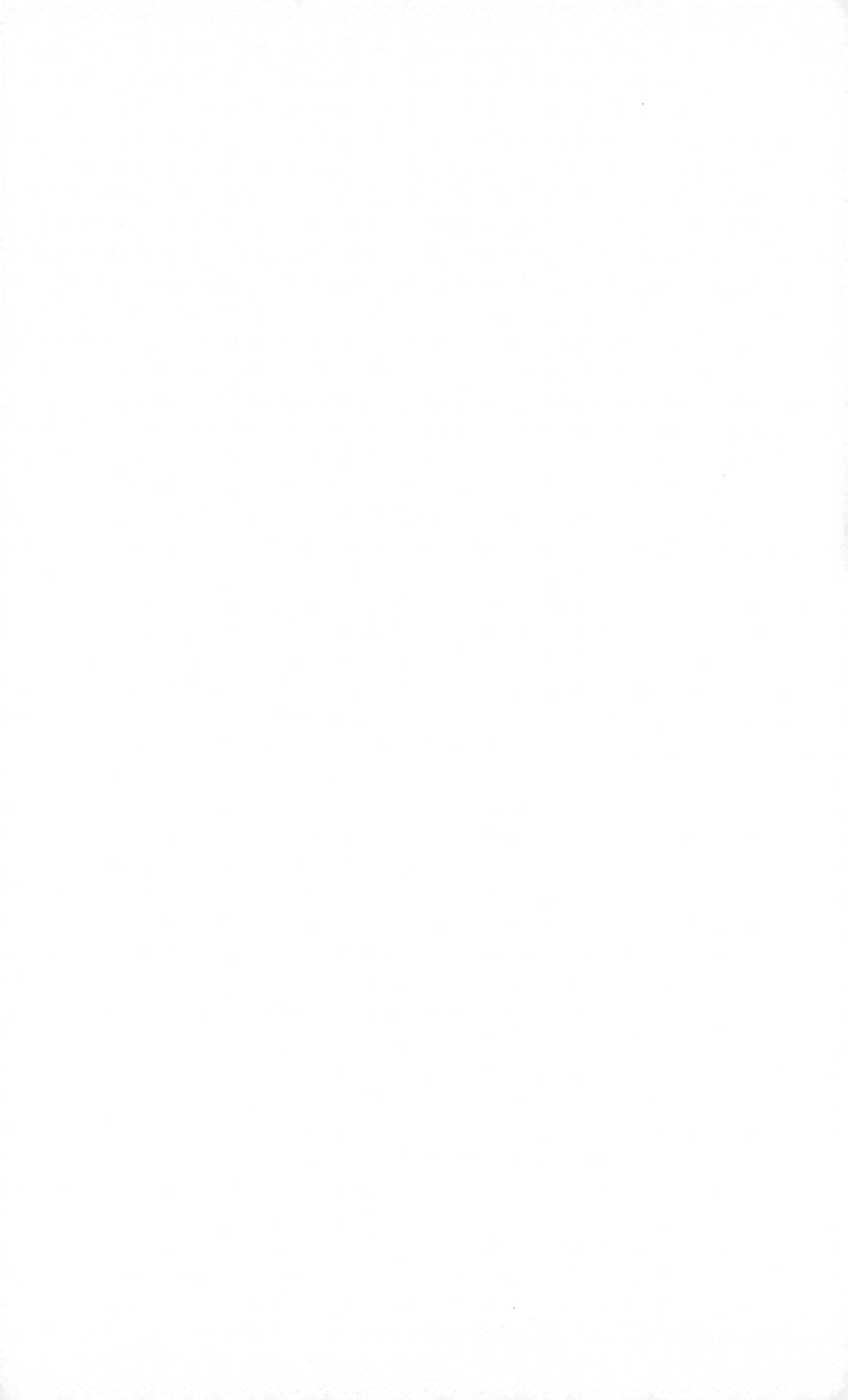

EU Authorised Representative:
Easy Access System Europe Mustamäe tee 50, 10621 Tallinn, Estonia
gpsr.requests@easproject.com

Printed and bound by CPI Group (UK) Ltd, Croydon, CR0 4YY
07/05/2026
02104604-0003